Her Side of the Story
•

FOR JACOB AND HARRIET

and the class of 1985 who ate the Caramello chocolate, smelt the marigolds, stroked the woollen socks and helped paste the gold stars on the wall as mnemonics in our reading of Janet Frame's *Faces in the Water*

Her Side of the Story

●

Readings of
Mander, Mansfield & Hyde

Mary Paul

●

University of Otago Press

Published by University of Otago Press
56 Union Street/PO Box 56, Dunedin, New Zealand
email: university.press@stonebow.otago.ac.nz

First published 1999
Copyright © Mary Paul 1999

ISBN 1 877133 71 X

Cover image is a detail from
the original cover design of
Kowhai Gold: An Anthology of Contemporary Verse,
edited by Quentin Pope (London: Dent, 1930)

Published with the financial assistance of the
Massey University Publications Committee

Printed by Otago University Print

Contents

Illustrations appear between Chapters 2 and 3 (opposite page 74).

•

Acknowledgements

Since this book began its life as postgraduate research at the University of Auckland, and because its approach relies on discussion of varied readings of texts, models for which often took place in tutorial and seminar discussions, it would be impossible to thank everyone who has contributed along the way. Many colleagues and friends have helped with specific material: Susan Ash, Alex Calder, Derek Challis, Geoff Chapple, Wystan Curnow, Liasa Docherty, Wendy Harrex, Robin Hooper, Michele Leggott, Sandra Moran, Ray Richards, Pat Sandbrook, Laurence Simmons, Peter Simpson, Robert Sullivan, Joanne Wilkes, Peter Wells, Briar Woods and Anne Zimmerman. Special thanks go to Roger Horrocks for his sustaining encouragement and detailed comments.

Thanks, too, go to my students and fellow students whose discussion stimulated so much of my argument, to Philip Armstrong and Kim Batten to whose essays I have referred, and especially to the students of the Australian and New Zealand Women Writers Paper 1993–95, at University of Auckland. Shifen Gong, Michele Leggott, Denny Little, Sue Simpson, Sarah Shieff and Terry Sturm were on-goingly supportive of the project, while Deborah Shepard, Morag Mackay, Sarah Dugdale, Rae McGregor, Aorewa McLeod, Liz Park and Sarah Schieff offered assistance in final stages of the preparation of this manuscript in its earlier (thesis) form. Thanks go to Nickee Sanders for formatting, while editorial assistance and valuable suggestions came more recently from Linda Pears and my publisher Wendy Harrex. For technical assistance, my thanks to Greg Bennett of the Centre for Film, Television and Media Studies at the University of Auckland. Most importantly, thank you to my husband, Murray Edmond, for his ongoing intellectual and personal support, and to our children Jacob and Harriet, without whom I might have written this book much earlier, but not in this way.

I gratefully acknowledge the assistance of the University of Auckland Research Committee for assistance with travel to the Alexander Turnbull Library, and Massey University Publications Committee for support of this publication.

A version of Chapter One on 'Bliss' has been published in an earlier, less elaborated, form in *Opening the Book: New Essays on NZ Writing* (Auckland: AUP, 1995) A first version of Chapter Three on *The Piano* and Mander's novel was presented as a seminar in the English Department of University of Auckland in 1995 and material on *Tutira: Story of a New Zealand Sheep Station* and *The Story of a New Zealand River* was presented as a seminar 'Stocking the Run with Men (and Woman)' at the Narrative and Metaphor Conference, University of

Auckland, in July 1996. Images from two films are reproduced with the kind permission of John Barnett (for *Iris*) and Peter Wells (*Desperate Remedies*).

MARY PAUL
Auckland, September 1999

●

Another Player
Enters the Court

Rather than a transposition of meaning from author to reader's reader, to reader, literary criticism [can be seen as] a process, a movement back and forth between text and critic for the benefit of the critic and all those who share in the textual commentary. There can be no completion of an interpretive process, but only a temporary pause necessary to allow another player to enter the court.[1]

This book explores contemporary ways of reading some important New Zealand texts, all produced between 1910 and 1940, except for a recent film and filmscript which are considered as re-readings of one of the earlier texts. Interpretations of these texts have had a significant impact on New Zealanders' ideas of themselves, an aspect to which I draw attention as I classify and cluster together types of readings. The overall argument of the book is that interpretation is a process which can never be completed; nevertheless, at any one time there will be certain readings that are imperative. Thus I attempt new readings that make me, in the terms of the above quotation, a 'new player entering the court'. As such, I need to introduce my own background as reader and interpreter.

FEMINISM AND READING

In 1974 in London (a New Zealander abroad) I completed an MA dissertation. My subject was what I saw as the political success and failure of English novelist Elizabeth Gaskell. Feminism was at that time getting a lot of attention in the popular press and was very much a topic of conversation amongst young people, but was not widely applied to academic discussion of literary texts.[2] I chose my topic on the work of a so-called 'minor' woman writer in order to challenge her designation as such, but my interest seems to have been primarily in recovering the social and political impact of her work. In arguing for this, I see in retrospect that I reproduced some standard assumptions about women and art. And I obviously held to these assumptions in spite of the fact that I had taken part in the women's movement in New Zealand – listening to and reading Germaine Greer and participating in suffrage commemorations. And in London I had encountered more of its manifestations in consciousness-raising groups, experimental film making, avant-garde art at the ICA, and 'wages for housework' collectives. Also at this time I read the recently published *Of Woman Born* by Adrienne Rich, though I was probably more informed by the liberal feminist tradition from Mary Wollstonecraft, Harriet Taylor and J. S. Mill.

My overall argument in the dissertation was to acknowledge the importance of political questions in Mrs Gaskell's novels and I tended to discard what I saw as the more female consolatory aspects of her work. However, it is interesting that I was anxious enough about the paradoxical nature of these judgements to spend the last page of my discussion on what could now be construed as a problem of gender and reading. First I outlined the problem sympathetically:

> There are still women who feel like Mrs Gaskell did, that the world of the arts is part of a sort of dream world a woman must inhabit while she rears her children and cares for her home. If because our world is changing this is not a satisfactory idea of art for us, it was still one which made a great many women's lives more bearable than they otherwise would have been.[3]

And then I finished with a quote from Mrs Gaskell:

> One thing is pretty clear, *women* must give up living an artist's life, if home duties are to be paramount. . . . I am sure it is healthy for them to have the refuge of the hidden world of Art to shelter themselves in when too much pressed upon by daily small Lilliputian arrows of pedaling cares; it keeps them from being morbid as you say; it takes them into the land where King Arthur lies hidden, and soothes them with its peace. I have felt this in writing.[4]

The subtext of my comments when I wrote 'there are still women who feel like Mrs Gaskell did' was, I think, a response to my mother's comfortable idea of 'art' and domesticity: I wanted to challenge its traditional conservative implications. Not everyone's mum has a theory of art, but mine had as my parents were figures in the New Zealand intellectual and art community.[5] My father was a bookseller and one of the first local publishers, my mother a painter and book designer, latterly an art historian. My father's ideas about the importance of culture were informed by a left-wing sense of social responsibility. But it was my mother who brought me up through my teens (after my father's death) and her tendency was to justify quality of life entirely in terms of ability to appreciate art and aesthetics. This was an attitude bound to enrage a young woman with political interests in the late 1960s and early 1970s. Probably I also perceived her emphasis on form over content as a subtle directive to me about the sort of woman I should be.

The contradictions lurking in my remarks not only indicate my personal background but also provide a good introduction to what happened generally in the succeeding twenty years in feminist thought. The kinds of judgements I was making were typical of that period. Buried in my way of speaking was the feeling that most of what women produced as cultural artefacts were signs of their subordination, and therefore not to be taken seriously. The corollary was that there is (or will be some day) a new woman who is free from these traces of subordination. Whereas in 1974 my dissertation, as far as it was feminist at all, assumed a discourse of equality, in the following years what became important in reassessing women's lives and women's cultural production was a discourse of difference – that is, a way of talking about what women are, not what they might be. The first and for me most important introduction to this new approach was Juliet Mitchell's *Psychoanalysis and Feminism*, which I was also reading at this time. I had heard Mitchell speak at Ruskin College, Oxford, and I knew she had lived in New Zealand as a child, but it was her radical approach rather than these anecdotal connections that interested me. Mitchell was the first English-speaking feminist to use Freud to explicate discussions about gender, to get away from the rhetoric of liberation, and to explain why all woman are not feminists. In France the 'Psych et Po' (Psychanalyse et Politique) groups coming from a similarly libertarian left background were revising Lacan to similar effect – but I did not know about them until the mid 1980s.

Mitchell argued that we enter culture in a complex way, either as a man or as a woman. In theorising about female identity (or what we call the female subject) she was wanting to show that 'the way that we live . . . the necessary rules of human society is not so much conscious as *unconscious*'.[6] And that the language of the unconscious develops in a specific way for women. Freud's formulations offered useful concepts which Mitchell and the contemporaneous group in Paris opposed to the 'bourgeois and idealist tendencies within, largely, American radical feminism'.[7] In literary terms Mitchell formulated an idea of women's writing as betraying the 'hysteria' that arises inevitably from the contradictions of femininity. The French feminists in a similar vein suggested a new way of valuing this female specificity beyond the terms of oppression.

Around 1985, when teaching undergraduates and studying, I revisited Juliet Mitchell's ideas and discovered how similar angles had been elaborated by French feminist thinkers. I became absorbed in the problems of how to apply these ideas to the texts that we discussed in tutorials and lectures. I enjoyed the performative and creative aspect of some of the most famous of those essays – Hélène Cixous's 'The Laugh of the Medusa', Luce Irigaray's 'When Our Lips Speak Together' and Julia Kristeva's 'Women's Time' – and the impact they could have in the university context.[8] These theorists had taken the terminology of Jacques Lacan and extended it. In their terms the female was considered not to be able to speak itself in the Symbolic but was instead a site of semiotic subversion to be found in writing, its presence signalled by absences, elision, and marginalia. Femininity was a dissonant presence on the margins, so dissonant (one line of argument ran) that it did not matter if a biological man or woman was the source. Textual experiment was *ipso facto* female – or, in an alternative formulation, the female spoke the body which the humanist rationalist tradition had suppressed through its exclusive binary categories: mind/body, man/woman.

But while I was fascinated with the possibilities of these new ideas, I was also frustrated with the cultish and imitative adherence to their vocabulary that I found appearing as literary criticism, and with the glib way in which these theories were absorbed into the standard academic discourse. I was worried, too, at the implied essentialism of the idea of writing the body, just as I had been worried by what seemed to me a naive idea of oppression in Dale Spender's work and in much American radical feminism.[9] I tried out a variety of angles that were emerging in the debates between these theories – trying to find a position. For instance, in a review of an anthology of New Zealand women's poetry I suggested that it might be a 'ghettoisation' to put all the women together.[10] Yet at the same time I was critical of the editor's failure to acknowledge her line of continuity with a previous all-women anthology. Again my paradoxical attitudes suggested that I was groping for an intellectual position that would be sufficiently complex to express my intuitive understanding. Similarly, in an introduction to a collection of women's new fiction, I tried to position myself outside the earnestness of debate about the specificity of women's writing and culture by being rather flippant and using food metaphors to explain our selection of stories.[11] In this case I was proposing a performative solution to a rather controversial and politically sensitive situation, where we were inundated with many stories whose themes seemed formulaic.

Just as productive as this struggle for a solution, though, was my teaching of a novel, *The Passion of New Eve*, by English writer Angela Carter.[12] This novel is a satire about the extremes of feminism and other ideologies. Typically, Angela Carter showed how old ideas come in new bottles. She portrayed a women's community where supposed truisms such as 'man is time' and 'woman is space' were chanted from a megaphone while a sex change operation was performed on the central male character to punish and re-educate him. Carter's opposing of one universalising and totalising discourse to another, shown in terms of late twentieth-century culture, helped me to reflect on the problems I was having in shaping my feminism and a feminist approach to reading. Instead of wanting to find a single solution, I became gradually more interested in the way that different types of reading are needed at different times. As well, I became increasingly fascinated by the complex and often tenuous relationship of reading to theory or ideology. I found I enjoyed exposing the way that readings tend to circulate often in opposition to each other. I found pleasure in discovering the ways that the same elements could be used to justify opposite interpretations. And I became interested in thinking about 'reading communities' and how they reinforced a particular way of understanding in relation to political and social aspects of a period.

An essay by Toril Moi written in 1988, but which I read in 1990, helped me to bring these ideas together. Moi too was trying to take a 'meta' look at feminism, explaining the shift from an emphasis on sameness to an emphasis on difference as typical of the cyclic logic to which protest movements were always bound. I particularly liked the way she explained what she called 'the impossibility of the idea of feminism':

> First, feminism is committed to the struggle for equality for women, a struggle which has often been seen simply as the effort to make women become *like* men. But

the struggle for equal rights historically and politically commits feminists to emphasise the value of women as *they are* (i.e. *before* equal rights have been won). For the very case for equal rights rests precisely on the argument that women are *already* as valuable as men. But given women's *lack* of equal rights, this value must be located as difference, not as equality: women are of equal human value *in their own way*. This logic, which avoids taking the male as norm, has been evident in Western feminism since its inception.

Moi went on to draw out the paradox:

My point is that under patriarchy even equal rights feminists have to assert the value of women as women, since it is the only way to *counter* the systematic devaluation of women and women's work under patriarchy. Equality and difference are not in this sense antitheses. But a discourse of female difference, even so, is not readily compatible with one of female equality. Articulated in isolation, the emphasis on female difference comes disturbingly to echo the very patriarchal prejudices against which the champions of women's equality are struggling.[13]

In this particular essay Moi also discussed the further theoretical solution, given this 'constraining logic of sameness and difference' that Julia Kristeva proposed: that of 'a third space' where the logic of identity and binary opposition are themselves deconstructed. This was the line also taken by English critic Mary Jacobus, who gave a guest lecture in Auckland in 1989. But again, this textualisation and dissolving of sexual difference worried me. It seemed that if it was not consciously anti-patriarchal it might simply coincide with traditional sexism. Thus a reading based on this theory would risk simply repeating and describing the status quo. My suspicion was increased by the fact that some of my male colleagues were delighted with these developments. They breathed a sigh of relief to see the naivety of radical feminism, its identity politics and presumably its aggression, coming to an end. What I was worried about was not so much the theory itself – which is certainly important and challenging – but its appropriation or convenient application in the academic context. Thinking about the importance of context or milieu further increased my interest in *why* one way of reading a text should be chosen over another – and *who* was doing the reading and for what purpose.

Gradually, out of these questions about feminism and reading, I came to the methodology of this book, which is designed to question and interrogate ways of reading. Each chapter proceeds by setting readings of a single text in opposition to one another, then it attempts the construction of another readin. This new reading is not the 'correct' reading but is currently for me the most relevant, self-conscious and historically aware interpretation. My first and last chapters are particularly concerned with the application of feminism to reading – the effects that its emphases and complexities (or inconsistencies) may have on what we make of texts. The opening chapter, on Katherine Mansfield's 'Bliss', could be said to directly illustrate the paradoxes of identity politics. The last two chapters, on reading the work of Robin Hyde, show how a feminist reading can get stuck in a kind of tragic essentialism and subsume ideas of different women at different periods into one idea of 'woman'. My effort is to interpret the writer's work in a wider cultural and social context and with a materialist feminist emphasis.[14] For example, the ambiguity of 'Bliss' is explained in terms of the jostling of ideas about sexuality and psychology at the time it was written, while new information about the 1930s allow me to position Hyde as an experimental modernist writer beyond the debate between nationalism and feminism.

The other chapters bring in questions of nationalism and culture which are also vital to understanding contemporary readings of these New Zealand texts. The chapter on Mansfield's 'Prelude' displays how a range of readings recycle certain textual elements. Particularly interesting is the recent emphasis on European 'heritage', which has emerged in the late 1980s and 1990s. Also included is a type of feminist account which leaves out history, specifically the history of European settlement; this can in turn be challenged by reading the story in relation to the history of women in colonial society. The chapters on *The Piano* and 'The River' suggest that the activity of interpretation can be wider and more vital than it has previously been. The impulse to contextualise leads me to emphasise what are sometimes considered peripheral elements – the conception and gestation of the film, its publicity and packaging as well as the film's effects on the New Zealand cultural scene. The controversial business of the 'other' film script that was being developed before *The Piano* is raised not as a matter of intrigue but to discover the significance of this veiled relationship in a postcolonial society, where local indigenous industries are vulnerable to being co-opted by a cultural mix-and-match school of film making.

THE GROWTH OF THEORY

When I was an undergraduate student in the early 1970s, other theories besides feminism were 'in the air' – for example, we read Michel Foucault, Claude Lévi-Strauss, Edmund Leach. But although I recall a friend writing a structuralist analysis of *Paradise Lost*, it was, I think, a rare example. Like feminism, these forms of theory – structuralism and post-structuralism – were for the most part not applied to the study of literature. Or, it might be better to say, their application did not seem to us a crucial issue – it was not acknowledged that new theory could have a dramatic effect on the reading, writing and discussion of literature.

In 1984, however, when I began to teach and study at Auckland University after some years spent working in the theatre, in an art gallery, and bringing up a son and daughter, it was a different story. The teachers were reading a lot of theory and pondering its relevance to their teaching and research. An MA course which I was invited to audit (in order to catch up with theory) was presented as disrupting the conventional English studies reliance on 'New Criticism' and Leavisite assumptions. This was an emphasis that reflected the backgrounds of the lecturers and perhaps was not so useful to the students who did not need to fight their way out of New Criticism. I was familiar with postmodern frag-mentation, both in the theatre and in the visual arts; for example, I had seen in London, and again when she visited this country, the work of visual artist Mary Kelly. Her *Post-Partum Document* aimed to show how sexual difference is produced through systems of representation, and her collection of objects (for example, stained nappy liners) contested the Madonna representation of mother and child by recording the physicality and social 'realities' of that relationship.[15] Also, in a 1983 essay on 'alternative' theatre in New Zealand, I had used the term 'trans-avant-gardeism' to describe the historical mix of styles utilised by the theatre company Red Mole – a term that has been overtaken by the idea of the 'postmodern'. And back in the 1970s on visits to Sydney and Poland I had attended workshops with Jerzy Grotowski and seen the company's production of *Apocalypsis*, which constructed its narrative out of a number of famous texts by writers from T. S. Eliot to Simone Weil.

As I recall, the works of theory discussed in that 1984 MA course were an eclectic mix. No one was able to give an overview because the teachers themselves were still struggling with the new material and its implications. The pedagogical answer was to suggest that theory had freed us from the idea of 'truth' and that therefore we could concentrate on expertise: that is, the only criterion for good criticism, interesting cultural analysis, excellent theses or excellent essays was the skill of application. The more difficult the concepts one could handle, the better. Theory had showed us that the performance of a certain ritual was probably always what academic writing in the subject of English had been about, and now we were able to acknowledge it directly. As someone who was always struggling for an overview or a 'meta' approach to my discipline, I found this approach impressive but also frustrating. I firmed my resolve to keep examining the politics of reading, asking what I suppose you could call committed questions (why, what, who and when) of any interpretation. I wanted to feel there was more relevance to interpretation than merely a fine performance and considered that unconsciously even fine performances would still favour certain assumptions or audiences, and in the long run make the study of culture irrelevant and disappointing.

There were, however, some other local aspects to the upsurge in theory. A magazine, *AND*, had appeared in 1983 in four issues. Two of its three editors were associated with the Auckland University English Department. The magazine was intended to shake up the orthodoxies of New Zealand literature and criticism. It aimed to encourage new ways of reading by new contextualisations and by the introduction of new theories. Its visual design drew New Zealand high culture into a relationship with popular culture and challenged the orthodox Romantic image of the artist as agonised, alone, and always struggling against the philistinism of the larger society. Several articles showed how the literary concept of New Zealand had been invented, exploring the idea of nation and national culture. My interest in the oppositional patterns I had found in feminist criticism were matched by these new discussions.[16] Again I found myself involved in rethinking my approach. I came to realise that I shared the assumptions of the intellectual subculture in New Zealand, which had defined itself against the wider society; in order to step back from orthodox ways of reading, I had to reassess those assumptions. One of the editors of *AND* magazine, Leigh Davis, was also a poet and latterly a merchant banker. His work showed me how a post-structuralist idea of language could influence writing as well as reading. For example, sonnet '62' from his series 'Willy's Gazette' was constructed out of found phrases, suggesting that identity does not precede language but is found within it; and also the 'idea that language is a commodity in which poems can be found'.[17] The collage technique which the poem uses goes back to the early days of modernism, but poets such as Eliot and Pound tended to contrast high culture with popular culture, emphasising the tensions between them. This poem ran references to that high culture together with snatches of advertising discourse, or clichéd language, collapsing what had previously seemed essential distinctions and suggesting that the images of poetry can be as commodified as fashionable garments.

Good-bye Matisse your paper collés
are OK its your occupation
art's such a nice place to bring up
your heroes wearing say
pushed up at the elbows a dark
blue sweatshirt in the wide chalky
world of exemplars where nothing happens its
water mark of a fools cap and bells
in the grain red harbour board
pilot cutters ply their lining up again the ACT IV
to port that I look upon cacoethes
scribendi a maze of figures tracking upon
their own plane the air
craft's here its the rest of your life.[18]

When in 1987 I co-edited an anthology of contemporary poetry with my husband, Murray Edmond, we included this poem and others by Leigh Davis. Theory, and discussion of the relativism of different poetics, had given us the freedom to look around at the diversity of contemporary poetry and made us interested in attempting some categorisations. We stressed that the 'majority of poets' in the anthology had 'responded to a break down of consensus, the loss of literary homogeneity, and traditional control of literary genealogy, with welcoming enthusiasm'.[19] In retrospect I think that what we were attempting in this anthology – a sense of freedom and taking a step back so that we could acknowledge diversity – is similar to what I am attempting in this book, in exploring different types of criticism.

Some major changes in teaching New Zealand literature came about in the late 1980s and early 1990s, partly because of theory and because of the increased consciousness of New Zealand as a post-colonial society. A new *Penguin Book of New Zealand Verse*, edited by Ian Wedde and Harvey McQueen with advice from Margaret Orbell, put Maori waiata and poems alongside the work of established European New Zealand poets. A whole new area of enquiry was opened up by the juxtaposition of, for example, Allen Curnow's 'House and Land' with Arapeta Awatere's lament 'He tangi mo Keepa Anaha Eehau', printed in both Maori and English.

Discussions in tutorials and lectures began to generate a range of new topics. We looked at the exclusiveness of literary history, and the need for certain communities to read texts in certain ways. We discussed oral cultures, and the problems of one culture describing another. We put early nineteenth-century New Zealand texts beside other accounts of Pacific exploration, for instance Herman Melville's *Typee*. And we compared the representation of Maori and Maori culture in Pakeha plays of the 1960s with the development of contemporary plays by Maori writers.

The common link that I was able to make amongst all these discussions was the idea that different readings or reading tendencies could be associated with different communities at different periods. Frederick Maning, for example, wrote *Old New Zealand* about his experiences as a Pakeha-Maori living in the north of New Zealand in the 1820s. We approached his account cautiously. We examined how it was read (when it was written and published) in the 1860s, and its relationship with the escalating conflicts between Maori and Pakeha. We looked too at how it was read later as a work of ethnography, and we updated our reading sceptically – Maori and Pakeha students and lecturers alike – for its unbalanced stress on the warlike character of Maori society. We even read the work psychoanalytically, finding symptoms of unease in its narrative.

These teaching experiences reinforced my interest in types of readings. They also made me aware of the interested (non-neutral) character of reading as a process for generating meaning. Questions about women, race and nation heightened my sense of searching for a way of talking about texts that was adequate for the end of the twentieth century.

My emphasis on reading was also a way of avoiding the emerging tendency to identify gender and race as competing candidates for being the most important factor in reassessing New Zealand writing and culture. Courses in the university and the department were, I thought, getting stuck on the perceived need to establish a priority. The editors of two significant 1990s publications, *The Oxford History of New Zealand Literature* and *The Writing of New Zealand* (an anthology of New Zealand non-fiction), both suggested that writing concerned with the legacies of colonisation was the most significant area of literary, historical, and theoretical innovation. Terry Sturm saw it as the 'most urgent' debate:

The new international discourses of post-colonialism and post-modernism, of linguistic theory, and of feminism, which have begun to find their way into debate about New Zealand literature, are also part of this contemporary context. 'Serious' writing by women has expanded dramatically in the past two decades . . . . It is a diverse, exploratory literature, written from a wide variety of perspectives, but its main tendency has been oppositional, challenging male accounts of New Zealand society and culture. Most urgent of all, however, have been the cultural questions posed, with increasing intensity throughout the 1980s, by debate about relations between Maori and Pakeha in New Zealand, fuelled by the resurgence of Maori claims to cultural self-determination under the terms of the Treaty of Waitangi.[20]

Alex Calder similarly asserted that an emphasis on any theme other than the 'intercultural' one would be mistaken:

I'm interested, not in some patriotic little flame that shines within, but in the kind of knowledge and perspectives being a New Zealander has entailed. To define those is to take part in a discussion that allows no one a last word; the best one can do is to have taken part in a timely enough fashion. Had this anthology not emphasised intercultural themes, had it supposed the action was elsewhere, it would seem to me to have been an inessential collection.[21]

Unlike Calder or Sturm I think that the 'action' needs to be seen more broadly, or less separately. Unless we look at our habits and types of reading, we will endlessly duplicate similar patterns – albeit on those important themes. We need to understand the conventions of reading and criticism, then we need new strategies to make our 'readings' fresh.

THEORIES OF READING

'Reader response' and 'reception' theory have been furthered over the last twenty years under the pressure of other forms of theory, and particularly because of a need to theorise mass media and media audiences. Early studies of reception tended to focus on historical response to literary texts. More recently, the study of reception has been the attempt to theorise what takes place when a text is read or a film is viewed. A variety of theories and approaches have been developed. Emphasis on readers (as against authors) has not necessarily meant a free-for-all concept of meaning. In fact, some critics have developed a new version of the determinability of the text by emphasising the ways in which the text tries to position the reader to approach it in a certain way.[22]

Many studies have had a strong philosophical and linguistic interest, but I am more concerned here with the multiple ways in which a text can be read and with the particular reading possibilities and constituencies clearly present in the New Zealand situation. Some post-structuralist approaches might be seen as undermining my methodology of comparing and contrasting readings. Stanley Fish, for instance, argues that every critic's reading of a text arises deductively out of a theory: whether of film, art, society or gender. Presumably Fish would also argue that there is no way of discussing readings in relation to each other because there is no Archimedian point, or neutral ground from which to conduct the discussion. In a related argument Roland Barthes has argued against the reading of readings, or the search for a 'meta' reading, because such an activity could only endlessly duplicate the subjectivity of interpretation. David Bordwell opens his book with a rejoinder to this position of Barthes:

> 'I do not know', remarks Roland Barthes, 'if reading is not, constitutively, a plural field of scattered practices, of irreducible effects, and if, consequently, the reading of reading, meta-reading, is not itself merely a burst of ideas, of fears, of delights, of oppressions'. Barthes's doubt seems to me too strong, a systematic meta-criticism of interpretation is a plausible project. Nonetheless the task does require some ground clearing.[23]

I acknowledge Barthes' complex interpretive *tour de force* in S/Z, but am more interested in the practical metacriticism of interpretation that Bordwell attempts. Also, I have found the explanations of post-structuralist philosopher Paul Ricoeur useful. Like Ricoeur, I see criticism as an ongoing dynamic; and like Bordwell I see 'readings' as made not found, but as having certain craft conventions: 'The perceiver is not a passive receiver of data but an active mobiliser of structures and processes (either 'hard-wired' or learned) which enable her to search for information relevant to the task and data at hand'.[24] This is how Bordwell describes the implications of this approach *vis-à-vis* film:

> Taking meaning-making as a constructive activity leads us to a fresh model of interpreting films. The critic does not burrow into the text, probe it, get behind its facade, dig to reveal its hidden meanings; the surface/depth metaphor does not capture the inferential process of interpretation. On the constructivist account, the critic starts with aspects of the film ('cues') to which certain meanings are ascribed. An interpretation is built upward, as it were, gaining solidity and scale as other textual materials and appropriate supports (analogies, extrinsic evidence, theoretical doctrines) are introduced. Another critic may come along and add a wing or story to the interpretation, or detach portions for use in a different project, or build a larger edifice that aims to include the earlier one, or knock the first one down and start again. Yet every critic . . . draws on craft conventions that dictate how proper interpretations are built.[25]

The implication of this for criticism is that we need to be aware of the 'craft conventions' involved in doing readings. My larger argument is also compatible with Bordwell's conclusion that the protocols of interpretation have become very tired and predictable and that we need fresh approaches. Again I enjoy Bordwell's familiarity with the academic world and the detached way in which he chronicles interpretive fashions. I hope to achieve a similar detachment in my accounts of readings, but I am also trying to develop a new approach (or 'poetics') of interpretation which may be similar to Bordwell's. Ricoeur suggests the possibility of a hermeneutics that would take in 'the parallel theory of the genesis of text, and of reading, and show the flow from one to another'. And while he acknowledges the 'tendency of French structuralism to treat a text as structure with its own laws that one may study objectively, not in the least mixing it with the expectations, preferences, prejudices, or the hopes and affinities of the reader, he is most concerned to make a case for a study that includes the different stages by which a reader becomes 'interested':

> Only, I would think that for me, this objective and absolutely disinterested study, in the right meaning of the word, therefore, without any relationship to our interest is merely an abstract and preparatory phase for an appreciation of the text from which we make our own flesh and blood through a sort of appropriation which makes from what was strange something appropriate and familiar. I don't believe that these two attitudes, one much more objective, which triumphs in structuralism, the other much more subjective, which triumphs in what I have just called appropriation, contradict each other, because they mutually bring each other forth. A completely objective study kills the text, because one operates on a cadaver. But inversely, reading which would be perfectly naive and would not have passed through all the mediations of an objective and structural approach would be only the projection of the subjectivity of the reader on the text. Consequently, it is necessary that subjectivity be held in some way at a distance and that the appropriation be in some way mediated by all the objectifying activities.[26]

The following chapters attempt to interrogate what David Bordwell has called 'the conventionality of criticism' and to develop a way of identifying and moving through typical readings in order to find one which seems to me 'right for now', but (inevitably) open to challenge from the next player.[27] The texts that provoke the readings I discuss are in some respects arbitrary but in other respects significant choices. They are works – fiction and some poems – that I taught in courses on New Zealand literature from the mid 1980s. As university texts they can all be regarded (even if only in a weak sense) as canonical texts. While discussing these texts with particular students I was also, as I have explained, reading theory and considering the relation of pedagogy and research methodology to the new ideas I was encountering. In the following chapters I try to keep in mind the methods that I have developed in my teaching. I have attempted to lead students to consider detail, to encourage close reading while also pushing them to generalise from those details, and then to make them aware of what they have just done – to identify, for instance, their own habits of interpretation, their assumptions, and their theoretical or ethical bases.[28]

The conventions of academic writing are also addressed in the style I have chosen to use. In order to evoke the experience of reading and not lose its sensuousness I put myself inside each reading, so to speak – inside its universe of discourse. This approach acknowledges that what are often thought of as theoretical or philosophical differences are in some respects aesthetic or taste preferences; or, in Bordwell's terms, readings are articulated through particular forms of rhetoric 'for rendering the conclusions of critical reasoning attractive to the interpreter's audience'.[29]

Toril Moi suggests, in the essay quoted earlier, that only 'a materialist analysis can provide a credible explanation of why the burden of Otherness is placed on this or that particular group in a given society at a given time'.[30] My feminism has taken a similar direction. And if in the more materialist readings here – the readings that I find most relevant to today's situation – one can find a preponderance of concern with the changing constructions of marriage, mothering, sex in marriage, childbirth and fertility, I am happy to acknowledge that when I began this book these were preoccupations. I wanted to consider them not in an abstract way, as a sort of 'gynaecological feminisim', but because there experiences were part of my own life. Other aspects of my intellectual temperament might be less obvious. Even as a child, round nine or ten years old, I can recall being preoccupied with 'sorting out' debates or feuds between my friends. I remember hurrying back from having lunch at home – we went home for lunch in those days – for that purpose. That preoccupation with identifying and sorting out differences has remained with me. New Zealand cultural criticism has seemed to me too diffuse; I like my feuds properly explicated. In fact, I have looked for opposition to make it easier for a clear exchange of ideas to take place. So this book is informed by the desire to distinguish differences, not necessarily to find a satisfactory synthesis (though that is sometimes attempted), but as a step towards understanding.

Anger about the perceived ownership of ideas and history, the sometimes arbitrary workings of academic power structures, as well as the desire to have what I say taken seriously have also provided an impetus for my work. But, not wanting my seriousness to become just another way of building a canon or a hierarchy, I have attempted a more pluralist, and perhaps humorous, strategy by which I make each act of interpretation serious unto itself, yet still open to challenge. Again, as a university teacher, in my working life I have been interested in the material and political situations of university English departments in a postcolonial society, and the relationship between gender and power in those departments. Yet if this account of my own position as a reader sounds like a purely personal analysis of my own bias or psychopathology, this introduction stands to identify the representative aspects of my development. This is the way in which I proceed, examining readings not in order to judge individual readers but to clarify possible 'subject positions'.

Looking at this project, I see that I am a facilitator and that what I am performing is a service, but also that I may be naive if I think that the facilitation and understanding (in these different readings) is powerful. May I not actually be fulfilling the role – often a woman's – of a servant? What can I say to this except that I acknowledge that naivety. Next time, perhaps, I shall do things differently. Or perhaps not.

CHAPTER ONE

•

'Bliss', and Why Ignorance Won't Do:
Current Reading Practices

[The critic can produce] really accurate, sharp, loving, descriptions of the appearance
of a work of art.
Susan Sontag *Against Interpretation* [1]

Perception is not a mere grasp of an abstract shape of a fiction or vivid sensations;
it is an effort after meaning.
David Bordwell *Making Meaning* [2]

This case study, comprises four different readings of a single story. Drawn
from student responses, they demonstrate the benefits (and pleasures) to be had
from multiple readings. Critical readers both inside and outside the academy are
so conscious now of the importance of the reception of writing – how a text is
interpreted according to the specific location, gender, and habits of the reader –
that we easily concur with the statement of Janet Staiger in her book *Interpreting
Film* that 'cultural artefacts are not containers with immanent meanings'.[3]

What, then, do we do with this awareness when we read, when we discuss
works with other readers or when we write criticism? In the case of criticism, the
idea that theory is always being exercised, that we are always reading from a
theoretical position, has led to some arbitrary pairings of 'reading with'. Sometimes
the theoretical position is explicitly identified and argued for within an essay or
article, but often it is not. As film theorist David Bordwell puts it, 'when interpreters
"apply" theory they do so in an *ad hoc* expansionist manner and theory often
functions as a black box; if it gets the job done there is no need to look inside'.[4] I
suggest that it *is* important to look inside – to look closely at the limitations or
political implications of 'reading with Freud' or 'reading with Chodorow'. This
can be done by putting such readings alongside one another, as in this chapter.
The presentation of opposed interpretations is a way of dramatising some of the
movements and changes which have taken place in the reception of cultural
products and in the application of cultural assumptions in the course of this century.

The sample text I want to discuss here is the well-known short story 'Bliss',
by Katherine Mansfield (1888–1923). Since it was published in 1918 this story
has elicited contradictory and heated responses from both writers and critics, so
it is an excellent candidate for this exercise. It was variously described by
contemporary writers as 'discordant' (Middleton Murry), a product of 'superficial
smartness', 'poor', 'cheap' (Virginia Woolf) and as a story in which 'the moral
implication is negligible' (T. S. Eliot).[5] Critical reaction in the 1970s and 1980s
has been more expository but not much more enthusiastic. Elaine Showalter has

used 'Bliss' as an example of Katherine Mansfield's 'brutality' in a fiction that she describes as typically 'punitive and cautionary' in a period when female writers emphasised female autonomy but then cut it down in a sleight of hand designed to protect themselves from their own failures and disappointments. This term 'punitive' concurs with C. K. Stead's description of Mansfield's theme of 'female identity fully realising itself only in a sexual relationship which at the same time is the source of pain, fear and ultimate destruction'. Kate Fullbrook, on the other hand, in a revalorisation of female modernism, values the painfulness of Mansfield's stories (and of 'Bliss' in particular) as a protest against oppression.[6]

The interpretations of this story voiced by my students do not have the scope of these comments, but are similarly intense and oppositional. Their interpretations tend to revolve around the main character, Bertha. Some of them see her as having a distorted state of mind, as being incapable of change, as someone who is locked into neurotic repetitions – continually getting herself worked up over nothing at all. Other students, influenced by feminist ideas, react to this as an attack on Bertha and argue that she is a marvellously alive and aware character, an isolated example of sincerity amongst the pretences and pretensions of the other characters. Moreover, these readers want to endorse the idea of woman as an artist of domesticity, which Bertha seems to epitomise. A third take by students is self-reflexive; it introduces the idea that both of the above attempts at interpretation are actually born of the emotional needs of the reader to resolve the story.

Three of my four readings are based, then, on student responses which I have extended by interpreting their philosophical bases into, respectively, a Freudian, a cultural feminist and a Lacanian reading.[7] The fourth reading, which I call modernist and historicist, is more stylistically and contextually based. Following that, I raise the possibility of other readings,and draw out the implications of my strategies.

READING ONE: THE TALE OF AN HYSTERIC

Many readers have understood 'Bliss' as a story with Freudian implications without really noticing their own presuppositions; I shall spell out the argument rather explicitly. At the same time, I hope to raise questions about the nature of such an approach. What exactly are we doing when we cite Freud in confirmation of the interpretation of a story? Does it make this story a case history? Does it universalise (as female) those qualities of underdeveloped ego and sexual identity which we see in Bertha? Freud certainly did draw out general points about femininity from the fact of female hysteria. These are questions to bear in mind, as they will provoke other questions and problematise the application of theory.

'Bliss' is the tale of an hysteric; that is, it is the story of a biologically adult woman whose repetitious and excitable behaviour suggests we cannot quite trust her version of events. It seems, in Freud's words, that some 'incompatible occurrence' has taken place in her 'ideational life' such that she has set up a complex chain of evasions and defences.[8] Bertha's infantilisation is also indicated by her name – Birth(a) Young, i.e. a very young child. (Incidentally, Bertha was also the name of the woman who was Freud's first subject in his study of hysteria, known in the case history as Anna O.) We can see Mansfield's Bertha as having similarities to the symptomatology and perhaps the 'aetiology' (causality) of what, in a number of famous case histories (written close to the time when 'Bliss' was published), Freud described as 'hysteria' and 'hysterical neuroses'.

Bertha Young is an intelligent woman and the story shows her searching for an explanation for her heightened mental and physical states. This search is initially constituted in a series of exclamations and questions about her life. These exclamations and questions are put in a series of constriction and release images – a fiddle in a case, not to be taken out; a coat enveloping a body, and then thrown off; a baby in the arms of a woman who is not her mother. The images set up and anticipate the denouément of the story – fur-coated Pearl in Harry's arms – almost as if Bertha's own metaphor was out to get her from the start. First there is Bertha's image for her own body: 'How idiotic civilisation is! Why be given a body if you have to keep it shut up in a case like a rare, rare fiddle?', which is echoed in the image of her baby: 'How absurd it was. Why have a baby if it has to be kept – not in a case like a rare, rare fiddle – but in another woman's arms?'[9]

Yet Bertha also sees herself as extremely privileged and happy. She has everything she could want: 'She was young. Harry and she were as much in love as ever, and they got on together splendidly and were really good pals. She had an adorable baby. They didn't have to worry about money.'[10] In a similar kind of explanation, she attributes her feelings of loss of control and emotional intensity – an intensity that is threatening to tip her over into hysteria – to the societal conventions. By speaking of 'how idiotic civilisation is', she implicitly criticises British society that pampers and protects middle-class women, but narrows their lives by making them give their babies to nurses to rear, making their loneliness and isolation a measure of their social status.

Is Bertha's explanation for her state of mind sufficient? Freud suggests that though one must always ask a patient how she herself would explain her neuroses, one must keep to the principle of not adopting the patient's belief without a thorough critical examination. In Bertha's case we come to realise that her euphoric descriptions of her life are a defence against acknowledging dissatisfaction and pain. Even her partial explanation is a further attempt at denial, which attempts to displace the reasons for her hysteria on to the societal circumstances of her life and the distant idea of civilisation. This second line of defence is akin to the initially very plausible explanation which Dora, in 'Fragment of an Analysis of a Case of Hysteria', gives for her anger with Herr K and her father.[11] Bertha's partial and fragmented explanation (she frequently corrects herself: 'No, that is not quite what I mean') puts the weight of responsibility on 'civilisation', and this can be seen as one of a series of associations which lead away from the real cause of her anxiety.

A part of Bertha's state of mind is characterised by her sense of her own fluidity. She identifies herself as being like particular objects in her house and garden, as if dissolving the limits of her self. When she goes upstairs to dress she discovers that her clothes laid out on her bed are the colours of the pear tree: 'A white dress, a string of jade beads, green shoes and stockings. It wasn't intentional. She had thought of this colour scheme hours before she stood at the drawing room window'.[12] She objectifies herself as a beautiful thing, and is more interested in herself as an object of love than she is in loving. Perhaps she is unable to bring together tenderness and sensuality – Freud's description of a normally adjusted sexuality – because of her narcissism.

The fact that she sees the pear tree, which she identifies with so closely, as non-generative, frozen in its beauty, with no sign of the prospect of future blossom ('not a single bud'), nor of decay ('or a faded petal'),[13] reinforces this interpretation. Although Bertha seems to be extremely aware of herself as a sensual being, this awareness is contained within herself in such a way that it, like the pear tree's richness, is unable to be acted on. For example, she thinks of herself as having 'a bright glowing place in her bosom' with 'a little shower of sparks coming from it' that is about to break into a fire, but is unable to acknowledge the association of this ardour and blissful sensuality with more explicitly sexual images.[14] Images of the pear tree rising against the moon, and the cats sneaking through the garden prompt a partial reaction in her, which again suggests a setting up of a defence against some repressed sexual memory.

> Down below, in the garden beds, the red and yellow tulips heavy with flowers, seemed to lean upon the dusk. A grey cat, dragging its belly, crept across the lawn, and a black one, its shadow, trailed after. The sign of them, so intent and so quick, gave Bertha a curious shiver.
> 'What creepy things cats are!' she stammered, and she turned away from the window and began walking up and down . . .[15]

In the study of an individual's symptomatic behaviour there is often an evasion or a supposed story which is put in place of the actual repressed memory. Bertha's focus on the attractiveness of Pearl Fulton, the single woman who is her latest 'find', can be seen as just such an evasion: 'They had met at the club and Bertha had fallen in love with her as she always did fall in love with beautiful women who had something strange about them.' Bertha's conviction that it is Pearl Fulton who is the reason for her excitement on this evening, and that Pearl is about to impart some marvellous secret to her, indicates a sensual interest in Pearl but one which is safe, diffused and not threateningly physical like the specifically sexual demands of the black cat for grey cat, or of her husband Harry for her.

Being close to Pearl and being aware of how 'beautiful' and 'strange' she is causes Bertha to think of her husband. Her words suggest that the hidden (until this moment) symptom of Bertha's hysteria is frigidity:

> For the first time in her life Bertha Young desired her husband.
>
> Oh, she'd loved him – she'd been in love with him, of course, in every other way, but just not in that way. And equally of course she'd understood that he was different. They'd discussed it so often. It had worried her dreadfully at first to find she was so cold, but after a time it had not seemed to matter.[16]

But even this truth-telling of Bertha's may represent a 'conversion' of affect: Bertha is able to fantasise about being alone with her husband because she is unconsciously aware that his interests are directed to Pearl Fulton. She is safe in her realm of fantasy.

Freud, in his 'Three Essays on Sexuality', suggests that cold women – women who are 'anaesthetic' to their husbands – are so because of a failure to properly reject their desire for their parents. Initially children's sexual impulses are directed towards their parents but this is overcome, rejected and repudiated by the time of puberty, and it is this detachment from parental authority that is so important for the progress of civilisation between the new generation and the old. Bertha Young is one of those who, as Freud puts it, is 'held back'. Freud describes such cases as being 'mostly girls' who 'persist in their childish love far beyond puberty' and later in their marriages 'lack the capacity to give their husbands what is due to them; they make cold wives and remain sexually anaesthetic'.[17] Bertha's relationship with Pearl Fulton can also be seen as belonging to this formulation – 'an exaggerated need for affection and an equally exaggerated horror of the real demands made by sexual life' which Freud characterises as evidence of a poorly negotiated Oedipus complex.[18] She, Bertha, can also be seen as unable to meet a real erotic demand because her behaviour is dominated by 'an opposition between reality and fantasy'.[19]

Towards the end of the story Bertha is anxious about the charged atmosphere in the room, a charge which she associates with her own frightening new anticipation of being alone with her husband and her new-found desire for him:

> . . . something strange and almost terrifying darted into Bertha's mind. And this something blind and smiling whispered to her: 'Soon these people will go. The house will be quiet – quiet. The lights will be out. And you and he will be alone together in the dark room – the warm bed. . . .'[20]

But, in order to cover or repress this frighteningly intense image, she jumps from the chair and runs over to the piano: '"What a pity someone does not play!" she cried. "What a pity somebody does not play"'. This cover-up is actually an expression of desire. It expresses what Bertha was trying to say earlier. It is not that it is sad that the rare, rare fiddle *is shut up in a case*. What is sad, what leaves an excess of desire, is that it is not *played*. Thus the word *play* occurs again associatively. Bertha wants to be played upon, to make music. However, Bertha's desire cannot find sexual expression, as the end of the story confirms. This final event of the story can be seen as a kind of restaging of the primal scene that has presumably been traumatic in Bertha's case.[21] The violence (or what Bertha perceives as violence) of the moment of assignation between her friend, Pearl Fulton, and her husband, Harry, indicates that she has repressed certain memories of sexual trauma or sexual experience which are repeated back to her here:

> . . . she turned her head towards the hall. And she saw . . . Harry with Miss Fulton's coat in his arms and Miss Fulton with her back turned to him and her head bent. He tossed the coat away, put his hands on her shoulders and turned her violently to him. His lips said: 'I adore you' and Miss Fulton laid her moonbeam fingers on his cheeks and smiled her sleepy smile. Harry's nostrils quivered; his lips curled back in a hideous grin while he whispered: 'Tomorrow', and with her eyelids Miss Fulton said: 'Yes'.[22]

This experience could be a changing point in the life of Bertha Young – an occasion where, in Freud's words, 'the barrier erected by repression can fall before the onslaught of a violent emotional excitement produced by a real cause; it is possible for a neurosis to be overcome by reality'.[23] But, in this story, we are left with an unknown outcome: Bertha may mature under this onslaught, or she may become even more traumatised, neurotic, hysterical, divided between fantasy and reality, unable to bring together tenderness and sensuality, suspended in a typically feminine immanence. In the words of an Ezra Pound poem of the period she may be a woman 'dying piecemeal of a kind of emotional anaemia'.[24]

READING TWO: A STORY ABOUT UNIQUELY FEMALE IMAGES OF CREATIVITY AND SHARED FEMALE IMAGINATION

Is it possible to change the centre of the story and read with Bertha instead of against her, to empathise with her instead of analysing her as neurotic? Bertha Young, with her vitality and ardent nature, can be seen as standing against a patriarchal society that stifles women into roles of wife, daughter, spinster and servant according to their relationships with men.

> Although Bertha Young was thirty she still had moments like this when she wanted to run instead of walk . . .[25]

Bertha undercuts expectations of the decorum appropriate to a married woman of her age. Her name, stated immediately, suggests the birth (Bertha) of a new (Young) woman. She is a woman who has discovered the power and beauty of things in themselves: 'she wanted to . . . take dancing steps on and off the pavement, to bowl a hoop, to throw something up in the air and catch it again, or to stand still and . . . laugh at – nothing – at nothing, simply'. Her spontaneity also indicates that she is resisting notions of progress and 'means to ends', which reduce the ability of individuals to fully experience themselves and others in the present time.

As Bertha enters the house it is as if she enters a place of female community, where few words are needed to convey meanings and where familiar and nourishing rituals are followed. On this particular day Bertha is full of a new kind of excitement which she doesn't properly understand. The excitement is exhilarating, making her unable to tolerate constrictions so that she throws off her coat ('she could not bear the tight clasp of it another moment') as soon as she enters the house.

The interior fits her mood: the dining room is described as 'dusky and quite chilly', suggesting a churchlike space, prescient with meaning. The arranging of fruit that takes place here is an aesthetic ritual associated with the female world. The servant, Mary, bears 'the fruit on a tray and with it a glass bowl, and a blue dish, very lovely with a strange sheen on it, as though it had been dipped in milk'. Bertha is a kind of high priestess of the art of fruit arrangement; her hands have not fetched or picked this fruit but she has chosen it and now she places it in the right way, in the beautiful bowls. Rather than seeming trivial or exploitative, this task is described in glowing, almost holy terms:

> There were tangerines and apples stained with strawberry pink. Some yellow pears smooth as silk; some white grapes covered with a silver bloom and a big cluster of purple ones.

and the lines that follow suggest another aspect of femininity celebrated:

> These last she had bought to tone in with the new dining room carpet. Yes, that did sound rather far-fetched and absurd, but it was really why she had bought them. She had thought in the shop: 'I must have some purple ones to bring the carpet up to the table'. And it had seemed quite sense at the time.

Bertha is using the vocabulary of an artist and though she is almost apologetic about her analogy, she is nevertheless convinced of it:

> When she had finished with them and had made two pyramids of these bright round shapes, she stood away from the table to get the effect – and it really was most curious. For the dark table seemed to melt into the dusky light and the glass dish and the blue bowl to float in the air. This, of course, in her present mood, was so incredibly beautiful . . .[26]

Susan Gubar in her essay 'The Birth of Artist as Heroine' describes Katherine Mansfield as 'redefining art so that it ceases to exclude women's crafts and instead pays tribute to the domestic mythology of the female community'.[27] From Gubar's angle this scene can be seen as depicting, even honouring, Bertha as an artist of interiors whose study of the tricks of perspective, and the aesthetic impact of her fruit arrangement, is as important as such questions are to a painter or sculptor. Gubar's argument is that modernist women writers created at this time a series of feminine utopias in 'a moment of exultant delivery' before the 'rapid acceptance of Freudian theory after World War One which coincided with the decline of the Feminist movement'. And she sees Mansfield's later work as containing 'key examples of these feminine utopias' and of 'the heroine as the artist'.[28]

Looked at in this way, Bertha can be seen as an artist who creates out of her fruitful medium an image of female generativity: the pyramid-piled fruit in the bowls stand up like a pair of luscious breasts – fecund, promising, flavoursome, with a lovely glow like the sheen of a woman's skin.[29] And the glass dish has the look of having been dipped in milk. The female symbolism further explains why

Bertha is so entranced – she herself has created this sign of femininity and it has a mysterious and powerful effect on her: 'This, of course, in her present mood, was so incredibly beautiful. . . . She began to laugh.' The powerful image and its association with glowing breasts naturally enough reminds Bertha of something: 'And she seized her bag and coat and ran upstairs to the nursery' where her baby – little B – is being given supper:

> The baby had on a white flannel gown and a blue woollen jacket, and her dark fine hair was brushed up into a funny little peak.[30]

The picture of the little girl baby recalls the intensity and colour of the breasted bowls on the table – 'blue', 'white' and 'dark', and again the generative power of connection between women, particularly mother and daughter.

The description of the dining room indicates the liminal state that Bertha is in. She stands on an edge where she could easily be absorbed into the *dusky* tableau in front of her. And as the narrative proceeds there are several more moments which suggest her 'plasticity' of character. It is, as Gubar suggests of the women in Mansfield's later 'Prelude', as if Bertha inhabits 'the blurred boundaries between shore and water, the perfect setting to represent the blurred demarcations between self and other during the "oceanic" time of infancy when the child thinks of the mother as itself'.[31]

The story can be seen as exemplifying the suggestion that women in their adult life preserve this powerful sense of blurring and fluidity, an erotic interdependence with others that 'endows female subjectivity with greater complexity, greater plasticity, and greater empathy'.[32] This latter quote refers to formulations about the psychology of women made by contemporary feminist psychologist Nancy Chodorow, who claims that women's psychology departs from men's because women do not need to separate from their initial identification with their mothers in the same way that men do.[33]

Bertha senses 'holiness' in her moment with Pearl Fulton. She comes to a consciousness of her female empathy and ability to erotically become one with the other woman, in a kind of psychic sensuality. Her interaction with Pearl seems rich in signs:

> And still in the back of her mind, there was the pear tree. It would be silver now, in the light of poor dear Eddie's moon, silver as Miss Fulton, who sat there turning a tangerine in her slender fingers that were so pale that a light seemed to come from them.
> What she simply couldn't make out – what was miraculous – was how she should have guessed Miss Fulton's mood so exactly and so instantly.[34]

It is as if the occasion is a beautiful thing created between Bertha and Pearl – an opera of moments, hiatus, signs, duet and solo or a canvas with a rich combination of foreground, background and chiaroscuro, but still a part of the fluid, plastic, female subjectivity that is constructed in the story. It is set in clear contrast to male characters whose ideas about identity and whose categories of experience are very cut and dried. Bertha's husband, Harry, enters the house and joins its female community late in the story, but he is bent on controlling, compartmentalising and avoiding the diffuse experience the women offer. This is shown in his movement from one discrete environment to another: office, taxi, home. His attempt, albeit humorous and sometimes deceitful, to reduce everything to a simple biological explanation also suggests that he reduces tenderness and sensuality to a matter of genital sex – an insight substantiated by the gesture of liaison and conquest we see him making at the end of the story.

Similarly Harry denies any relationship with his baby daughter whom he claims he will be interested in only 'when she has a lover'. Again, this statement is jokingly made but suggests that a professional man of his type can think of a woman only in terms of male-oriented relationships. In 'A Society', from her collection of essays *Monday or Tuesday*, Virginia Woolf sketches in a portrait of such a man:

> . . . they teach him to cultivate his intellect. He becomes a barrister, a civil servant, a general, an author, a professor. Every day he goes to the office. Every year he produces a book. He maintains a whole family by the products of his brain – poor devil! Soon he cannot come into a room without making us all feel uncomfortable; he condescends to every woman he meets, and dares not tell the truth even to his own wife; instead of rejoicing our eyes we have to shut them if we are to take him in our arms. True, they console themselves with stars of all shapes, ribbons of all shades, and incomes of all sizes – but what is to console us? . . . Oh, Cassandra, for Heaven's sake let us devise a method by which men can bear children! It is our only chance. For unless we provide them with some innocent occupations, we shall get neither good people nor good books . . . [35]

In Woolf's description we see perhaps a measure of sympathy for this man who is excluded from an experience of innocence and commonality, who is forced by circumstance into lonely self-importance, which in turn forces him into deceitfulness. This man is locked out of relationships by status and gender, and because it is women who mother, it is only women who can retain that wealth of experience and relationship. Men are unable to enter the freedom of women's time which is time outside history – because history itself is a male construct.

Male jealousy can also be seen as determining the end of the story when Bertha witnesses her special friend in a moment of assignation with her husband. The male system of power, with its need to control women, has intervened even here (or especially here) in this moment of intimacy between two women. What will be the outcome? Will Bertha understand this betrayal as trivial alongside the fluid radiance of women and the merging identities she has experienced? Or will it destroy her, as so often women are destroyed by the forces of patriarchy?

READING THREE: 'BLISS' AS ENDLESS DEFERRAL

Both the readings we have looked at so far seal up the meaning of the story, locking its ambiguities safely away from the reader. So goes the argument of a completely different perspective on Mansfield's story produced by Philip Armstrong, an MA student in the year I put forward my original case study, containing only three readings, as a seminar. I felt impelled by the very difference of this approach to include it.

Armstrong's reading of 'Bliss' was produced as course work for a theory paper and is Lacanian (informed by the ideas of psychoanalyst Jacques Lacan, who conjoined a semiotic theory of language to Freudian theory), suggesting that we come into being-as-ourselves only as we speak, and are spoken, in language. Language is construed as constantly capable of slippage (in meaning) because all words are meaningful only in relation to other words; identity, because it emerges in language and naming, is seen to be equally fluid. This, then, is obviously a more sophisticated approach because it brings in reflexive questions about language and fiction. It is an approach usually taken by advanced students, as it is less accessible to undergraduate students who make the Freudian and cultural feminist interpretations because these understandings are a part of their cultural background.

The discourses that Armstrong attaches to 'Bliss' are those of Lacan and Shoshana Felman (writing on 'The Turn of the Screw'). Armstrong argues that Mansfield's story can be seen as being like Henry James's 'The Turn of the Screw' in that it is a literary work that has a 'ghost effect' because it 'exerts a seemingly magical power in demanding from the reader a reading act, a critical re-action which tends always towards repetition of the action of the story'. The story is capable, therefore, 'of implicating and interrogating its own readers'.[36]

Armstrong describes the story 'Bliss' as one 'full of presence that is absence', and that the reader's temptation is 'to fill in the empty spaces'. But instead of doing this 'in-filling' he suggests there are other possibilities. He draws attention to Felman's contention that Lacan's new type of analysis opens up a radically new assumption that what can be read (and perhaps should be read) is not just meaning but lack of meaning; that significance lies not just in consciousness, but specifically in its disruption Armstrong suggests reading 'Bliss' as Felman read 'The Turn of the Screw', 'not to *capture* the mystery's solution, but to follow, rather, the significant path of its flight', to ask how does the meaning of the story, whatever it may be, rhetorically take place through permanent displacement, textually take shape and take effect: *take flight?*[37]

Armstrong goes on to argue that the meaning of 'Bliss' cannot be closed round sexuality. This is something both of the earlier readings could be said to do. In the Freudian reading the explanation is frigidity, fear of sex and lack of release; in the cultural feminist reading, the explanation is Bertha's polyvalent and therefore subversive female sexuality. But when we read the story in these ways, he suggests, we push its problems of inscription away from us. Attempting to tie down meanings, are we perhaps avoiding the ambiguities it has generated? Are we frightened of the story's aporia, its erasures, elisions, gaps and unanswered questions?

But could we not take another step, suggesting that the ambiguity of meaning in this story matches the ambiguity of sexuality? This would be in line with Felman's idea that 'sexuality is rhetoric, since it essentially consists of ambiguity: it is the coexistence of dynamically antagonistic meanings. Sexuality is the *division and divisiveness of meaning*; it is meaning *as* division, meaning *as* conflict'.[38]

The story opens with Bertha's grasping for words: 'she wants to stand still and laugh at – at nothing – at nothing, simply'. That 'nothing, simply', which forms the climax of the first sentence, is the first of a series of lacunae which give, in Lacan's words, a 'punctiform' shape, a form filled with holes. Philip Armstrong introduces his 'glance' at the story with the acknowledgement of the presence of an absence:

> The temptation is to fill that empty space with something – to say, as Dunbar does, that this represents Bertha's repression of her lesbian desires for Pearl. But to do so is to repeat what Barbara Johnson calls 'the gesture of blankfilling' . . . So I will leave the gap gaping, and note its progress through the text; as repeated only by words like 'nothing', dashes (–) which show a failure of words, a hesitation before signification; or the ellipses (. . .) suggesting a slide into the abyss of the wordless; or space between paragraphs (   )[39]

Armstrong sees other critics as closing down even the aporia of the story by regarding them as 'connections in disguise'.[40] He questions whether or not a blank is only, or always, a connection in disguise. He reminds us of Bertha groping for words and at the same time feeling in her bag for the key' to her front door.[41] He then goes on to parallel our reading the story with Bertha looking for her key: 'a key of course being something that fills a hole to open a door that allows the continuation of an itinerary'. But in this case the key is lost. So, how to continue with this reading when the text itself refuses to discover such a key'?[42] Armstrong's suggestion is that the entry point to the story must then be not via the key, but via the letterbox at which Bertha keeps rattling; that is, the reader must keep pushing at the openings, at the gaps, where messages come through.

When the story is read this way, other gaps and elisions appear. Armstrong suggests a new way of reading the 'fruit bowl' passage. Instead of seeing images of female fertility, he notes something about language. Commenting on that 'most curious space' that opens up between the fruit bowls and the ground where 'the dark table seemed to melt into the dusky light and the glass dish and the blue bowl to float in the air', Armstrong notes the detachment of the signifier from the signified: 'Those fruit bowls, so obviously symbols of something or other, take on such autonomy that they fly off into the air by themselves'.[43]

We can also point out that the adjectives 'glass' and 'blue', applied respectively here to the bowl and the dish, are reversed on the next page. What else are we observing here than the endless shifting of a chain of signifiers? What we become suspicious of is the attempt to possess the signifiers, or to fix them to one particular locality: for these are always only signifiers which are continually misappropriated and repeatedly misplaced, elements in the dimension of the Symbolic, not the Real. As Armstrong puts it:

> Later in the story Eddie Warren, who is a poet and therefore supposed to exercise some kind of mastery over words, tells of the fear of 'travelling through eternity in a timeless taxi'. Another expression, like Bertha's hysteria, of the anxiety occasioned by what Derrida calls the 'endless drifting off-course' of language, the potential for the letter to always already not arrive at its destination. In Mansfield's story, this wayward itinerary of the signifier is represented by slippage in time as much as place . . .[44]

And the 'most significant slippage of all is that effected in this story by the Pear Tree'.[45] The combination of understatement and superlative, so characteristic of Bertha's social milieu, becomes a symptom of unfocused uneasiness about the inadequacy of words. For the reader and for Bertha, the pear tree seems to put an end to all this uneasiness – to the endless itinerary of expectation and disappointment. The pear tree is superlative: 'in fullest, richest bloom; it stood perfect, as though becalmed' and 'it was so still it seemed, like the flame of a candle, to stretch up, to point, to quiver in the bright air, to grow taller and taller as they gazed – almost to touch the rim of the round silver moon'.[46] Its stillness offers a denial of exchange, a resistance to the continuous slippage of signification. Here there seems to be a congruence of signifier and signified – that longed-for reaching of the Symbolic through to the Real. And its phallic description gives it the position of a transcendental signifier. This would seem to be the privileged term – the key to fill all the gaps.

But the pear tree proves to be as subject to dispossession and misappropriation as any other signifier – and the division of the pear tree is paralleled in a pattern of duplications and duplicities of the characters. Bertha's disappointment at the pear tree's refusal to be a symbol of her life temporarily parallels the reader's disappointment at not finding the key or centre to the story. At first Bertha seems to be imaged in the pear tree. And in a shared equation Pearl is like the moon – with her silver colours and her 'moonbeam fingers', but Eddie too is like the moon with his white socks and tie, and Pearl's name links her with the pear. The signifiers are involved in slippage. Bertha's attempt to identify with the pear tree and to attribute absolute meaning to it is a quixotic attempt undermined by the multiplying meanings. And at the end of the story even Bertha's own 'lovely pear tree' is appropriated by Pearl in 'the purloining of a letter, the prolonging of the itinerary of a signifier'.[47]

Pearl's appropriation of the tree can be seen (among other things) as castration of Bertha through symbolic theft of the phallic signifier. In these Lacanian terms this castration is the primordial moment when the body senses its split from the Real – because the Real is that which is not expressible and so is known only in moments of stress. Elizabeth Wright explains the notion of such a trauma:

> This experience cannot be included in the Imaginary, the realm of illusory wholeness, nor can it be part of the Symbolic, the domain which grants a conditional identity. This traumatic moment can return in psychosis as the experience of the 'fragmented body', unique for every subject, remainder and reminder of this fracture, appearing in art as images of gross dismemberment.[48]

Narrative as the compulsion to tell a story, or the attempt to catch up retrospectively on this traumatic separation, is thus a universal desire, the consequence of being a subject in the world. We need to tell the happening (of loss/castration) again and again – a happening which (in the case of 'Bliss') we see briefly implied in the lips of Harry and the eyelids of Pearl before we are forced on in the itinerary of the story. Thus, Armstrong concludes:

> Mansfield leaves us dangling at the edge, refusing to show us whether the writer, like the critic, sees everything after all or has some critical blind spot which will keep her/him trapped forever in that circuit, that triangle, repeating endlessly the blindness of writing and reading, which thereby become again the repeat of the repeat.[49]

Armstrong's reading discovers 'Bliss' to be a story that is not only ambiguous but about ambiguity. And this is not only the ambiguity of particular signifiers and signifieds, but about the very process of making meaning in a world where there is only an endless slippage of signifiers because meaning can be generated only by one signifier's difference from another. And access to 'reality' is only at best a glimpse of wrongness and fragmentation.

•

The addition of Lacanian theory to the reading of the story has a curious effect – it is as if it enlarges the story's moody regretful tone to take up all the space of interpretation. It has been suggested that Lacanian theory particularly suits literary critics because the themes of ambiguity and loss implied in the slippage of signifiers fits in with a tone of nostalgic sexualised sadness that has been part of literary studies since Romanticism. Even impressionistically used, as in Armstrong's account, this Lacanian discourse also makes certain assumptions that become relentless in their own way. And although the Lacanian account is less normative than the Freudian, because it adds a complex theory of language, it is still as 'phallogocentric'.

READING FOUR: A MODERNIST READING

The first two of the three readings I have put forward concentrate on the question of the subject. They argue over Bertha – whether she is maimed or whole. It is interesting to see how the same details can be read differently, according to changing fashions and perceptions. Bertha is a character who provokes questions of interpretation because she is in a liminal or on-the-edge state, and the interpretation of that as hysteria and neuroticism, or as special insight and perceptiveness, can be a touchstone to individual and social values. But is there a way out of these oppositions?

Certainly the Lacanian reading shifts the ground of our understanding. But if it shows 'Bliss' to be 'about' the fragile construction of subjects in language, then couldn't a great many stories be similarly described? The playfulness of the reading is revealing (not least because it problematises its own status as interpretation) but it seems a very specialised procedure. An approach that focuses on social and cultural specificity retains a strong use-value. One such approach is an attempt to read the story in terms of intellectual history, in a reconstruction of modernist thinking. This has the advantage of shifting attention away from questions of subjectivity.

What follows, then, is a reading that instead of favouring any of the characters, or a combination of the characters, distances them all in a satire on the construction of their perceptions. Middleton Murry didn't like this story because of what he called its mixture of 'lyricism and satire'.[50] He must then have seen it in two parts: the serious (if poetic) evocation of character and situation, and the overstated easy digs made at the fashionable crowd of aesthetes and dilettantes in the latter part of the story ('white socks', 'Why must it always be tomato soup?', 'Eternity in a taxi'). I would suggest, however, that the story uses the obvious satire at its centre as a kind of metonymy for its whole method. Thus I would argue that both the Freudian and cultural feminist readings that I have carried through – in a kind of 'masquerade' – are in themselves targets of satire in the story.

First, the Freudian reading: here the real explanation for Bertha is her 'sexual anaesthesia' and her inability to uncover and satisfy her feelings, while Harry and Pearl Fulton are examples of functioning normalcy. But, does not the story, within itself, undermine Harry and call into question his actions and words, particularly the hearty physical explanations of character that he 'turns on' for Bertha? Harry's caustic asides are efforts to reduce and explain behaviour in terms of 'good stomach', 'liver frozen', 'pure flatulence' or 'kidney disease' but they turn out to be cover for his real motives. In short, Harry's physical explanations about women are so patently an excuse or disguise, a way of controlling and impressing them, that by association this tends to undermine other physical or medical ways of explaining Bertha's behaviour, including a Freudian reading of the story.

By this I mean that Freud's explanation (of femininity and desire) was based on a first principle of biological difference. And this suggests a genital base to behaviour, all conventional behaviour being able to be seen as governed by a complex web of desire, displacement of desire, association (and so on) but proceeding from the physical difference. It can be argued that in his case histories Freud was attacking contemporary prudery by focusing especially on the interpretation of women's behaviour and psychic lives. The impulse was liberatory but it also sprang from seeing women as paradigmatic examples of repressed sexuality.

Mansfield, I would argue, is aware of how the language of subjectivity and morality, particularly associated with women, was at this period being exposed (by the new science of psychoanalysis) as a language of repressed genital desire. Nancy Armstrong, writing about the power of domestic fiction from the eighteenth to the twentieth century, argues that 'the turn of the century preoccupation with the unconscious' was part of a new emphasis on the scientific as against the personal which aimed to undermine a morality of personal choice and sexual refusal which had been developed through the previous century in fiction by both men and women – a morality very much associated with femininity.[51] Seen in this way, Freud's 'discovery' of the hysterical characteristics of femininity could be regarded as another sortie in the war of the sexes, aimed to undermine female influence.

Mansfield's story shows up the new language of analysis in the way feminist criticisms of the Dora case study have shown up Freud.[52] Both expose the one who makes the analysis as implicated in his own scenario, and with personal gain to make from seeing the women in question as not in control of their bodies or their minds, not to be trusted to know themselves. In the story Bertha's own self-diagnosis – 'she was so cold' – could be seen as words put into her mind by Harry (as is the 'list' of material happinesses) as a convenient explanation which sanctions his behaviour. Indeed, the Freudian idea of sexuality as an ultimate explanation and of 'coldness' as a problem that women have (nothing to do with the man) seems to have entered both Bertha's and Harry's thinking. Bertha seems to have taken on the idea of her lack of sexual response being her own fault, and is pathetically thankful for her husband's willingness to discuss 'her' problem: 'they were so frank with each other. They were such good pals. That was the best of being modern.'

So, the story satirises the milieu, and part of that milieu's new interest was in frankness about sexual matters and psychological explanations for behaviour. Their taste in ideas is shown alongside their taste in clothes, food and entertainment. Two years after this story was written Mansfield commented: 'I am amazed at the sudden "mushroom growth" of cheap psychoanalysis everywhere. Five novels one after the other are based on it: it's in everything. And I want to prove it won't do – it's turning Life into a case.'[53]

The story can be seen as setting the sexual explanation of behaviour up for contemplation, rather than presenting it as a given. This can also be related to Mansfield's comments on D.H. Lawrence's work. In her letters Mansfield reacts against Lawrence's sexual explanation of everything not because she is prudish (as we have seen there is desire in her story and sexual imagery) but because she is not satisfied with his 'exaggerated insistence on sexual differences'.[54] She wrote in 1921 about Lawrence: 'When he gets on to the subject of *maleness* I lose all patience. What nonsense it all is. And he must know it is. His style changes – he can no longer write. He *begs the question*. I can't forgive him for that it's a sin'.[55] The question that he is begging appears to be: 'Is there such a thing as maleness?' For Katherine Mansfield, when she reads Lawrence, that question hovers unanswered between her and the writing. It gets in the way, because he doesn't attempt to answer it, because he assumes an essential 'maleness', and, when he writes about women, a 'female principle'.

A more famous comment of Mansfield's about Lawrence is this one:

> I shall *never* see sex in trees, sex in running brooks, sex in stones & sex in everything. The number of things that are really phallic from fountain pen fillers onwards! But I shall have my revenge one of these days – I suggested to Lawrence that he should call his cottage The Phallus & Frieda thought it was a very good idea . . . [56]

In 'Bliss', though, Mansfield does see sex in trees – the pear tree which, as Pearl and Bertha watched, 'seemed, like the flame of a candle, to stretch up, to point, to quiver in the bright air, to grow taller and taller as they gazed . . .' So the avowal of 'no sex in trees' seems to support my suggestion that she is in fact parodying a certain newly fashionable attitude to the world – that tendency to see sex in everything.

Here I am calling more attention to the intense ambiguity of the sign, for if this is the masculinist version (Lawrence's), then the idea of a female principle (ethos, prose) is also parodied in the story in the image of those luscious heaps (pyramids) of grapes: breasts in fruit. This parody is important because the feminine aesthetic values that I put forward in the second reading were also part and parcel of the period round 1918 when the story was written – ideas of a feminine prose and a feminine aesthetic. So, again we can argue that we are looking at Mansfield's questioning of versions of reality which were fashionable ideas of the period.

This satire is also shown up by the plot Bertha's idea that she had a special relationship with Pearl is shattered by the betrayal at the end of the story. The high expectation about relations between women – 'I believe this does happen very, very rarely between women, never between men' – is exposed as Bertha's illusion. This exposé is crafted as an ironic comment on the romanticisation of women in terms of a female principle. This latter is a theme in much of Mansfield's work. An early story, 'The Advanced Lady', mocks the lady novelist who gushes about women as 'beautiful gifts'. At the end of the story, the narrator leans over to correct that irritating lady, whose actions constantly contradict her words, and says: 'But you know, that theory of yours about woman and Love – it's as old as the hills – oh, older!' The story ends with the narrator's comment: '"Ignorance must not go uncontradicted," I said to the Advanced Lady.'[57]

Though this kind of narrator disappears from Mansfield's later stories, the same impulse to comment ('ignorance must not go uncontradicted') on the self-servingness of different versions of reality remains important. (Mansfield also says in relation to Dorothy Richardson, 'People today are simply cursed by what I call the personal.'[58]) A connection can be made between this questioning of the personal and Mansfield's uneasiness about the idea of true feminine style – and also with Mansfield's determination to distinguish herself from writers such as Dorothy Richardson and Virginia Woolf.[59]

Another modernist approach which complements my sense of the story as satire is to insist on its perspectivism. The narrative weaves in and out of the characters' minds so that we can't trust a single image as authoritative or authorial. For instance, even the symbolism of the moon and the tree, a powerful and beautiful image, can be called into question. Seen in this way, the story suggests that it is a deceit, a self-deception, to believe (in an objective way) in this symbolism which involves only a moment – albeit a powerful, poignant and beautiful moment – of intense subjectivity. Sexual symbolism often compounds a dangerous illusion, and can be a prelude to self-deception.

Thus in 'Bliss' (and I would argue in other Mansfield stories) moments of insight and perceptiveness are often seen as tricks people play on themselves or others. Moments of identity, though they are to be admired for their beauty and persuasiveness, fall away. The realisation is that supposed unities are tricks of self-deceit, or even possibly the effect of another person's mind control. Some of the most dangerous of these tricks are played around the idea of masculinity and femininity: and this is different from a Freudian reading discovering symptoms of denial and repression. A picture of oneself or another as the embodiment of female or male qualities can shore up that sense of hollowness and meaninglessness, but it can also lead into some tricky situations. Thinking of oneself as a modern woman is a typical illusion that Bertha and other Mansfield characters labour under and it makes them vulnerable.

Mansfield is showing women not as tragic victimised figures (vulnerability incarnate), but as prey (as men also are) to myths which immobilise them. Thus one could see Mansfield, as Kate Fullbrook does, as 'one of the darkest of the modernists'.[60] Fullbrook may be correct in making the important distinction that for Mansfield the analysis of gender, the oppression of women and female sexuality, though it may be 'the central instance', is not to be seen as an apotheosis of corruption.

•

With these four readings I have raised a number of points. One is that theory, and identifying a theoretical basis upon which one interprets a piece of writing, is in itself subject to questions of fashion and taste. Another is that there is a value in being perspicacious about criticism, and that it is worthwhile elaborating and explaining different views of a work. The implications for feminist criticism are that we have to be aware of the cultural and historical context of psychoanalytic readings and the strategic significance of cultural feminist approaches (and I hope that I have shown they are intimately related).[61]

My modernist reading may have a special appeal today because it shows a writer at the beginning of the twentieth century deconstructing certainties about gender and identity in what we think of (at the end of the century) as a very contemporary way. One could turn for an explanation of Mansfield's parodic distance to her position as a 'colonial subject', her exclusion from that cloistered (perfumed) bourgeois world 'behind the closed curtains', and her ambiguous situation as an emigré in a bohemian group.[62] But the contemporary (1910s) ambivalence in the literary world about questions of gender should also inform our understanding of her satirical stance. Let me give an example of what Rachel Blau du Plessis calls a 'symbolic moment in September 1913':

> A group of young men of letters, including Allen Upward, Ezra Pound and Richard Aldington, petitioned the editor Dora Marsden for a name change of the journal in which that circle of artists was regularly appearing. The name to which the men objected was *The New Freewoman*.
>
> They felt that the present title of this paper caused it to be confounded with organs devoted solely to the advocacy of an unimportant reform in an obsolete political institution. In two words – female suffrage. Which of course had not yet been won. The literary men proposed a change in agenda by limiting the social allusions Marsden's title made.
>
> The political high handedness appealed to Marsden. She approved and their journal became *The Egoist* in 1914.[63]

This account is interesting, because it shows us how much intellectual women – women in the arts and a bohemian intellectual circle – may have regarded the struggle for women's rights as over, and the 'banalities of gender' (in du Plessis's words) as *passé*. Marsden proposed that women 'can be as "free" now as they have the power to be' and that those who insisted on speaking of social formations were 'controversialists'.[64] This frame on female modernism reveals yet another way in which the period of Mansfield's story had a complexity and ambivalence equal to that of our own, and may usefully locate this chapter's effort to meet such complexities.

This chapter does not attempt to exhaust possible readings; for instance, a Marxist reading of the story could make a class analysis of the relationships portrayed in the story, arguing that male bourgeois desire from the nineteenth-century on was associated with power and was aroused by women of lower status or questionable reputation, such as the ambiguously free Pearl. This association, it has been argued, comes from the fact that middle-class boys were brought up largely by servants and nannies. For middle-class women, on the other hand, fear of sexuality and frigidity could be seen as caused by the association of female sexual activity and desire with the danger of a fall in social status. Female heterosexual desire was frozen by the need to preserve status. Read with this in mind, 'Bliss' is the story of a typically middle-class sexual quandary. (Or, to take a completely different tack, critics familiar with the field of narratology may see the story as echoing the pattern of female resistance to, and explanation of, serial monogamy, which occurs in the many versions of the fairytale *Bluebeard*.)[65]

Jerome McGann, in the last words of his *The Romantic Ideology*, stresses the importance of specific readers and writers rather than a fetishised insistence on 'text' which turns 'works of art into passive objects, the consumer goods of a capitalist world'. He describes his alternative:

> To return poetry to a human form – to see what we read and study are poetic *works* produced and reproduced by specific men and women – is perhaps the most imperative task now facing the world of literary criticism.[66]

Though in this discussion I have used typical readings, I too am addressing the production and reproduction of works of literature and seeing this as importantly tied to individuals, modes of interpretation and reading technologies, and sets of values as they occur at particular periods, rather than as a phantomised process of text and theory.

Chapter Two

Conjunction and Renewal:
Reading Katherine Mansfield's 'Prelude'

The starting point of my last chapter was the acknowledgement that texts are produced by readers as well as writers and that all readers (though they may not realise it) bring theories to what they read. [1]

There are other interesting and complex ways in which criticism and reading are co-opted. David Bordwell, in his book about the interpretation of films, *Making Meaning,* gives a very useful analysis of this. He stresses that reading has certain conventions that are common to much inferential discourse, and that like most 'craft' discourses reading is affiliated with a certain community of interests, such as those of academic institutions. Its conventions entail certain habits of meaning-making. And it is the different application of such conventions that shapes the particular range of readings, not the infinite variety of readers and texts, or the mysterious unknowableness of the text.[2] Bordwell makes a taxonomy of the ways spectators or critics 'make sense of a film', which is useful to my attempts to be self-conscious about interpretation. He outlines it as follows:

> I suggest that when spectators and critics make sense of a film, the meanings they construct are of only four possible types.
> 1. The perceiver may construct a concrete 'world', be it avowedly fictional or putatively real. . . . This very extensive process eventuates in what I shall call *referential* meaning, with the referents taken as either imaginary or real. We can speak of both Oz and Kansas as aspects of referential meaning in *The Wizard of Oz*: Oz is an intratextual reference. Kansas an extratextual one.
> 2. The perceiver may move up a level of abstraction and assign a conceptual meaning or 'point' to the fabula and diegesis she constructs. . . . The film is assumed to speak directly. . . . When the viewer or critic takes the film to be, in one way or another, 'stating' abstract meanings, he is constructing . . . *explicit* meaning.
> 3. The perceiver may also construct covert, symbolic or *implicit meanings*. The film is now assumed to 'speak indirectly'. . . . Units of implicit meaning are commonly called 'themes', though they may also be identified as 'problems,' 'issues,' or 'questions.'
> 4. . . . the perceiver may also construct *repressed* or *symptomatic* meanings that the work divulges 'involuntarily'. . . . If explicit meaning is like a transparent garment, and implicit meaning is like a semiopaque veil, symptomatic meaning is like a disguise. . . . symptomatic meaning may be treated as the consequence of the artist's obsessions. . . . Taken as part of a social dynamic, it may be traced to economic, political or ideological processes . . . .[3]

In the following readings of Katherine Mansfield's story 'Prelude', it is possible to see Bordwell's schema in operation when certain textual features are identified first as referential, and latterly as implicit, or even symptomatic, thus changing the interpretation of the story in a kind of recycling mode – a recycling which is of course also tellingly influenced (via the choice of meaning-making) by the concern (humanist, feminist, nationalist, etc.) of the different periods. Here I don't use Bordwell's 'types' in any strict order, but proceed with an awareness of the kinds of distinctions he is drawing.

'Prelude' is a long short story set in colonial New Zealand in the 1890s and written by Katherine Mansfield, before 'Bliss', in 1916. Most readings of the story have not centred around a single character (as with Bertha) but have tended to see the whole story as having a particular significance in terms of humanity, nation or femininity. My chapter juxtaposes three typical readings before moving on to a new interpretation which is 'postcolonial', in the sense that it reassesses nationalist versions of New Zealand society and identity assumed in some of the other accounts, and attempts to come up with a more comprehensive view of the story.

READING ONE: RENDER NOT TELL – THE NATURALISM OF 'PRELUDE'

'Render not tell' could be described as the aesthetic catch cry of naturalism which informs this first reading. Specific quotations come from an essay by Ian Gordon, a Scottish expatriate and Professor of English at Victoria University from 1936 until 1974. His essay 'Katherine Mansfield, New Zealander' was published in 1944.

Applying the ideas in this essay, the story 'Prelude' can be seen as capturing the world of a colonial middle-class family in Wellington at the turn of last century in all its complex, impressionistic intensity. The fact that there are twelve sections in this long short story (about fifty pages in most editions) which are not linked narratively (their time is consecutive but not continuous) is seen as evidence of the capturing of that world. This is not to say that the story has no sense of narrative, but that the complexity and subtlety of the narrative is closer to the experience of real time than in a conventional fast moving (more eventful) story, and thus allows a more complex scene and more complex characters to be built up. The fact that each section of the story turns on the perspective of a different character means that the reader has 'the sensation of living with living people, not just hearing about them, but really entering into their lives and their actions.'[4]

The kind of detail appreciated in such a reading would be the way in which Kezia's grief at the killing of the duck dissipates when she sees Pat the handyman's earrings. This sequence bears witness to the simultaneous depth and fleetingness of emotion, which the reader recognises as truthful. Kezia's traumatic confrontation with what appears to be meaningless violence is mediated by adult pragmatism and results in an epiphany: betrayal of one loved object in favour of another is the only way to keep on living. The passage runs from:

But Kezia suddenly rushed at Pat and flung her arms round his legs and butted her head as hard as she could against his knees.
'Put head back! Put head back!' she screamed.

to:

Pat dragged Kezia up into his arms. Her sun-bonnet had fallen back, but she would not let him look at her face. No, she pressed her face into a bone in his shoulder and clasped her arms round his neck.

to:

She put up her hands and touched his ears. She felt something. Slowly she raised her quivering face and looked. Pat wore little round gold ear-rings. She never knew that men wore ear-rings. She was very much surprised.
'Do they come on and off?' she asked huskily.[5]

Discussing 'The Aloe' (an earlier version of 'Prelude') in his essay, Gordon makes a point of the fact that it was written in London during the First World War shortly after Katherine Mansfield heard of her brother's death.[6] But Gordon stresses that it shows her subtlety that she does not write directly about war: 'Her reaction was not, as it would have been with so many writers, to write a story of wartime bereavement.'[7] Instead, she deflects her emotion into a story about childhood in New Zealand and in this 'aloofness from outside events and ability to write of people rather than movements' she is, he suggests, 'curiously akin to Jane Austen'.[8]

Another New Zealand critic and Katherine Mansfield scholar, C. K. Stead, develops a similar point about her pension sketches (*In a German Pension*) set in a German spa town Mansfield had travelled to to escape gossip about a pregnancy. Stead asserts that the clever conversion of personal crises into fine writing confirms Mansfield's talent: 'under the pressure of so much experience [she] wrote her first book . . . not at all in the confessional manner most young gentlewomen in like circumstances would have chosen, but converting it all into "black comedy".'[9] He makes implications here (familiar from New Criticism) about the need to transcend the personal and to create something more objective.

Read in this way, another important quality of 'Prelude' is its eschewal of moralising and didacticism: '. . . too often', Ian Gordon comments, 'it is demanded of the writer in New Zealand that he [sic] should share the New Zealand passion for reforming the world. Katherine Mansfield reformed nothing in her stories. She was interested in human beings as human beings, not in economic and political man.'[10] Gordon is asserting that Mansfield sees humanity and the individual as always more important than issues of class or inequality. Her evenhandedness with the privileged and the underprivileged would be an example: they are both possible objects of satire or affection. The story mocks Alice, the servant girl, just as firmly as it inspects the foibles of Beryl, Linda Burnell's lovely unmarried sister, and even shows the two young women as similarly anxious about their romantic futures. First Beryl is fantasising and Alice interrupts:

> 'If I were outside the window and looked in and saw myself I really would be rather struck,' thought she. Still more softly she played the accompaniment – not singing now but listening.
>
> ... 'The first time that I ever saw you, little girl – oh, you had no idea that you were not alone – you were sitting with your little feet upon a hassock, playing the guitar. God, I can never forget. . . .' Beryl flung up her head and began to sing again:
>
> Even the moon is aweary . . .
>
> But there came a loud bang at the door. The servant girl's crimson face popped through.
>
> 'Please, Miss Beryl, I've got to come and lay.'
>
> 'Certainly, Alice,' said Beryl, in a voice of ice. She put the guitar in a corner. Alice lunged in with a heavy black iron tray.[11]

Then, when Alice is similarly preoccupied in her own private musings, it is Beryl who interrupts:

> Alice was making water-cress sandwiches. . . . But propped against the butter dish there was a dirty greasy little book, half-unstitched, with curled edges, and while she mashed the butter she read:
>
> '. . . . Spiders. To dream of spiders creeping over you is good. Signifies large sum of money in near future. Should party be in family way an easy confinement may be expected. But care should be taken in sixth month to avoid eating of probable present of shellfish. . . .'
>
> How many thousand birds I see.
>
> Oh, life. There was Miss Beryl. Alice dropped the knife and slipped the *Dream Book* under the butter dish. But she hadn't time to hide it quite, for Beryl ran into the kitchen and up to the table, and the first thing her eye lighted on were those greasy edges. Alice saw Miss Beryl's meaning little smile and the way she raised her eyebrows and screwed up her eyes as though she were not quite sure what that could be.[12]

In short, in such a reading 'Prelude' is foregrounded as about a concrete world (demonstrating what are seen as universal values) in which different qualities of individuals can be appreciated without blaming or moralising. The writer maintains a clear eye, seeking to do justice to the complexities of reality, not telling her readers what to think. She presents, rather than asserts or emotes. Similar kinds of remarks are made about another of Mansfield's late stories by Ian Gordon:

> Imagine her story, 'The Garden Party,' which is largely a contrast between the happiness of the wealthy family and the tragedy that takes place in a poor-home in a nearby lane – imagine this story re-written by most of the present generation of New Zealand writers and it is difficult to see how they would keep out of the story a certain resentment that one family should be wealthy and the other poor. Not that Katherine Mansfield is not critical. The callous selfishness of the mother in the story is contrasted with the tender sympathy of Laura, the child-heroine. But Katherine Mansfield's attention is all the time on people as individuals not as symbols of a social class.[13]

•

Let us look at this reading of 'Prelude', for example. The meaning of the story seems embodied in its respect for reality, its desire to give a subtle, complex, clear account of life in the world it constructs. For Gordon, a particular moral philosophy does seem to emerge from this – as though such a writer or such an observer will necessarily be a humanist, valuing the individual above all else.

Gordon's essay on Mansfield was published in the fourth volume of Progressive Books' series *New Zealand New Writing* (1944), a series which he also edited. Progressive Books was a left-wing publishing company particularly active in the 1930s, and *New Zealand New Writing* was modelled on the English *Penguin New Writing*.[14] This was perhaps rather paradoxical as Gordon was, as Rachel Barrowman has pointed out, a 'self-confessed Tory' who described himself as an 'alien cuckoo' in the Progressive Publishing Society's 'nest'.[15] Whatever the reason, Gordon's comments seem to be a response to the didactic context; they are offered as a corrective. He argues that Katherine Mansfield's work is of an international quality because it evokes scenes without moralising. He refers specifically to the nineteenth-century tendency to preach and moralise but he is clearly also thinking of the 1930s and 1940s pressure on writers to be on the side of the working class. For Gordon, Mansfield's formulation of individuals transcends social and historical contexts, and has a truth value that cannot be achieved by those writers who make people into types or 'symbols'.

Ian Gordon's theoretical assumptions here seem a mix of naturalism and New Criticism. Ironically, his desire to transcend the social and historical was very much of its time. We can see the same influences at work in our next reading, which may be categorised as 'cultural nationalist'. The difference lies in a shift away from the 'timeless' and 'universal' to an urgent desire to situate oneself in a 'new' country. This way of reading brings a sense of history, while retaining a faith in naturalism and realism. In effect it kidnaps what have already been identified as Mansfield's positive qualities on behalf of New Zealand. Allen Curnow's well-known remarks about Mansfield's early poem 'To Stanislaw Wyspianski' (in his 1960 introduction to *The Penguin Book of New Zealand Verse*) are the most influential formulation of this approach but there are elements of it in Ian Gordon's essay, indicating the persuasiveness of cultural nationalism by this time (1944). My nationalist reading draws on comments by Gordon and Curnow (and can be paralleled with Eric McCormick's comments on Hyde, with which I deal in a later chapter).

READING TWO: A LITERARY NATIONALIST READING

'Prelude' can be seen as capturing the ambivalence and drama of being a New Zealander. A nationalist reader can make much of the fact that Katherine Mansfield was able to write about her own country only in the last years of her life. This seems to be the topic that allowed her to make the innovations that mark her as a serious writer. The story was chosen to open the Penguin collection of her fiction and according to its cover note: 'in 1916 Mansfield wrote "Prelude" and from that time onward . . . was master of her own style'.[16]

Ian Gordon also engages in this way of reading. For instance, he stresses that 'Prelude' was developed from an earlier story which was 'a very lovely reconstruction of her life as a child among brothers [sic] and sisters in Wellington'. Her eye for local detail is seen as adding force to the concreteness of her later work. In a slightly different vein, he suggests that painful exile and embarrassing memories of her native land were part of Mansfield's experience as a New Zealander and that only in the last period of her life, when she was dying, could she finally acknowledge herself as inescapably 'the little colonial'.[17] Gordon also notes that: 'one of the major ideas revolving in her mind in her final months was the plan for a New Zealand novel' of which she considered this story, as developed from the earlier version 'The Aloe', an important sequence.[18]

A nationalist reading can co-opt other formal and textual elements. For instance, the episodic structure of the story can be seen as reflecting the fragmented quality of New Zealand landscape and life. This argument is reinforced by the fact that Mansfield's other major New Zealand story, 'At the Bay', has a similarly episodic structure. However, this nationalism is seen as having nothing to do with unsophisticated patriotism or mechanical accumulation of facts. Gordon comments: 'She [Mansfield] has no need to give laboured descriptions of bush or Wellington streets and winds . . . the atmosphere is there [in a] phrase or a half sentence . . .'[19]

Read in this way, a passage such as the following can be understood as an example of the use of local detail to evoke the loneliness and isolation of the characters in the midst of a 'strange' environment:

> In the garden some tiny owls, perched on the branches of a lace-bark tree, called 'More pork; more pork.' And far away in the bush there sounded a harsh rapid chatter: 'Ha-ha-ha . . . Ha-ha-ha.'

And this same detail is seen as well handled – and not an example of exotica – because it sits alongside a plain unpretentious description of everyday events:

> Kezia thrust her head under the grandmother's arm and gave a little squeak. But the old woman only pressed her faintly, and sighed again, took out her teeth, and put them in a glass of water beside her on the floor.[20]

This kind of writing (or reading) is in line with the New Critical assumption that every detail should have symbolic implications but that it should also be 'real.' The writer should observe a particular decorum in giving his or her images a concrete reality or objectivity.[21]

Another assumption of this kind of reading is that a nation (and a childhood sense of place) has a mysterious power. Thus being a New Zealander is seen not as a question of conscious choice but is involuntary:

> . . . [KM] had no memories of an English childhood, nor, to use Mr Holcroft's fine phrase, any memories of a voyage. . . . She fought hard to leave [NZ] and having won

free at last she never returned. . . . But in spite of all she was a New Zealander. She could no more escape from her birthplace than from her heredity. When she put pen to paper it framed the words New Zealand. When her mind played round with scenes and characters and incidents for her stories, the scenes and characters and incidents rose unasked from her New Zealand childhood.[22]

In these remarks we can see Ian Gordon's assumption that the best New Zealand writers were (inevitably) caught in a drama of being and not being New Zealanders, and that an involuntary tangle of acceptance and denial characterised their works. This idea was most influentially formulated by Allen Curnow in his comments on Mansfield's 'To Stanislaw Wyspianski', which he saw as powered by this typically New Zealand mixed emotion, thus dating the moment ('as early as 1910') of the 'emergence of New Zealand as a characterising force in the work of a native poet'.[23] Curnow included this previously unanthologised poem in his *Penguin Book of New Zealand Verse* (1960). The poem is addressed to a Polish poet and mourns his death 'from the other side of the world' and 'from a little land with no history'. Curnow's reading provides such a good example of the nationalist approach that I shall quote the poem in full:

From the other side of the world,
From a little island cradled in the giant sea bosom,
From a little land with no history,
(Making its own history slowly and clumsily
Piecing together this and that, finding the pattern, solving the problem,
Like a child with a box of bricks),
I, a woman, with the taint of the pioneer in my blood,
Full of a youthful strength that wars with itself and is lawless,
I sing your praises, magnificent warrior; I proclaim your triumphant battle.
My people have had nought to contend with;
They have worked in the broad light of day and handled the clay with rude fingers;
Life – a thing of blood and muscle; Death – a shovelling underground of waste material
What would they know of ghosts and unseen presences,
Of shadows that blot out reality, of darkness that stultifies morn?
Fine and sweet the water that runs from their mountains;
How could they know of poisonous weed, of rotted and clogging tendrils?
And the tapestry woven from dreams of your tragic childhood
They would tear in their stupid hands,
The sad, pale light of your soul blow out with their childish laughter.
But the dead – the old – Oh Master, we belong to you there;
Oh, Master, there we are children and awed by the strength of a giant;
How alive you leapt into the grave and wrestled with Death
And found in the veins of Death the red blood flowing
And raised Death up in your arms and showed him to all the people.
Yours a more personal labour than the Nazarene's miracles,
Yours a more forceful encounter than the Nazarene's gentle commands.
Stanislaw Wyspianski – Oh man with the name of a fighter,
Across these thousands of sea-shattered miles we cry and proclaim you;

> We say 'He is lying in Poland, and Poland thinks he is dead;
> But he gave the denial to Death – he is lying there, wakeful;
> The blood in his giant heart pulls red through his veins.'[24]

Curnow uses the opening lines to suggest that it was only those writers (and perhaps painters and readers) who, torn emotionally by their colonial situation, and registering that division in their work, would be able to create a genuine New Zealand cultural tradition. He identifies Mansfield's feeling as 'something like shame for her country: for its childish clumsiness, for its merely physical pre-occupations' and suggests that the 'taint' of New Zealand, at this stage of its incubation, 'offended a child of the nineties, where the colonist of the sixties had breathed fresh air'. He also contrasts Mansfield with William Pember Reeves who, safe back in England, 'made romance out of the old pioneer'. What Curnow's reading does not do is relate the poem adequately to the Polish context, nor does it see that the New Zealand content is perhaps being used merely to raise broader issues (about the complex emotional situation that must be negotiated by the East Europeans).

A nationalist reading of 'Prelude' would focus attention on the pressure of location. And a sign of the pressure of location may be an emphasis on childhood. Seen this way, Mansfield's writing is suffused with antipathies as well as loving creation and this is part of the effect. The imagistic and impressionistic technique involves the rising up of images in her mind that can be compared with the peculiar intensity of childhood sense experiences:

> The fat creaking body leaned across the gate, and the big jelly of a face smiled. 'Dod't you worry, Brs Burnell, Loddie and Kezia can have tea with by chudren in the dursery, and I'll see theb on the dray afterwards.[25]

The vulgarities of such intense sense experiences overwhelm, but their particular beauty is also powerful:

> . . . she trailed through the narrow passage into the drawing room. The Venetian blind was pulled down but not drawn close. Long pencil rays of sunlight shone through and the wavy shadow of a bush outside danced on the gold lines.[26]

The theme to be discovered in this story is belonging, or the lack of it: witness the characters' dreams, fantasies and longings. The fact that the minimal narrative is about leaving one house to move to another serves to enlarge the theme. Loneliness and isolation are experienced, along with a sense of emotional desolation or distance. The child is at a distance from her mother, as husband is from wife. Isolation and emptiness are also emphasised in the darkness of the journey from one house to another:

> It was the first time that Lottie and Kezia had ever been out so late. Everything looked different – the painted wooden houses far smaller than they did by day, the gardens far bigger and wilder. Bright stars speckled the sky and the moon hung over the harbour dabbling the waves with gold. They could see the lighthouse shining on Quarantine Island, and the green lights on the old coal hulks.[27]

Focusing on the rootless nature of New Zealand experience, we can see the dreams of characters such as Linda (and her brother-in-law, Jonathan Trout, in 'At the Bay') and even Beryl as reflecting a Chekhovian desire for a more sophisticated society, where imagination is as important as material things. This is what Allen Curnow calls Katherine Mansfield's 'intuition that New Zealand's obstinate social hedonism, marching with the littleness and the isolation and already taking shape in its laws, stood between her and the knowledge of life (and death) she needed'. He continues: 'She rejects the "stupid hands" which were shaping the social order, the callousness inherited from the gain-hungry colonising, and the political high-mindedness which would make the state each man's brother's keeper.'[28] Stanley serves to represent one version of the settler superficiality, the shallow optimism, that Mansfield turned her back on.

•

The two ways of reading that I have just outlined (naturalist and nationalist) have been very persuasive in New Zealand criticism. The first is not particularly interpretive. Its ideas of quality are the modernist truisms of the period – writing which keeps its eye on the object, which is not hijacked by political or moral causes, which is true to reality and individual complexity, etc.

The nationalist reading, particularly Curnow's account of the Mansfield poem, uses these critical orthodoxie, retaining the emphasis on reality, but it is most interested in a text's relevance to *local* reality. This approach uncovers a hidden national drama, which involves a colonial situation of creative malaise. In some respects, it is implied, this colonial drama parallels an oedipal drama, so that coming to live in this country is like a boy tearing himself away from his mother (country) and finding a way to live with the harsh words of his father – his native land.[29]

More recently there has been a rather different nationalist reading of 'Prelude'. This emblematic (or heritage) nationalism, as I shall call it, is more generally associated with popular culture. It is exemplified in an essay by Lydia Wevers, 'The Sod Under My Feet'.

READING THREE: EMBLEMATIC NATIONALISM – 'PRELUDE' AS PASTORAL

Lydia Wevers makes sense of the story 'Prelude' in terms of its iconography of New Zealand – images which help us to inhabit our own country imaginatively (as well as physically). In David Bordwell's terms, Wevers is doing more recycling – 'interpretation can generate a cycle of meaning-production.'[30] She is taking the explicit world of the story and discovering (or generating) new implicit meanings.[31]

In this reading, images can be enjoyed for their conjuring power: the creek, the paddock, the old colonial (heritage) villa with its coloured glass in doors or windows are all evocative. When they read about Kezia looking through the coloured glass, many New Zealanders can relive their own childhood experience:

> The dining-room window had a square of coloured glass at each corner. One was blue, one was yellow. Kezia bent down to have one more look at a blue lawn with blue arum lilies growing at the gate and then at a yellow lawn with yellow lilies and a yellow fence. As she looked a little Chinese Lottie came out onto the lawn and began to dust the tables and chairs with a corner of her pinafore. Was that really Lottie? Kezia was not sure until she had looked through the ordinary window.[32]

Katherine Mansfield's companion story 'At the Bay' lends itself to a similar reading. Bathing suits hung over verandah rails and sandshoes left out to dry provide a quintessential image of days at the beach:

> Over the verandas, prone on the paddock, flung over the fences, there were exhausted-looking bathing-dresses and rough striped towels. Each back window seemed to have a pair of sand-shoes on the sill and some lumps of rock or a bucket or a collection of pawa [sic] shells. The bush quivered in a haze of heat; the sandy road was empty except for the Trouts' dog Snooker, who lay stretched in the very middle of it.[33]

The corrugated iron in 'Prelude' – a familiar icon of 'heritage' New Zealand– can also make readers feel a sense of belonging to the same community as the writer:

> The windows of the empty house shook, a creaking came from the walls and floors, a piece of loose iron on the roof banged forlornly.[34]

and could, read in this way, be considered a linking signifier with Allen Curnow's image poem 'Wild Iron':

> Sea go dark, dark with wind,
> Feet go heavy, heavy with sand,
> Thought go wild, wild with the sound
> Of iron on the old shed swinging, clanging:
> Go dark, go heavy, go wild, go round,
>   Dark with the wind,
>   Heavy with the sand,
> Wild with the iron that tears at the nail
> And the foundering shriek of the gale.[35]

Such poems are close to imagism in their technique but criticism can make explicit their value as icons of New Zealand. This 'feel of place' is also found in a passage from 'Prelude' which uses the New Zealand terms 'creek' and 'paddock' and names local flora:

> Dawn came sharp and chill with red clouds on a faint green sky and drops of water on every leaf and blade. A breeze blew over the garden, dropping dew and dropping petals, shivered over the drenched paddocks, and was lost in the sombre bush. In the sky some tiny stars floated for a moment and then they were gone – they were dissolved like bubbles. And plain to be heard in the early quiet was the sound of the creek in

the paddock running over the brown stones, running in and out of the sandy hollows, hiding under clumps of dark berry bushes, spilling into a swamp of yellow water flowers and cresses.[36]

Characters as well as scenes produce typical or emblematic images. Thus Wevers sees 'Prelude' as depicting a prosperous 1890s family and Stanley Burnell as representing a 'common colonist', typical of members of the Liberal Party who had won their status through hard work, not simply by privilege of birth. She identifies him as the type Keith Sinclair refers to when he writes:

> The democracy was in power and the politician had to be, or at least seem to be, if not a common man, then one of the common colonists. He should be big, preferably loud, certainly hearty; nor, on any account, should he be suspected of feeling superior to the voters by reason of culture or fastidiousness.[37]

This man is the head of the family whom the story celebrates. Thus the story is, as Wevers puts it, emphasising 'the family as a location of productivity, collectivity and difference, as a meaningful set of relationships ordered by gender and class-based structures of power' and related to a certain period in history.[38] 'Prelude', read in this way, is a prediction of present-day New Zealand prosperity and national character ('this is/was our society'):

> What is most striking about Mansfield's stories is their reiteration of the patriarchal family . . . as a basic institution of social order. Whatever she may have thought about 'pa-men', there is no question but that Stanley Burnell supports and structures his family in a way that is simply not available to a character like Dick Harmon [in 'Je Ne Parle Pas Français'].[39]

What makes the difference, and makes the portrayal of the New Zealand patriarch so positive, is that:

> . . . Stanley's patriarchy is firmly based on his material success, and indeed that all the things which characterise his family and make it, in its expansiveness, openness and relative benevolence, so very – in the context of Mansfield's fiction – un-European, are produced by Stanley's ability to keep making money, to literally expand the territory the family occupies, 'the children and the gardens will grow bigger and bigger'. While the household carefully preserves its strata – Beryl hangs the bankrupt Chinaman's pictures in the kitchen where 'nobody need gaze at them but Pat and the servant girl' thereby enacting the exact location of class, race and material difference on the edges *but inside* the large house of white middle-class New Zealand – it is a patriarchal order which strives for some inclusiveness, some humanising . . . of the boundaries . . . .[40]

According to this reading, the story also shows how appropriate European settlement is for this country. It has been, and will be, right because it is so obviously successful:

> In a quite literal way the Burnells' property draws attention to its own visibility and particularly its possession of a landscape. As Kezia and Lottie travel to their new

house in Karori the whole of Wellington harbour spreads itself under the night sky and the unknown country they travel leads them to a house whose 'soft, white, bulk' lay 'stretched upon the garden like a sleeping beast', a simile which suggests the naturalness (and lack of threat) of the house's occupation of its territory.[41]

In this successfully negotiated contract, Wevers' explains, women 'look after and work for the environment that represents Stanley's ownership of wealth in the New World':

> . . . Linda by having babies until she finally manages to produce the boy who inherits the empty place at the top of the table; Mrs Fairfield by setting things in order, the kitchen all in pairs, replicating Linda's old bedroom in the larger one she moves into; Beryl both by her household labour and more subtly repaying Stanley's support with companionship while he eats a dish of fried chops or plays cribbage; the children by acknowledging, as does Isabel, the most 'grown-up' of the little girls, that they have their father to thank 'for liking it better than town'.[42]

The food on the table, even the duck they eat, is 'a home product'. In the colonial society, produce and comfort are the obvious result of labour. Material wealth and affluence are seen differently here than in Mansfield's European stories, where they deform character and turn women, in particular, into beautiful objects who are not allowed to demean themselves by association with the lower classes (Wevers uses the example of the story 'A Cup of Tea'). Here, in the New Zealand stories, 'the wealth of the Burnell family is wealth they work for' and therefore its plenitude can encompass even 'its disagreeable or dissenting elements, the poisoning presence of Mrs Kember, like a rat, or the melancholy of Jonathan Trout whose labour imprisons him'.[43]

Wevers concludes that 'Prelude' achieves an extraordinary balance, where Stanley Burnell's 'amazing health, vigour and energy' which 'speak volumes for the state of the nation as a material enterprise, expanding, profiting, populating' are offset by 'the rest of the household' which 'speaks for the contrary and often opposing drives and ambitions that the nation is heir to'. The whole is bathed in 'the fact of collectivity and shared territory [which] surrounds each separate member of the Burnell household and its larger community'.[44] And for Wevers this is a satisfactory compromise that makes it possible for Linda to laugh in a light and bantering way at her own over-developed self-expectations:

> What am I guarding myself for so preciously? I shall go on having children and Stanley will go on making money and the children and the gardens will grow bigger and bigger, with whole fleets of aloes in them for me to choose from.[45]

The overall preoccupation in this approach to the story seems to be to identify it as a symbol of the 'New Zealand' of the 1890s. In doing so, however, the reading inevitably becomes involved in valorising Pakeha culture of the period, sharing some of its assumptions about itself. Wevers' essay, from which I have selected only one line of argument, does complicate itself to some extent by placing this interpretation within a kind of frame which makes this picture of New Zealand possibly Katherine Mansfield's 'dream of nation'. In spite of this, the central emphasis seems revisionist, since Wevers appears to be rescuing the story from extreme (particularly feminist) interpretations in favour of a more moderate understanding – reclaiming 'Prelude' on behalf of a positivist history of New Zealand. (Her essay post-dates accounts of the story by Kate Fullbrook, Carolyn Heilbrun and Sydney Kaplan.[46]) Its reading, particularly of the last lines of the story, is in sharp contrast (for instance) to Kate Fullbrook's feminist account. The suggestion is that Linda's tone is not bitter, nor even resigned, but frank and warmly humorous.

This more optimistic (even ingenuous) reading of 'Prelude' makes Mansfield's work much easier to commodify than the earlier more troubled and questioning nationalist version. The last decades have seen a growing desire for national icons. Mansfield has become part of a heritage industry.[47] One can pay a nostalgic visit to the restored house where she was born or buy garden ornaments from a shop named after one of her stories. Wevers cannot be blamed for the excesses of the 'Kiwiana' industry, but the general tendency in her essay and its desire to be positive does seem to provide an opportunity for smugness. One might take from it, for example, that Stanley represents the New Zealand 'bloke' with qualities much more promising than his European counterparts because he is a self-made, hands-on man in a productive economy.

Kate Fullbrook proposes a diametrically opposed account of 'Prelude' (and she also includes 'The Aloe' in her discussion). Looking at it from her point of view, a reading that delighted in the contrast and textures of the Burnell household, that saw the difficulties of the household as a part of the dynamic plurality of the family in colonial society, and that accepted the idea of its unity being guaranteed by a man who represents 'the fullest possible consummation of individual life', would have to be totally taken in by the story and even complicit with the power it critiques.

READING FOUR: A FEMINIST READING
– SEXUAL BATTLEFIELD DISGUISED AS A PASTORAL

Has Wevers' approach mistaken the disguise for the reality, has it missed the violence of the story in admiring 'Prelude' as another 'home product'? Isn't this similar to Stanley's blindness in not recognising the violence that simmers beneath the surface of his home? Is the violence that Pat the handyman directs towards the duck not an analogue for the hatred that Linda feels towards Stanley? A feminist reading is likely to see the story preoccupied not with nation, but with 'the Burnells' destructive marriage'. It is also likely to take Linda's 'languor and sickly delicacy' (understood as sensuousness by her husband) as signs of a complete retreat from life, and to see Linda's version of sexuality as an experience of 'bondage'.[48]

These are the elements Kate Fullbrook discovers in a chapter on 'Prelude' in her book *Katherine Mansfield* (published in 1986) which constitutes part of a larger argument about Mansfield. In her reading, 'Prelude' uses a poetic version of an impressionist style to defamiliarise the ordinary. The many sections, the lack of linearity, and the changing angles of perspective ('Identity in the story is as impermanent as the dappled moments in a Renoir or a Manet') suggest that life cannot be seen in one way, and that the unexpected will always intervene.[49] The story begins with the Burnells moving to a new house, and Fullbrook sees this move as a metaphor for the possibility of change, 'as the characters are temporarily dislodged from their habits and set roles'.[50]

The change of houses, the dislodgement, serves to reveal the ways in which feminine roles are constructed. For example, Kezia finds the servant girl's hairpin left behind in her room, but can find nothing in her grandmother's. We see these marks of gender and class being interpreted by the little girl. The sections are each about 'education into dominance and submission in terms of class, sex and age and are punctuated with moments that deny the permanence of such divisions'.[51]

Read in this way, certain incidents become more significant. For example, at the beginning of the story when Kezia and Lottie, who have been left in the care of the Samuel Josephs, are made fun of over the afternoon tea table:

> Moses grinned and gave her a nip as she sat down; but she pretended not to notice. She did hate boys.
> 'Which will you have?' asked Stanley, leaning across the table very politely, and smiling at her.
> 'Which will you have to begin with—strawberries and cream or bread and dripping?
> 'Strawberries and cream, please,' said she.
> 'Ah-h-h-h.' How they all laughed and beat the table with their teaspoons. Wasn't that a take-in! Wasn't it now! Didn't he fox her! Good old Stan![52]

This act of humiliation sends ripples of meaning through the story, suggesting a 'persistent identification of eating with cruelty' and particularly male cruelty:

> The little boy, Stanley, is indulged in petty bullying by his mother just as the adult Stanley Burnell, Kezia's father, is indulged in his corresponding appetitiveness by the women who are likewise humiliated by him. Stanley Burnell is closely associated with devouring things too – the cherries that he pretends to share with his wife but gobbles himself; the pork chops he smacks down while Linda is unable to eat; the duck, sign of mortality and human destruction for Kezia, that he carves with artistic sadism. In delineating this calm, everyday world, Katherine Mansfield, like Sylvia Plath, pairs destruction and desire as the most ordinary of associations. Both of the Stanleys offer sustenance to women that they not only fail to deliver, but offer falsely in the first place. Kezia, not yet bowed, eats her own tear as her mother consumes herself in response to the appetite of her husband.[53]

Linda's stories and nursery images of children as fluffy chicks, and of her husband as a bounding dog, go with her infantilised and enervated state, in stark contrast to Stanley's energetic affectionate selfishness. Her very passivity sustains his performance of masculinity. Linda's nursery images are tokens of defence constantly in danger of being destroyed by a monstrous reality, the silly mask of the middle-class matron who knows nothing about anything and who lives within a frilly myth of femininity.

Linda's paranoia (that 'THEY were there. . . . THEY knew how frightened she was')[54] has been increased by her dream:

> She was walking with her father through a green paddock sprinkled with daisies. Suddenly he bent down and parted the grasses and showed her a tiny ball of fluff at her feet. 'Oh, Papa, the darling.' She made a cup of her hands and caught the tiny bird and stroked its head with her finger. It was quite tame. But a funny thing happened. As she stroked it began to swell, it ruffled and pouched, it grew bigger and bigger and its round eyes seemed to smile knowingly at her. Now her arms were hardly wide enough to hold it and she dropped it into her apron. It had become a baby with a big naked head and a gaping bird-mouth, opening and shutting. Her father broke into a loud clattering laugh and she woke to see Burnell standing by the windows rattling the venetian blind up to the very top.[55]

This fearful vision of sex (and its consequences) becomes more explicit in Linda's picture of the ugly aloe plant. She expresses a rare enthusiasm: 'I like that aloe. I like it more than anything here. And I am sure I shall remember it long after I have forgotten all the other things.' But the affection she expresses is associated with negative thoughts of her husband because the aloe provides her with a rare image of female strength against a male predator. The ugly sharpness of its leaves express her desire for protection from things that 'rush at her' (such as her husband, dogs, and children):

> If only he wouldn't jump at her so, and bark so loudly, and watch her with such eager, loving eyes. He was too strong for her; she had always hated things that rushed at her, from a child. There were times when he was frightening – really frightening. When she just had not screamed at the top of her voice: 'You are killing me.' And at those times she had longed to say the most coarse, hateful things. . . .
>
> 'You know I'm very delicate. You know as well as I do that my heart is affected, and the doctor has told you I may die any moment. I have had three great lumps of children already. . . .'[56]

Kezia has this same fear of 'rushing animals', which indicates mother and daughter's common female hatred of 'the orthodox polarity that designates male as active predator and female as prey to things that "rush" and things that "swell"'.[57] Both mother and daughter are 'searching for sexual rhythms of life that are other than mere animal pouncing'.[58] But (as Fullbrook sees it) Linda is still thoroughly trapped in this game of reluctance and pounce – 'a classic portrait of the condition and response of a Victorian mother and wife to the sexual configurations of her age'.[59] Linda cannot accept the way her life is turning out, but neither can she revolt against it. Her feelings are unable to be spoken to herself or others. In her one moment of exchange with her daughter Kezia she cannot communicate the 'inchoate private meaning' that she gives to the aloe.[60]

•

Read in this way, by foregrounding certain elements and finding implicit violent meanings in them, 'Prelude' is only deceptively a pastoral, and is perhaps even a parody of pastorals. Linda's seemingly sensible compromise with the future, the acceptance that she will have more babies and Stanley will get richer and there will be whole fleets of aloes, is, in Kate Fullbrook's words, an expectation of a future in which 'spiked emblems of hatred' will bind 'the woman whose mask will remain in place'. This is a woman who owns nothing, neither her body nor the courage to communicate about it. Her apparent commonsense is actually a horrible (and perverse) embrace of hopelessness:

> The children like the horrid bird will grow without her love or consent; her egotistical husband will remain unaware of her distress and discontent; and the money that will also grow will be part of the obscene equation. Sex, cash and death will create 'whole fleets of aloes', spiked emblems of hatred binding the woman whose mask will remain in place.[61]

LIMITATIONS OF READINGS THREE AND FOUR

Wevers finds an example of an historical 'type' to support her reading. But the problem is that in showing Stanley Burnell to be a typical liberal – loud, optimistic, self-made – she is drawing on a narrowly formulated, and in this case male-oriented version of history. What about other versions? A feminist version of history? Does Wevers have complementary female types? Fullbrook's reading has provided such a type but she does not offer the historical specifics that Wevers suggests. Her interpretation seems at times overly judgemental, as if the Linda she describes is a post-1960s feminist projected back into the 1890s. Both readings illuminate some aspects of the story but seem incomplete. They can be seen as distinct discourses; Fullbrook's modern feminist discourse and Wevers' emblematic nationalist discourse each assimilate 'Prelude' to a different rhetoric and a different conceptual system.

How then to proceed? We need to bring yet another discourse into conjunction with Mansfield's text in order to construct a reading adequate to today's ideas about the period in which she was writing (and the one she was writing about). Another theorist of reading, philosopher Paul Ricoeur, describes the process in this way:

> If reading is possible, it is indeed because the text is not closed in on itself but opens out onto other things. To read is, on any hypothesis, to conjoin a new discourse

to the discourse of the text. This conjunction of discourses reveals in the very constitution of the text, an original capacity for renewal which is its open character. Interpretation is the concrete outcome of conjunction and renewal.[62]

My next approach takes the need for a new and not 'co-opted' history as its starting point.

READING FIVE: FEMINIST HISTORY
— A STORY ABOUT CONCEPTION AND MOTHERHOOD

What aspect of colonial New Zealand history is missed out in defining the 1890s as a newly optimistic decade in society when the hard work of the pioneer families was being rewarded in the creation of new family dynasties? Such a history is modelled around the careers of individual men, with women being included only as part of their families. What was life like for women then? What was specific to women?

To answer this question one has to think about the beginnings of colonial settlement. European society in New Zealand was at first a predominantly male society of individual European explorers, travellers or traders whose social and sexual relationships were founded within, or on the edge of, Maori communities. The church and the military constructed their own communities. Settlement represented a new stage beyond the fluidity of frontier living. Though there were at first many more male settlers than female, one of the important rhetorics of settlement (from the 1840s on) was the exhortation to marry and create a family. Only out of this would national prosperity develop and good habits be inculcated in the citizens of the new nation. It was considered important to attract a good quality of female immigrant, the right sort of girl to make a go of it. It was a common assumption that a settler must marry a European woman in order to succeed, and such women were spoken of as being 'in demand'. Comments by Edward Gibbon Wakefield, architect of some of the original colonial settlements, are typical of this discourse: 'A colony that is not attractive to women is an unattractive colony' and 'as respects manners and morals it is of little importance what colonial fathers are, in comparison with what the mothers are'.[63]

Historians are in dispute about the effect of this history on women (or, as we might put it today, how this society constructed women). Some historians, such as Raewyn Dalziel, seem to have changed the emphases of their interpretations in the course of their careers. At first Dalziel stressed the increased opportunities for immigrant women to marry, to participate in joint business and farming ventures with their husbands, and to take ad hoc leadership roles because of the incomplete nature of the society:

> The colonial environment opened new doors. It gave, within the context of an accepted role, a sense of purpose, a feeling of usefulness and a greater degree of independence than the women migrants had experienced before. To reach the same

end in England they would have had to break out of the shell of home and family and emerge into the world as rebels against position and role. Such escapes were often preceded by nervous breakdowns and illness and were accompanied by personal traumas. For colonial women the break-through was accomplished in the migration process – an escape carried through in the bosom of the family, and which, though accompanied by discomfort, hardship and often personal misery, held in the end significant material and emotional rewards within an accepted framework.[64]

However, the story that Dalziel constructs here she has also construed as having some down sides. Her later work, for example, on the New Plymouth settlement indicates that working-class female immigrants from areas of Devon, Cornwall and Dorset 'may well have experienced a contraction of opportunities in a colony where lack of economic infrastructure meant that women had few employment opportunities outside the home'.[65]

Recent publications, both of historical and fictional works, tend to stress the social surveillance of women immigrants, the strong discourses around conformity, the homogeneity of the female population (all young with children), and the common pattern of women's lives in terms of childrearing and choice of employment. A certain flexibility of sexual and family mores associated with the British working class seems to have disappeared in migration.[66] Charlotte Macdonald's *A Woman of Good Character* looks demographically at a sample group of immigrant women.[67] These women, whose obligation was to create the children and culture of the nation, did so prodigiously. Most of the women settlers who married and came to New Zealand (or came to New Zealand and married) between 1860–70 had large families, some having as many as twelve, fourteen, and sixteen children. They were literally the bearers of the society. However, by 1880 it had taken a turn the other way. The number of children and size of families decreased to below that of Europe – women were bearing fewer children and legislators and government were decrying this trend.[68]

Charlotte Macdonald suggests that the changing attitude to birth control brought about a profound change for women:

> Women who married or started their families in the 1850s, 1860s and early 1870s were among the last who would have expected to spend most of their adult lives pregnant or looking after young children. In this way their reproductive experience was more likely to resemble that of their mothers than their daughters. Sheila Johansson believes that the end of intensive child bearing and the shift from traditional to modern fertility patterns, deserves to be regarded as the BC/AD of the history of women.[69]

What this means in terms of the unwritten history of the later nineteenth century is that a lot of discussion must have been going on about conception, contraception and sex in marriage. This probably took place alongside the better documented discussion about drunkenness and family violence.[70]

Historians suggest that it was as a consequence (or side effect) of their meetings about unionism and temperance that women got together to talk to each other about birth control, abstinence, contraception and abortion. But perhaps the fiction of the time, and about the time, can also be seen as a method of formulating the subject, an acceptable forum in which women could consider how the control, or not, of fertility and sexuality affected their lives.

Reading Katherine Mansfield's most famous New Zealand set fictions ('At the Bay', 'The Doll's House', 'The Garden Party', as well as 'Prelude') in this way retains Wevers' sense of the importance of the settler society setting but removes the stories from being seen as idylls of family life at an optimistic period. (The 1890s was also a decade of sustained economic depression, when many men abandoned their families and went to Australia.) Instead, the reading gives a specific character to how women's lives were constructed in the time in which Mansfield was writing (1900s–1910s), as well as the time about which she was writing (1890s). These stories suggest that relationships between mothers and daughters from 1870 to 1910 must have been (poignantly) marked by the fact that a daughter's life was unlikely to turn out like her mother's.

In *Culture and Imperialism*, Edward Said discusses the movement from imperialism to an awareness of imperialism (and resistance to it).[71] We can think analogously about changes in women's lives, about the movement from the idea of reproductive inevitability to the idea of reproductive choice. It is not that one period ends and another begins, but that there develops an awareness of the outlines of the previous model – if we can call it that – and therefore of another possibility. This change disrupts the relationship between the generations of women and may intensify or prolong a disruption that has already taken place in the process of emigration. Perhaps the idea of choice and control is particularly assimilable in a population who were always forward-thinking in the sense of struggling to achieve a different and better life.[72]

These ideas suggest that Katherine Mansfield's story 'Prelude' may have a connection with the work of contemporary women writers in Australia and New Zealand, a context that our other readings have not looked for. In an essay 'Portrait of the Artist as the Wild Colonial Girl', about Australian Miles Franklin's novel *My Brilliant Career* (1901), Australian critic Susan Gardner argues similarly that there is a need to contextualise Miles Franklin's first novel. She asks: 'to what extent will concepts worked out with regard to mainstream European or American writers illuminate the emergence and characteristic concerns of an adolescent female writer from an extremely sex-segregated, rural, colonised society?'[73] Noting the prevalence of sexual rejection and marriage resistance in women's prose fiction about adolescence between 1896 and 1927, Gardner points to a description (by Michael Cannon) of the rural Australian woman's situation at that time:

> Since the farmer could rarely afford to hire labour, he relied on breeding a large family to relieve his physical burdens. To the wife's other problems, therefore, must

be added the fact that she was practically always pregnant or nursing new babies, often in filthy conditions which meant that half of them died and the effort must have been wasted to that extent. Breeding of farm animals 'was carried out more efficiently than that.[74]

Thus Gardner infers that the time in which Franklin grew up was 'even less a period of sexual and reproductive self-determination for rural Australian women than today', and suggests that response to these actual conditions of infant mortality and death in childbirth could well explain Franklin's theme of marriage reluctance. (Franklin's own family was depleted by childhood deaths, and the youngest of her three sisters died in childbirth.)

Gardner is writing to correct what she obviously perceives as the absurdity of puzzled academic comments about the 'irrational' or 'neurotic' association Franklin makes between 'death and childbirth [which] was to govern her attitude to marriage and to be a source of inner conflict which depressed her deeply'.[75] Gardner's point is persuasive but what I am most interested in here is the use of historical 'fact' to contextualise the reading of a writer of the time.

While the historical contextualisation is important, it is equally important that it should be related to fiction. The novels of the period suggest that there *was* talk going on about women's lives, about issues of power, sex and reproductive choice. We can acknowledge the extratextual evidence, but still adopt a different model, from the one Gardner used, to show the relation between literature and fact. So, instead of seeing *My Brilliant Career* as an attractive but romantic escape from social conditions (thus privileging literature by placing it outside social construction), we can see this novel and also 'Prelude' as acts of participation in the emerging discourse about sex in marriage and fertility. As texts they cross the gap between conversation (or even gossip) and literature. And it may be that it is this discourse that is new to the period, not the fact of birth and infant mortality in trying physical conditions, which was nothing new for women.

The Australian farm situation of constant pregnancies in trying physical conditions may seem far from the comfortable, well-regulated household of 'Prelude' and 'At the Bay', but in order to understand the period we have to take in the range of accounts and constructions of family types. As I noted earlier, by the 1880s the colonial family in New Zealand and Australia was smaller. This may not have been true of all families – we are talking averages – but the fact that such a change was taking place meant that the experiences of different women could be contrasted. There were different stories to tell. Gardner writes of the lack of sexual and reproductive 'self-determination'. But 'self-determination' is not so much an outcome as a process, a process that is still evolving today, though today the decreasing number of accidental pregnancies may be just as significant in altering the pattern of women's lives.

Jean Devanny, in her autobiography *Point of Departure,* contrasted the mores of two country districts she grew up in. She was recalling a period from 1905 to around 1911 and her move from the country district of Ferntown to the mining community of Puponga, both on the West Coast of the South Island:

> . . . the traditional sociability of the mining fraternity was tremendously enlivening to us after the dull, almost non-existent community spirit of the farmers. . . . No ceremony about visiting here as in Ferntown. The women popped in and out of each other's houses at any time of day, to drink tea and gossip.[76]

The teenage Jean understood the women's conversations (often about sex and unwanted pregnancies) because when only thirteen and still living at Ferntown, she had assisted a young woman friend (her former teacher) through the physical trauma of a self-induced abortion:

> Nothing this day either, though Rose took a double dose. At dusk, there came indications of movement but it was slow, slow, and as time ticked away remorselessly, we were faced with the fact that again I would have to leave her. . . .
> By lunchtime she was brought to bed by the severity of her pains; but as the afternoon wore away our hopes once more faded. Determined, her face ablaze with fever, Rose got off the bed with the intention of taking the remainder of the mixture – and the movement brought about the crisis. At the sight of the embryo, an inch long and dead white, I retched, then fell into uncontrollable weeping. But Rose was jubilant. . . . 'As soon as it's dark,' she cried joyfully, 'we'll carry it up to the bridge and drop it into the creek. The tide will carry it out.'[77]

In the mining village the girl's knowledge was expanded:

> The favourite and constant topic, over tea or beer, was sex; and especially those aspects of it having to do with procreation. Methods of birth control, their success or failure, and the procuration of abortion, was ever under review.[78]

But for herself, the young woman was unconvinced:

> My own interest in these matters was, so far, abstract: for somehow I had become possessed of a smug, pseudo-virtuous notion regarding artificial means of prevention. Never, I would snobbishly state, would I 'degrade' myself by using these methods of family limitation. The older women would laugh derisively. 'Wait till you've had a few kids! Then you'll change your tune.'[79]

The period Devanny is recalling not only falls within the time frame Gardner is referring to, but also within Mansfield's life. (Devanny was born six years later than Mansfield in 1894, and both were in their teens in the early 1900s.) Such passages show that something like education in 'reproductive self-determination' was very much a feature of these years even if it was whispered in some communities (probably depending on class) and talked about openly in others. News travels, by rumour or – in this case – when one young woman moved a couple of miles on the West Coast of the South Island. In saying this I am not disputing the depressing statistics; at this time an education in such techniques as described above could be a desperate remedy, and an education in dangerous practices. 'Reproductive self-determination' sounds so sanitised and safe, but to be meaningful it has to refer not only to more recent times when a woman can choose safe legal abortion, but also to earlier times when ideas about limiting pregnancies were spread informally. The consequences of this – for example maternal mortality from dangerous abortions – could perhaps be thought of as eventually leading to expanded contraceptive information and the legalisation of abortion. Seen in this way, reproductive self-determination is an idea as much as a practice, a revolutionary leap in thinking.

So how does 'Prelude' manifest this 'BC/AD' shift and how can it be seen as part of the contemporary discourse on 'self-determination'? Heterosexual relationships, where unprotected sex is the norm and not discussed, are still familiar territory but that this should be mostly the case in long-term marriage relationships marks the shift. In middle-class marriages conversation about sex or birth control was often taboo, or at least extremely strained. Such a marriage would have had a different character from most middle-class marriages in the 1990s, when explicit discussion of sexual topics occurs everywhere from women's magazines to party conversations. We should also consider the situation of Katherine Mansfield as a young woman in the 1910s who has rebelled against the conventional notions of female desire, who has had a number of extra-marital relationships (probably with women as well as men), who has been pregnant and lost an unborn child, who has suffered from infections associated with venereal disease and is possibly sterile, and who in her writing life is pursuing an artistic ambition to convey sensuality and desire outside the conventional limits of romantic narrative or family romance.[80] She also wants to question stereotypes of masculinity and femininity. How would she write about women characters similar to her mother and women of her mother's generation, and with what motives would she do so?

First, Mansfield's 'Prelude'can be seen as taking a speaking position similar to that of Jean Devanny, who commented on the Puponga women's preoccupation with the topic of sex: 'especially those aspects having to do with procreation'.[81] The young Devanny could say: 'Never . . . would I degrade myself with these methods of family limitation', but the older Devanny and the older Mansfield have obviously learnt differently. This is already implied in Devanny's retrospective account of her adolescence – labelling herself 'snobbish' and recalling the older women warning: 'Wait till you've had a few kids.' There is thus an ambiguous play of perspectives between past and present, which allows the reader to put herself and her own experience into the mix.

The Mansfield story can be seen as a similarly retrospective account. The author is a woman looking back on herself as a young girl and recollecting the advice or information she was once given by her mother, being told (albeit obliquely) about sex and pregnancy. It is interesting here to consider some more extratextual evidence about the author's life. When Katherine Mansfield wrote this story her brother had just died, and we have already seen how other critics have found grieving for him as obliquely shaping the story, but I want to go one step further and argue that the conception of Katherine Mansfield's brother coincides with the exact days on which Mansfield set this story. The story can thus be seen as a daughter's piecing together of an unrecognised moment in her mother's life – the occasion and circumstances of the conception of her son, the writer's brother.

This idea makes the story much more linear and a little like a detective fiction – closer to another Mansfield story about a New Zealand woman, 'Woman at the Store', than we perhaps thought.[82] If 'Prelude' is a detective story, it can be read in the following way (and I use the loaded term 'clue' rather than Bordwell's 'cues' because I am consciously constructing a reading of 'Prelude' as inviting the reader to play detective):

> Textual clues
>
> *First clue*: Prelude: something coming before. In music, a prelude to the main part. If the main part is life, then the prelude is the conception.
>
> *Second clue:* Overheard dialogue: *Him*: 'I'm so confoundedly happy.' *Her*: 'Are you?' Perhaps he is very pleased about her being pregnant. Whereas she is unsure. (Of course he can't possibly know she is pregnant but he may surmise and, yes, it could be another daughter but there is the possibility of a son.)
>
> *Third clue:* Stanley is very happy on ride home.
>
> *Fourth clue (extratextual):* Leslie Stephen, Katherine Mansfield's brother, was born on 21 February 1894. If Easter was late that year (the two families are recorded as moving just after Easter 1893) then the days of that move would correlate with the probable date of his conception (a sum Katherine Mansfield could also have done).[83]
>
> *Fifth clue (extratextual):* Katherine Mansfield said of the story 'The Aloe,' which was the draft for 'Prelude' and from which she hoped to develop a novel: '"The Aloe" is lovely. It simply fascinates me, and I know that is what you would wish me to write' (the 'you' being her dead brother). 'And now I know what the last chapter is. It is your birth. . . . That chapter will end the book.'[84]

As we have seen, Ian Gordon wrote that Mansfield's subtlety as a writer was revealed in the fact that mourning her brother's death she did not write directly about him. The present reading would challenge this kind of assertion. An admiration for distance and objectivity were characteristic of an earlier period of criticism. A post-colonial interest in settler society turns us as readers back to the past in a different way, eager to (re)construct intimate details of an earlier way of life in order to see how ideas of individualtiy are produced. Some other readings stressed fragmentation; but now we are looking to linearity and the literal. Relatedly, Linda Burnell is a figure who suggests a portrait of Mansfield's own mother, not only because Kezia her daughter is associated with the author in this and other stories, but also because the character of Linda Burnell, like Mansfield's mother Annie Beauchamp, was apparently more interested in the social side of life than in rearing children, a task often left to the grandmother and servants.[85] This woman, we can assume, was bearing children in the 1880s and 1890s at the time births started to decline, but she was also the wife of a newly affluent businessman whose move to the outskirts of the city implied success – and visions of dynastic growth. At the beginning of this story this man does not have a 'longed-for' son. It may be that by the end he does (perhaps?). Certainly, in the later story 'At the Bay' we know the Burnells have a baby boy.

'Prelude' opens with Linda, mother of three daughters and wife of Stanley Burnell, setting off in a loaded buggy for their new house. The buggy is crammed with 'absolute necessities' and the two younger girls, not considered as such, have to be left behind with neighbours. 'We shall simply have to cast them off,' their mother exclaims. This abandonment of, significantly, two daughters is the beginning of a story which can be seen as opening up an ambiguous area between the idea of femininity and motherhood, eroticism and fertility, a story which puzzles about whether or not there is a necessary relationship between female sexuality and pregnancy, even between sex and marriage, and what it would mean if there is not. These questions are opened up through the portrait of a strained marriage.

The girls are not taken to their new home until evening. It is dark when they first see the house: 'The soft white bulk of it lay stretched upon the green garden like a sleeping beast.' This choice of metaphor for the house suggests its animality, perhaps the beast within, within people and within the house. The 'bulk' of the sleeping beast might be associated with the man of the house, though 'soft and white' might suggest a woman's body. The mysterious life inside is confirmed when 'one and now another of the windows leaped into light. Someone was walking through the empty rooms carrying a lamp'.

Kezia is the first to see the house, but the sensual atmosphere is continued in the description and sensations of Lottie, as she awakens in the new environment:

> 'Where are we?' said Lottie, sitting up. Her reefer cap was all on one side and on her cheek there was the print of an anchor button she had pressed against while sleeping. Tenderly the storeman lifted her, set her cap straight, and pulled down her crumpled clothes.[86]

This sensuous mood is belied inside the house. Kezia's exuberance ('"Ooh," cried Kezia, flinging up her arms') has to be curbed because 'Poor little mother has got such a headache.' There is little tenderness from her mother: '"Are those the children?" But Linda did not really care; she did not even open her eyes to see.'

The action at the table is more sanguine. Stanley Burnell and Linda's sister, Beryl, are eating: 'Have another chop, Beryl. Tip-top meat, isn't it? Not too lean and not too fat,' Stanley suggests euphemistically. The children having been rebuked and his wife silent, Stanley strolls over to the fireplace still chatting to Beryl while he waits for his mother-in-law to find his slippers:

> Burnell got up, stretched himself, and going over to the fire he turned his back to it and lifted his coat tails.
> 'By Jove, this is a pretty pickle. Eh, Beryl?'
> Beryl, sipping tea, her elbows on the table, smiled over the cup at him. She wore an

unfamiliar pink pinafore; the sleeves of her blouse were rolled up to her shoulders showing her lovely freckled arms, and she had let her hair fall down her back in a long pigtail.

Stanley needs attention from his lovely sister-in-law. Linda's lack of participation on the first night in the new house is depressing him; ignoring him and the children, she lies with her eyes closed. Beryl provides the feminine warmth and composure required. However, Stanley's interest in Beryl has ramifications. It gives Beryl the confidence to tease him when she describes the hard work she has been doing to get the house straight: 'The servant girl and I have simply slaved all day.' It also makes her vulnerable to his irritation:

> '. . . We have never sat down for a moment. We have had a day.'
> Stanley scented a rebuke.
> 'Well, I suppose you did not expect me to rush away from the office and nail carpets – did you?'
> 'Certainly not,' laughed Beryl. She put down her cup and ran out of the dining-room.
> 'What the hell does she expect us to do?' asked Stanley. 'Sit down and fan herself with a palm leaf fan while I have a gang of professionals to do the job? By Jove, if she can't do a hand's turn occasionally without shouting about it in return for . . . .'[87]

This exchange has an adverse effect on Stanley's digestion; it is a moment where his wife needs to step in, to reclaim him from her sister and to alleviate all his testy agitation which will do no good to her or the rest of the family:

> But Linda put up a hand and dragged him down to the side of her long chair.
> 'This is a wretched time for you, old boy,' she said. Her cheeks were very white but she smiled and curled her fingers into the big red hand she held. Burnell became quiet. Suddenly he began to whistle 'Pure as a lily, joyous and free' – a good sign.
> 'Think you're going to like it?' he asked.

Linda is still white faced, not feeling well, but she knows the importance of quietening Stanley. At this point she offers him physical affection. Perhaps she promises to offer more of herself, offers some 'fun' tonight when she curls her fingers into the big red hand – certainly it starts him whistling.

Linda's role as wife and mother requires her occasionally to carry out certain moves and give certain speeches. Similarly his sister-in-law, another of Stanley's dependants, must do 'a hand's turn occasionally' and be very nice to him in return for being accommodated in his house. No wonder Beryl's sensuous and sexual feelings get linked with her anxiety about lack of financial independence. In this mood she undresses in a pool of moonlight, fantasising a male gaze outside the window ('letting her clothes fall back, pushing with a languid gesture her warm, heavy hair. . . . The window was wide open; it was warm, and somewhere out there in the garden a young man, dark and slender, with mocking eyes . . . '). But then her thoughts turn to Stanley as a reminder of her actual situation ('"How frightfully unreasonable Stanley is sometimes," she thought, buttoning. And then as she lay down came the old cruel thought – ah, if only she had money of her own.'). Before she goes to sleep, Beryl's fantasies become more specific, about a future husband with money ('A young man, immensely rich, has just arrived from England. He meets her quite by chance . . . ')[88]

In this sequence where all the night-time scenes are linked together, Beryl's moment at the window leads into a scene between Stanley and Linda. The heat that Beryl and Stanley have stirred up around each other is being neatly transformed by Linda, who is willing to listen to Stanley's boasting from the calm depths of their bed:

> 'The thing that pleases me,' said Stanley, leaning against the side of the bed and giving himself a good scratch on his shoulders and back before turning in, 'is that I've got the place dirt cheap, Linda. I was talking about it to little Wally Bell to-day and he said he simply could not understand why they had accepted my figure. You see land about here is bound to become more and more valuable . . . in about ten years' time . . . of course we shall have to go very slow and cut down expenses as fine as possible. Not asleep – are you?'[89]

Whether Linda has been asleep or not, she knows the appropriate response: 'No dear, I've heard every word' – and how to flatter and soothe him:

> 'Good night, Mr Business Man,' said she, and she took hold of his head by the ears and gave him a quick kiss. Her faint far-away voice seemed to come from a deep well.

She also knows that this is the time that she is required to give him that anchoring of sex. So that when he draws her to him, not assuming too much ('Good night, darling,'), she responds: 'Yes, clasp me.' ('"Yes, clasp me," said the faint voice from the deep well.') If this is read as the time of sex and conception, what follows is a dream about the consequences.

Linda dreams of metamorphosis, and the swelling 'of a tiny ball of fluff . . . a tiny bird', into a baby with 'a big naked head and a gaping bird-mouth, opening and shutting'.[90] No doubt Linda is anxious about the consequences of the sex she gave, whether with enjoyment or not, and aware of a possible pregnancy.

Stanley Burnell, on the other hand, is delighted with himself: he has become more than he was. For a man having a son is very special. Not only will the son be his heir but creating a son cements the father's place in a patriarchal society. By virtue of his successful marriage and career and now with the possibility of a son and heir, he has successfully negotiated the oedipus complex – and has a whole new oedipal relationship awaiting him with his son. In theorist Nancy Armstrong's words 'the penis goes in as just another penis but it comes out of the mother as a phallus'.[91] Nancy Armstrong's argument is interesting to us because it is about Freud's model of the family which was so influential at the period Mansfield wrote this story. Freud's model, she argues, transformed (and mythologised) a previous relatively transparent gender contract between economic and emotional power. Whereas marriage was formerly a contract that 'translated money into love and converted the competitive operations of the marketplace into family relations', Freud's theory recast it so that 'the places of the family provide the ultimate explanation for all power relations'. The contract also gets recast as one of presence and absence and in 'somatic terms' as masculinity represented by the penis. But, in this model, to become the phallus the penis has to be desired by the mother. Armstrong's conclusion that 'this theory offers the ultimate mystification of middle-class power' is an apt description of what is unfolding in the story, at least in the representation of Stanley.[92] He becomes powerful when desired by Linda and when he looks forward to being the father of a son.

The contrast between Stanley and Linda is pinpointed when Linda's dream is broken into next morning by Stanley's cheerful rattling of the blinds:

> . . . she woke to see Burnell standing by the windows rattling the venetian blind up to the very top.
> 'Hullo,' he said. 'Didn't wake you, did I? Nothing much wrong with the weather this morning.'

There was nothing much wrong with anything as far as he was concerned. Last night his wife had conceived, he's sure of it, their son. (That night he will look at the empty place at the top of the dining room table and say to himself: 'That's where my boy ought to sit.') Now everything is going to be all right. He will have acquired all that he needs for his expansion of family and business – 'He felt somehow that he had bought the lovely day, too, got it chucked in dirt cheap with the house and ground' (and the women). He feels virile and satisfied as the result of Linda's embraces. He dashes off to his bath and comes back to exercise while Linda, 'raised on one elbow', surveys the room:

> Back came Stanley girt with a towel, glowing and slapping his thighs. He pitched the wet towel on top of her hat and cape, and standing firm in the exact centre of a square of sunlight he began to do his exercises. Deep breathing, bending and squatting like a frog and shooting out his legs. He was so delighted with his firm, obedient body that he hit himself on the chest and gave a loud 'Ah.'[93]

But for Linda the knowledge of a possible conception and the memory of the previous night have made her even more remote: '. . . this amazing vigour seemed to set him worlds away from Linda. She lay on the white tumbled bed and watched as if from the clouds.' Yet she is good-humoured towards his posturings when he shows off his fitness: '"I haven't a square inch of fat on me. Feel that." "It's rock – it's iron," mocked she.'

Stanley can now also enjoy Beryl's attentions – he scored his own victory last night, the categories of things are in their places. The right people are making money. The right man will have a son. In this frame of mind he can't be ruffled by Beryl:

'Breakfast, Stanley.' Beryl was at the door. 'Oh, Linda, mother says you are not to get up yet.' She popped her head in at the door. She had a big piece of syringa stuck through her hair.

'Everything we left on the verandah last night is simply sopping this morning. You should see poor dear mother wringing out the tables and the chairs. However, there is no harm done – ' this with the faintest glance at Stanley.[94]

He can now take her flirtatiousness as a token of esteem, something that is owed to him.

For Linda the day that follows is punctuated with hints of the night before. From bed she hears her children playing in the garden. She resents the celebration of the blinds pulled up to the very top by Stanley. She traces the flowers on the wallpaper and imagines them swelling up. She remembers her dream. She thinks of inanimate things coming alive. When she finally gets out of bed, she goes to the kitchen for something to eat. There she sees everything arranged in a way typical of her 'mother' (all in pairs) and Beryl singing about birds (birds again): 'How many thousand birds I see/ That sing aloud from every tree.' And when, at her mother's instruction, she goes into the garden to see the children and comes across Kezia regarding an aloe (planted in an island that lay in the middle of the drive – a drive that has previously been described as a 'whiplash'), it is quite predictable that she should find this plant symbolic of what has been happening to her:

'Mother, what is it?' asked Kezia.

Linda looked up at the fat swelling plant with its cruel leaves and fleshy stem. High above them, as though becalmed in the air, and yet holding so fast to the earth it grew from, it might have had claws instead of roots. The curving leaves seemed to be hiding something; the blind stem cut into the air as if no wind could ever shake it.

'That is an aloe, Kezia,' said her mother.

'Does it ever have any flowers?'

'Yes, Kezia,' and Linda smiled down at her, and half shut her eyes. 'Once every hundred years.'[95]

While Linda ponders her probable pregnancy, Stanley as reward for her tenderness and attention purchases some sumptuous, sensuous gifts of food:

On his way home from the office Stanley Burnell stopped the buggy at the Bodega, got out and bought a large bottle of oysters. At the Chinaman's shop next door he bought a pineapple in the pink of condition, and noticing a basket of fresh black cherries he told John to put him in a pound of those as well.

As a husband, businessman, and now landowner, Stanley Burnell is delighted with his world. Pat the handyman has been handling the mare and buggy on this trip home: '"Did she satisfy yer, sir?" said Pat getting off the box and grinning at his master', reminding him perhaps of the fact that his wife 'satisfied' him the previous night but also intensifying his anxiety about the possibility of his wife not being there to welcome him, or not fully reciprocating his feeling for her.

The Burnells' move to the country would have been typical of successful families of the period but a symbol of new affluence creates new pressures. Stanley's sense of identity, his ambition and his success are dependent on his womenfolk, his children and his house, but now he has put them at a point remote from him. He's worried at what will have become of them while he is gone; he is full of anticipation of Linda's gentle greeting.

> A sort of panic overtook Burnell whenever he approached near home. Before he was well inside the gate he would shout to anyone within sight: 'Is everything all right?' And then he did not believe it was until he heard Linda say 'Hullo, are you home again?'

He is relieved when he does hear her familiar greeting:

> Linda came out of the glass door; her voice rang in the shadowy quiet. 'Hullo! Are you home again?'
> At the sound of her his heart beat so hard that he could hardly stop himself dashing up the steps and catching her in his arms.
> 'Yes, I'm home again. Is everything all right?'[96]

It is as if Linda Burnell does not belong in the world that her husband and other men are developing. Her cool, drifty, half-hearted response to Stanley Burnell's enthusiasm is noticeable to the reader but not to Stanley, as if he would be too hearty and bluff to understand any but the most crass rebuff. He offers the presents as tokens of gratitude; she is cautious, teasing, unresponsive; but he is now the one who knows he will get what he wants.

> 'You seem pretty snug, mother,' said Burnell, blinking at the light. Isabel and Lottie sat one on either side of the table, Kezia at the bottom–the place at the top was empty.
> 'That's where my boy ought to sit,' thought Stanley. He tightened his arm round Linda's shoulder. By God, he was a perfect fool to feel as happy as this![97]

With the possibility of a son in his mind, Stanley is no longer frightened of the women in his family. Both the desires they arouse in him and their superior powers of management are less threatening now. Upstairs in the bedroom with his wife he 'put his arms round her and pressed her head into his shoulder. "I'm so confoundedly happy," he said.' But his wife is contemplating how her body has been taken over, the patterns of pregnancy and birth to come. 'Are you?' she responds, and her distance is implied by her sensitivity to the dark world outside:

> It was quite dark outside now and heavy dew was falling. When Linda shut the window the cold dew touched her finger tips. Far away a dog barked. 'I believe there is going to be a moon,' she said.
> At the words and with the cold wet dew on her fingers, she felt as though the moon had risen – that she was being strangely discovered in flood of cold light. She shivered; she came away from the window and sat down on the box ottoman beside Stanley.[98]

The following morning the children are playing again; this time playing at giving a luncheon party with geranium-leaf plates. In their grown up roles they discuss babies and servants: 'Yes, I've brought my twins. I have had another baby since I saw you last, but she came so suddenly that I haven't had any time to make her clothes, yet. So, I left her.'[99] The day continues with games, and betrayals – Pat killing the duck for the dinner table, the children's response to its killing, and tensions between Alice, the servant, and Beryl.

At dinner that night – their third in the house – Stanley Burnell asks rhetorically about the duck: '"Is this the first of the home products?" he asked, knowing perfectly well that it was', but he also knows that another home product will one day soon be sitting at this table – his very own son, conceived and born on this estate. The connection between baby and bird is drawn once again, and making a biographical leap we as readers are also aware of another veiled parallel – the fact that when Katherine Mansfield wrote the story her own brother was already dead.

But Stanley's new confidence is cemented; he can enjoy his sister-in-law's cleavage and her conversation, over a game of cribbage:

> In the front of her dress Beryl wore a bunch of pansies, and once when the little pegs were side by side, she bent over and the pansies dropped out and covered them.
> 'What a shame,' said she, picking up the pansies. 'Just as they had a chance to fly into each other's arms.'
> 'Farewell my girl,' laughed Stanley and away the red peg hopped.[100]

On this third evening in the house (and the last in the story) the moon and the aloe, the two images that match Linda's awareness of having conceived a child (or should I say our awareness of her having conceived a son), appear together. Linda goes outside with her mother, who is bathed in the dazzling light of the full moon while contemplating the aloe: '"I have been looking at the aloe," said Mrs Fairfield. "I believe it is going to flower this year".' Once again, our attention is drawn to Linda's fertility.

What follows is Linda's contemplation of her marriage, her future, her husband ('he was awfully simple, easily pleased, easily hurt'), her sexual relationship with him, and her strategies in the relationship, alongside her sense of her own delicacy. She thought about how she 'hated him'. But she also thought about how after times when he frightened her 'how tender he was, how submissive, how thoughtful'. These thoughts are punctuated by dreams of escape, and of aggression: 'She dreamed that she was caught up out of the cold water into the ship within the lifted oars and the budding mast. . . . How much more real this dream was than that they should go back to the house where the sleeping children lay and where Stanley and Beryl played cribbage.'[101]

The ship and the aloe are linked because the aloe's thorns are seen as protection against impregnation and fertilisation: 'she particularly liked the long sharp thorns. . . . Nobody would dare to come near the ship or to follow after.' But she knows she has no other possible solution but to accept the birth of this child.

•

This reading of the story in terms of the conception of a son should not encourage one to see it only from Linda's point of view; it is also the story of a father investing his pride and prosperity in the idea of a son. The inspiration was the author's real brother who, when the story was written, was already dead. This accounts for some of the cynicism with which the habits of the characters are presented, particularly the way in which Stanley's optimism is portrayed. What can be deduced from this? That the story suggests the transience of happiness, of material (and marital) success? Perhaps yes, but more specifically it presents the colonial project – the invention of a society, the need to get somewhere, building one's reputation with the right house and family. The story observes this project from a cynical distance, from the distance of the 'mother' country at war, and whose imperial ambitions (albeit elsewhere) have ended in the trenches. It also suggests the prescience of ungrateful daughters of the colonists, who were aware of their prescribed role as breeders for the benefit of the British Empire. One might draw the conclusion that the story is, like 'Bliss,' partly a satire on the new Freudian mystification of gender relations, particularly with its stress on the rule of the father.

CONCLUSION: THE GIRL ON THE VERANDAH

– AN UNGRATEFUL DAUGHTER?

All over this country, brooding on squatters' verandahs or mooning in selectors' huts, there are scattered here and there hundreds of lively, dreamy, Australian girls whose queer, uncomprehended ambitions are the despair of the household. They yearn, they aspire for what they know not; but it is essentially a yearning for a fuller, stronger life – the cry of their absorbed, imprisoned sunlight for action, action, action![102]

My final reading of 'Prelude' does (like some nationalist readings) see it as about ambivalence towards the optimistic materialistic colonial project, but other readings have not always noticed how decidedly female that ambivalence is. A case in point is Allen Curnow's focus on the self-description of the poet in Mansfield's poem to 'To Stanislaw Wyspianski.' 'I, a woman, with the taint of the pioneer in my blood,' he quotes, but doesn't notice the 'woman', only the 'taint of the pioneer'. He sees her sense of shame as characterising the emergence of a New Zealand psyche. It can be argued, however, that there is special meaning to being a woman and having a 'taint of the pioneer' in one's blood. It could mean not only the memory of physical hardship and sacrifice, persistent focus on future material prosperity, and a taint that disallows a person from valuing the life of the mind, but also, for women, a taint of physical submission from having had to bear the children of the future while simultaneously struggling to keep the European conventions of the family alive (the pioneer women's role).

Katherine Mansfield, in her writing about her family and particularly her father, repeatedly stressed the vulgarity of their habits. It was as if, for her, escaping the taint of the pioneer was escaping male crudity and female practicality – the two sides of the coin in this gender-divided society, in which people followed their assigned roles in a docile and almost childlike way.

In the poem she wrote: 'They have worked in the broad light of day and handled the clay with rude fingers; /What would they know of ghosts and unseen presences'/ . . . And the tapestry woven from the tragic dreams of your childhood/ They would tear in their stupid hands'. In her notebooks she records of her father on meeting him again after her time at school in London: 'His hands, covered with long sandy hair are absolutely cruel hands. A physically revolted feeling seizes me.'[103] And: 'Damn my family. Oh, Heavens what bores they are. I shall certainly not be here much longer. Thank heaven for that! Even when I am alone in a room, they come outside and call to each other, discuss the butcher's orders, or the soiled linen and I feel wreck my life.'[104]

Fig. 1. 'Wellington's Heritage'. Advertisement, *Evening Post*, 12 October 1994, page 5.

Fig. 2. 'Katherine Mansfield Birthplace, Te Puakitanga'. Pamphlet of the Katherine Mansfield Birthplace Society, 1996.

Katherine Mansfield left New Zealand in 1908, when she was 19, impatient to seek her fortune in London. She never returned, but in her stories she came back, time and again, to all the places she had known as a little girl and to the house where she spent her earliest childhood.

KATHERINE MANSFIELD'S
Muse House

Fig. 3. 'Katherine Mansfield's Muse' is assumed to be her Thorndon birthplace in this *Belle Design and Decorating* article celebrating settler heritage. *Belle*, June/July 1991.

recent

books

Mary has made up her mind

she can not and will not be

a governess, a teacher, a

milliner, a bonnet-maker nor

housemaid ... so she is

leaving [England].

Charlotte Bronte (on the decision of
her friend Mary Taylor to emigrate to
New Zealand)

Fig. 4. An evocative literary reference on the catalogue cover of Bridget Williams Books, 1995. The feminist publisher's use of Charlotte Brontë's words of advice to British immigrant Mary Taylor accord with the received idea of New Zealand as a place of opportunity for women.

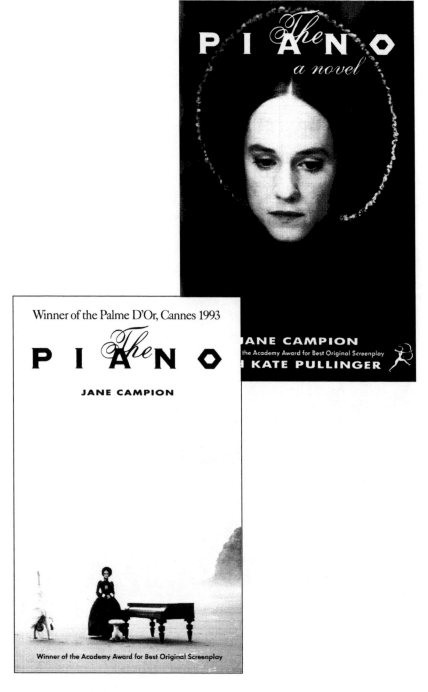

Fig. 5. Covers of *The Piano* screen play, novel (top) and publicity publication were uniformly packaged.

Fig. 6. The mise-en-scène of the Theatre at Large historical drama *Savage Hearts* (1994) echoes Campion's *Piano*.

Fig. 7. Still from *Desperate Remedies* with Kevin Smith and Peter Brunt. This sequence of men washing, shaving and socialising in a communal washhouse plays with the ambiguities of male comradeship characterising settler society.

Fig. 8. Cover of *The Story of a New Zealand River*, 1960.

Fig. 9. Still from *Iris*. Helen Morse, as the actress who plays Iris, and Derek Challis, Hyde's son, as himself, discuss the sensitive task of re-creating Iris's life.

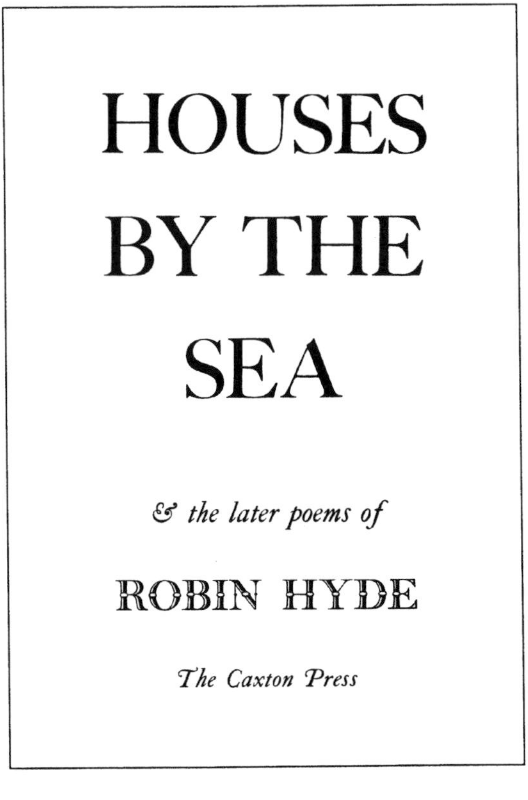

HOUSES BY THE SEA

& the later poems of

ROBIN HYDE

The Caxton Press

Fig. 10. Cover of Robin Hyde's *Houses by the Sea*, 1952.

THE MENACE OF JAPAN
Professor Taid O'Conroy

Professor O'Conroy's book is a startling revelation of the soul of modern Japan. He portrays a country that is corrupt from one end to the other. He shows that the power is in the hands of a few strong men. In this volume are authenticated stories of the debauching of Buddhist priests, unutterable cruelty, sex orgies, of trafficking in human flesh, of baby brokers. The book is not mere sensationalism ; it is a cold, logical thesis compiled by the author during his fifteen years in Nippon. George Bernard Shaw referred to it as "a work of great importance."

This new edition has been thoroughly revised and brought up to date.

Paternoster Library. 3s. 6d. *net.*

MY AUTOBIOGRAPHY — Benito Mussolini

Parallel to the meteoric rise of Adolf Hitler, is the astonishing career of Benito Mussolini, Italy's great dictator. The story of his humble beginnings, his activities as a socialist and a soldier in the Great War, his subsequent rapid accession to power provides a most interesting comparison to his counter-part beyond the Brenner Pass. It is a book that is historically valuable, giving us, as it does, intimate pictures of Fascism in theory and practice.

In the heat of the recent political discussions at Geneva and elsewhere, there has been a widespread tendency to belittle the magnificent achievements of a man, who, whatever may be said of his political ideology is undoubt- e saviour of

MY STRUGGLE — Adolf Hitler

as "Extra-
to it as a
ronicle said

It would not be exaggerating to say that no more important autobiography than this has been published since the War, and certainly no autobiography has been issued for decades over which controversy has raged so bitterly. Whatever one's political views may be, it is a book everyone should read, for it reveals the forces and circumstances which went to make a remarkable character, whose intense belief in his ideals won over a mighty nation, and changed the course of history.

net.

The *News Chronicle* called it "an astonishing book"; the *Evening News* said : "It commands attention." *Morning Post :* "We recommend a close study of this book." The *Evening Standard* said : "The whole of the political Hitler is in these brutally candid pages." Major F. Yeats-Brown wrote : "I hope 'My Struggle' will be published in a cheap edition."

First published (18/6 net) . . .	October,	1933
Second, Third, Fourth, Fifth and Sixth Impressions	October,	1933
Seventh and Eighth Impressions . .	November,	1933
Ninth and Tenth Impressions .	January,	1934
Cheap Edition	October,	1935
Cheap Edition	December,	1935

Paternoster Library. 3s. 6d. *net.*

Fig. 11. Advertisements from the end pages of Robin Hyde's *Passport to Hell*, 1936, remind us of the international context in which Hyde was published.

CHAPTER THREE

•

The Piano:
Listening for Echoes

The reading issue that I shall discuss next is one which commanded enough popular attention locally to be featured in a television current affairs programme in the same week that it was the topic of a university seminar. This suggests that it has a peculiar significance for local viewers or readers. It concerns a novel and a film.

The feature film *The Piano* was released in 1993 to enthusiastic audiences in America and Europe, and later in Australia and New Zealand. It received a very positive press and was the winner of many awards, notably sharing the Palme d'Or at Cannes. (Jane Campion was the first woman director to receive this recognition.) At the Academy Awards in the United States, Jane Campion won the award for Best Screenplay and young New Zealander Anna Paquin for Best Supporting Actress. The film was appreciated as an *auteur* movie set in a wildly beautiful location, 'a visually sumptuous, psychologically complex and often troubling story dwelling on familiar Campion themes of communication and passion.'[1] Advertisements for the film in the *New York Times* and *Los Angeles Times,* written to boost the film as an Oscar contender, emphasised the spirit of community in the making of the film with 'glowing comments from those involved . . . about their colleagues' and also stressed 'the role of women' in the project.[2] Publicity by Miramax spoke of 'the cross cultural quality' as 'one of the most deeply moving aspects of being on the production.'[3] Associating the film with the history of high culture, Jane Campion described the storyline as 'a transposed version of Emily Brontë's Gothic classic, *Wuthering Heights'*.[4]

Academics also took up discussion of the film immediately after its release: for example an issue of a periodical about the film was published in Italy in 1994 and a book of essays *Piano Lessons* was compiled in 1995; critical essays have since proliferated.[5] Many of these critics see the film as going beyond the gestures of liberal feminism in a 1990s feminist (or 'post-feminist') exploration of nineteenth-century sexuality.[6] A reviewer in *Sight and Sound* contrasted it with the more straight-forward equality-based feminism in the film of *My Brilliant Career*, while Jane Campion and her producer commented that though *The Piano* evolved from romantic fiction and has a nineteenth-century setting, it also has a 'modern' and daring dimension where the romantic focus shifts 'for Ada from her lover Baines to her husband Stewart', and 'Ada actually uses her husband as a sexual object'.[7]

I want to discuss the film from a perspective other than any of the above. An exchange from a film magazine correspondence column will help explain the approach I am proposing. A moviegoer writes to a columnist:

> Dear Pat: I almost had a heart attack when the writer in the movie *Stand by Me*, played by Richard Dreyfus, turned off his word processor without pushing the key to 'save' the story. Now a friend insists that this was meant to be symbolic, that he was putting the past behind him. What are the facts?
>
> Hacker, Marina del Ray, California.

> Dear Hacker: It was ignorance, not philosophical. Neither director Rob Reiner nor Dreyfus uses home computers – nor apparently did anyone else connected with the picture.[8]

This is an example that David Bordwell uses to explain different ways in which we make meaning from film and text. The anomaly in the film, interpretable in a formalist way as having a special symbolic meaning, could on this occasion also be explained by means of extratextual information. The director and actor were quite ignorant about computers. Bordwell draws certain inferences from the example:

> The first tactic encourages the critic to ask, 'What does the referential anomaly contribute to the text. . . . The second tactic invites the critic to ask, 'How did this anomaly get in the text?'. . . . The disparity is between the functionalist and causal explanations, and more notoriously between a 'formalist' criticism and a 'historical' one.[9]

The strategy of my reading involves in a general way this movement from a question about what referential uncertainty contributes (to the film) to a question about how it got in. This is a movement that Bordwell explains as generally a shift from formalist to historical criticism. I do not wish to imply that one approach is right and the other wrong. However, formalism did certainly take aggressive forms at the height of New Criticism – readers were warned to avoid the intentional fallacy, the misconception that the writer's real intentions could be any more finally located in a writer's comment on the text than in the text itself – whereas the last twenty years has seen a swing back to various contextualising approaches.

In the case of *The Piano* I am proposing a reading which is informed by a cluster of extratextual elements because I want to incorporate the kind of local experience which I think informs New Zealand understanding of the film. In particular I show how extratextual information led me to a connection with another text, a 1920s novel, Jane Mander's *The Story of a New Zealand River,* which can be seen as a 'pre-text' for the film, and one which has been overlooked and suppressed. This 'pre-text' shows the film in a new light. I draw on information, now in the public domain, for the movie having this relationship with this novel, and suggest that the implicit and thematic meanings that other critics have ascribed to Ada's muteness (a marvellously ambiguous silence, a sign of repression, etc.) can alternatively be seen, by someone familiar with both novel and film, as half-hidden or partly transformed references to that novel – connections that one could interpret as disguised because of the embarrassing presence of another production company's adaptation and prior ownership of film rights to the novel.[10]

I am also suggesting that *The Piano* is, in more ways than one, a palimpsest. Not only does it erase the realist approach and character motivations of the 1920s novel, but also it is unable to bring it fully into the 1990s. It is able to go only so far as the nationalism of the 1960s. The result is a 1960s view of New Zealand and its race relations; but the palimpsest (or pentimento effect) is strong because one can also see nineteenth-century elements, traces of the 1920s novel, and inevitably also elements of 1992–93.[11]

My discussion is importantly intertextual since there are a large number of primary sources involved. There is the novel *The Story of a New Zealand River,* the film *The Piano,* and the filmscript 'The River'. Other 'texts' include the Beethoven sonatas played in *The Story of a New Zealand River* (the *Appassionata* and the *Pathétique* for piano, and the *Kreutzer* sonata for violin and piano) and *The Piano* score and bestselling film-music CD by Michael Nyman. There is the published screenplay of *The Piano.* There is even a novelised version of *The Piano,* co-authored by Campion and Canadian novelist Kate Pullinger. There is also a little book about the making of *The Piano* (elegantly printed on expensive parchment) published by the film's distributors, Miramax, and sent to all members of the Academy, as well as the promotional video made for the movie and another made to promote Nyman's film music.[12] This proliferation of texts is not unusual for a successful film. A successful novel may also generate film, television and audio texts. To ignore all these surrounding texts, as we tend to do when we study only the 'primary text', is in some respects a narrow approach that exaggerates its uniqueness and also tends to ignore its extensive links with the 'market'.

Let us begin with some anecdotes. During the summer of 1992 two movies were being filmed locally with nineteenth-century New Zealand settings. Little information was released about them but Aucklanders came to know about them in various informal ways. For instance, I saw Sam Neill at the première of another New Zealand movie, *The End of the Golden Weather* (adapted from the Bruce Mason play by director Ian Mune).[13] He had remarkably greasy long locks which I was told were being grown for one of those movies.[14] Not long after, I met Michael Hurst and Jennifer Ward-Lealand in the Grey Lynn supermarket; both had period hairstyles and dyed hair and Michael was 'sporting' sideburns. One of these movies was of course *The Piano* (at that time referred to under its original titles *The Piano Lesson* or *The Piano Player*); the other was Peter Wells and Stuart Main's *Desperate Remedies.*[15]

I recalled these meetings when in early 1993 I saw a small notice in the local paper about a soon-to-be-released Jane Campion film, 'The Piano Lesson', and was particularly interested because I was teaching a new postgraduate course on Australian and New Zealand women writers – a course which included some late nineteenth-century writers and a number of early twentieth-century historical novels depicting colonial society in the late nineteenth-century.[16] In this class we discussed our anticipations of this movie and concurred with its use of 'piano' in the title because we had already touched on pianos as signifying the civilised customs that women were seen as bringing to a rough male colonial territory. And we concurred that the absurdity and difficulty of bringing an object as unwieldy as a piano to unknown and inaccessible areas intensified the powerfulness of the image. We were also aware that pianos had a peculiar significance in nineteenth-century European society. For instance *A History of Private Life*, a compendium based around studies of French society and literature, mentions a researcher who has discovered 'two thousand scenes in nineteenth-century novels in which a piano appears' – justification enough for the piano being called 'the lady's hashish'.[17] The chapter 'The Secret of the Individual' itemises the ways in which the piano was used to construct femininity in nineteenth century literature. They include the piano as a marker of familial intimacy and a sanctioned expression of female passion ('. . . the piano serves as an outlet for irrepressible passions … It is a piano that calms tumultuous feelings. . . . In this role the instrument replaced the horseback ride and the walk through a storm'). As a gift, it could be a sign of a man's rejection of a woman: according to some sources 'it was customary for a man to send a piano to a woman he had jilted'. Also, the rapt description of a woman playing at a candle-lit piano is described as encapsulating a male view of woman in this period.[18]

This is clearly not new territory and neither is it new in discussions of colonisation. Anyone familiar with New Zealand writing and colonial history will have thought about the significance if not the signification of pianos, which might explain the ironical effect in Janet Frame's *The Carpathians* when she has one of her characters remark: 'Oh, we used to be a great piano country! The early settlers, the families hoping to find paradise with acres of land, a mansion, servants, leisure, all brought their pianos and sheet music. The early battles to get land at all costs were fought by furniture and writing desks as well as by people.'[19]

We, my group of students and myself, thus accepted that the piano could be used as an important symbol of female character and migration, but a closer connection with any of the novels on the course wasn't suggested until one winter afternoon in 1993 when a friend had arranged to come round to (of all things) play the piano. While she played I watched her baby in the sun in the kitchen and reread (for my lecture) Jane Mander's *The Story of a New Zealand River*. Talking afterwards over a cup of tea, she noticed the novel and I asked about film producers Brigid Ikin and John Maynard and their work on it (I already knew that there had been plans to make a movie of the novel). I also expressed my interest in seeing the novel back in print.[20] She remarked that work on the film project was being discontinued because of too much similarity to Jane Campion's new movie. What she reported was that Brigid Ikin had begun development in 1985 on a film 'The River', an adaptation of *The Story of a New Zealand River*. An option on the rights was purchased from the nephew of the author via literary agent Ray Richards. She had shown the novel to Jane Campion as a possible director. My friend recalled that Campion had read the novel and not liked it, and had made negative remarks about the cold repressed figure of Alice, its main character. Then, she had gone away and written something very similar. My friend told this as a sad story, because it meant 'The River' could not be made: there was no audience for two such similar movies. It also meant that Mander could not be acknowledged by Campion.[21]

The difficulty of making 'The River' when 'The Piano' was already in production is a fact of film marketing – although a successful film generates a number of related *texts,* there is nevertheless not room for two similar *films.* A New Zealand film such as 'The River' could not compete with an overseas film such as *The Piano,* with a huge marketing budget, and would suffer greatly for being seen as imitative or derivative. The film market has its own reasons (as academics have theirs) for creating a mystique around the 'primary text' as unique, original, pure, etc. People go to see a film as a special 'one-off event' in contrast to television which is mass produced (or so the film marketers tell us) and a 24-hour continuous flow.

There was obviously the potential for legal and personal animosities over this incident. However, issues of copyright are notoriously difficult to prove; one has to make a case for something like 90 per cent similarity. The protagonists had clearly decided, for the sake of future professional and personal relationships, to resolve the matter privately. Brigid Ikin had after all been the producer of Campion's *Angel at My Table* and was no doubt keen to work with her again.

The anecdotal evidence above was subsequently given additional support by a number of newspaper articles by journalist Geoff Chapple, one of the authors of 'The River' script, and by an item on a current affairs programme *20/20* (TV 3, 19 July 1994). In this television programme Russell Campbell, an adviser on the script development of 'The River', confirmed that Jane Campion had been thought of as a possible director for the movie and shown its script. (Campbell, who teaches film at Victoria University, Wellington, recalls looking at nine drafts of 'The River').[22] The *20/20* programme also drew on, and quoted from, letters between the Film Commission, and John Maynard and Hibiscus Films. These letters (available under the Official Information Act) spoke of a 'release' document the producer of *The Piano,* Jan Chapman, wanted signed by Ikin and Maynard. The nature of this 'release' is not clear but apparently Maynard and Ikin were seeking the agreement of the Film Commission before signing. The Film Commission declined to release further letters discussing legal opinions obtained by Maynard and Ikin, on the grounds that legal opinions needed to be protected.[23]

My interest in this possible connection between film and novel, and film and filmscript, was not (either when I first came across it, or now) a judgemental one. However, I was intrigued by the complex intertextual web. I was also curious to see if the film would take part in the current reconsideration of what colonial experience meant for both European and Maori women, to which specifically I felt a new reading of Mander's novel could add. This reconsideration of women's history has been late coming in New Zealand and broadly speaking, as I suggested in my last chapter, the conventional view of colonial society, in as much as women figured in it at all, has been that it gave opportunities to European women. For example, migration has been seen as giving women the opportunity to marry, to escape restrictions of class, to learn new skills, escape roles, take joint management responsibilities in farming or business. In Australia, books such as Anne Summers' *Damned Whores and God's Police* and Miriam Dixson's *The Real Matilda* replaced the absence of women in the national tradition with stories of their oppression, as long ago as the 1970s.[24] But in New Zealand we missed out on this feminist challenge to the 'received' history and, as far as an overview goes, we had to rely on implicit arguments on behalf of women in the work of two male historians. In the 1980s Jock Phillips's *A Man's Country* suggested that the mores of colonial society were based on masculine competitiveness, physical prowess and ability to consume vast amounts of alcohol (with the obvious corollaries for women), while in the 1990s Miles Fairburn's *The Ideal Society and Its Enemies* similarly developed the argument that colonial society was atomised, lonely and often violent.[25]

A rereading of Jane Mander's novel could see it as showing the downside of migration for European women, in Alice's experience of a hurried and arbitrary marriage, physical isolation, loneliness and despair. Alternatively, if the focus of rereading was on the reconciliatory ending, the book could be seen as challenging the self-satisfied colonial narrative that wrote the woman's life happily into the story of the future and ignored the implied oppression of Maori and control of women. Did Jane Campion's rereading of some of the elements of the Mander novel propose a similar revision of nineteenth-century 'women's history'? This was the question with which I anticipated the movie. In order to answer it in any depth here, I need to establish the context by outlining the main features of the novel and the film, their receptions and a little about their authors.

JANE MANDER'S THE STORY OF A NEW ZEALAND RIVER

This novel, the first by Jane Mander (1877-1949), was written in New York during the First World War and accepted for publication by John Lane in 1918 before its 1920 publication in London and New York. The novel's title echoes that of Olive Schreiner's *The Story of an African Farm* and Mander saw parallels between her background and that of this other colonial woman novelist:

> Perhaps this nomadic life . . . made me want to write. Olive Schreiner once said she had to write *The Story of an African Farm* because she had looked so long at tigers crawling along the horizon against a fretwork of dead trees that something worked inside her. I rowed a flat-bottomed punt about the creeks and lagoons watching for a white heron that I never saw, and 'something' worked inside me.[26]

Both novels, bred in wild territories, show how aspects of femininity considered natural in a European context look strange or constructed in the colonial environment. They use the colonial experience to suggest that women should and can change. But though Mander's *Story* clearly has a feminist slant, hers is a much more optimistic narrative than Schreiner's. It is a love story and a family saga set in North Auckland, on the Kaipara Harbour, where Mander had herself lived – a late European settled area of tidal river, mudflat and bush, on the west coast fifty miles north of Auckland (a coastline not far from where *The Piano* was mostly filmed). The novel spans twenty years from around 1880–1901. It recounts the life of a family, a business, and a village; but the most important relationship is, as in *The Piano*, the one between mother and daughter.

The action takes place in the context of European settlement. One man's success as a timber merchant (cutting and shipping kauri) and his development of a new sawmill creates a thriving small settlement and eventually a family fortune – the family progress from camping in a tiny wooden house – only two finished rooms with a sack on the floor – to a (renovated and expanded) fashionably decorated family home. The story concerns the woman, Alice, lifted out of an ordered, defined, middle-class existence in Britain (sometimes she is English, sometimes British – but definitely Presbyterian) and placed by an obligatory marriage in an isolated bush community where conditions and people's ways are rough and strange. However, by the end of the novel, twenty years on, she is able to make a new marriage with the man she loves and to find her own voice.

Alice has a daughter, Asia – the other main character. There is a history outside the time frame of the narrative. At the beginning of the novel we know only that Alice, supposedly widowed, arrived in Christchurch with her piano and a child. Later in the book this history is recounted: Alice tells how she had been seduced and abandoned by 'the handsomest man ever seen in [her] town' when only eighteen years old, then thrown out of the house by her father when it was found that she was 'going to have a child'. Emigration seemed to be Alice's only solution. Asia was born in Sydney: 'It was wrong done to the child that obsessed me – it nearly drove me mad. I felt I had to save her. I would have told any lies to save her – I knew I was damned anyway – so I came to Christchurch with my piano …'[27] She considered her piano her most important possession, as it was both her livelihood (she becomes a piano teacher) and her passion.

In New Zealand, financial desperation and despair lead Alice into accepting help from businessman Tom Roland (he urges her to travel North to Auckland where he said he could get her pupils) and eventually into marriage. They have had two children, and have lived in a boarding house in Auckland, before he takes her into the wilds of Northland, at Kaipara. (The novel uses the real placenames.) The family are to live on the edge of the virgin bush that he is felling. And it is worth remembering that because of the different periods at which different areas of New Zealand were settled and cleared by the European, this part of the North was in 1880 as new to European habitation as other areas would have been twenty years earlier.

The novel opens with Alice and Asia, who is nine years old, and three-year-old Betty, a new baby, the household goods, and a piano loaded on a punt and heading up river towards their new home. The man who ferries them is David Bruce, the other man in the love triangle, at this moment looking rather rough and degenerate as he has been on a binge in town. Bruce is what we know as a remittance man, sent away from his English home because of some 'unwholesome' or tragic incident in his past, but he is not totally marked by this – he is also a doctor, Tom Roland's business partner, and a fine fiddle player, well-read and able to converse about education, religion and psychology. (Asia plays the *Kreutzer* sonata for violin and piano, and David Bruce's violin is implicitly complementary to Alice's piano playing. It is interesting to note that there are also some string instruments accompanying the piano in the soundtrack of *The Piano*.) Early in the novel we see Alice as David Bruce sees her:

> As they moved on towards him he suspected that Alice Roland was what the washerwoman called 'a real lydy,' and he saw that in spite of a hard black hat, and a rather ugly brown cloak, she was a young and very good-looking one too. . . . As Alice turned her grey, day-of-judgment eyes upon him, with a look that instantly judged him and dismissed him from her consciousness, he realised how much she resented being formally introduced to him as to an equal. He did not know that never before had she been presented to anyone who looked as unprepossessing as he did at that moment.[28]

Another passage from the opening pages gives more of the picture:

> Meantime, in the punt, Alice occupied herself with the immediate problem of coping with the cold, which was to be considered before the remoter issues of this dreaded excursion into unknown wilds. Betty, who was three years old, and the baby, who had just had her first birthday, both chose the occasion to howl piteously at this dislocation of accustomed ways. Alice, who could not bear that anything belonging to her should misbehave in public, exerted all her forces of comfort and cajolery.
>
> Asia heroically helped her mother with 'the children,' as she always called them. But she burned to investigate this wonderful adventure. Presently, when the baby was soothed to sleep on an improvised bed in a bath-tin, and when Betty was pacified, she felt she was free. Then she darted with the spasmodic rapidity of a squeezed wet bean from one part of the punt to the other, scrambling over the tarpaulin, and calling every few minutes in gasping whispers to her mother to look. Her life, spent so far only in cities, had contained no hints of the wonders of silence and space, of the mysteries of forest depths and rustling trees, of the strange ways of the free creatures of the air and earth. She clasped her hands, electrified and speechless, as startled wild duck rose from hidden places or ungainly shags flapped an erratic course down stream, or gawgaws croaked from the heights.[29]

Asia seems immediately at home in that wilderness. Even the image for her, 'squeezed wet bean', is vegetable in a domestic way but also links her with the surrounding bush vegetation. Later on, in her enthusiasm, Asia falls from the boat into the river and is baptised a New Zealander, making (as Dorothea Turner puts it) one of her 'waterborne exits and entrances'.[30] However, it is Alice in her *dis*-location who makes the still centre of the action. In the following paragraph Alice is shown to have a special relationship with her piano:

> Then Alice stood up. The only thing that seemed to belong to her, in that incongruous setting of boxes and mattresses and common furniture, was a piano which was packed in a heavy case. It had cost Bruce an anxious hour the night before, till with the help of chance riders he had got it safely aboard. Against the end of it she now leaned, her proud profile clearly visible to Bruce, who kept looking away from it and back again. He wondered if the scenery was getting her as it had got him the first time he came down that magic river. . . . He wondered once, as he saw Alice's face turned towards the gorge in the mountains, if she felt about it all as he had done. He knew that one might well forget the petty facts of life in the midst of that tremendous scenery. . . . Round each bend there was a fresh gully, a new and stimulating vista. And everywhere there was a vibrating silence, a terribly lonely silence, but rarely broken by the note of a singing bird.[31]

David Bruce is fascinated by Alice's 'impenetrability'. His explanation for Alice's reserve is that it is produced by an impossible insistence on the conventions of her class in an alien environment. Notice, for instance, her behaviour with her babies: she could not bear that 'anything belonging to her should misbehave in public'. David Bruce notes her superior manner towards himself and ambivalently admires her confidence, her absolute unbendingness – but wonders how she will adapt to this place. His fascination, noted at this point in the narrative, indicates that this apparently rough man will become the one who appreciates that Alice has a passionate nature often in conflict with her conscious mind – the one able to understand why she tortures herself with embarrassment and self-reproof.

The novel is concerned to explain Alice's character: she belongs as her husband also acknowledges to 'the class that rules the world', but the female version of that class is not adaptable. Being used to certain very precise conventions she is humiliated by the lack of privacy and formal spaces in her new home, by her husband's bluntness and discourtesy, and by the fact that other people know about the difficulties of her life. The gossip in her neighbourhood about another woman (her husband's mistress) who runs the local pub humiliates her, as does the vulgarity of her neighbours. She is frightened by her daughter's independence, and on one occasion she beats her for going on an innocent excursion into the bush with a boy whom she regards as 'unsuitable'. She hates other people educating her daughter. Her 'principles' form a shell of resistance and reserve around her. But they don't make her strong. She is dominated by the abruptness and sexual demands of her husband because she thinks that is the way it must be. Mander is quite explicit about this. After Roland's flirtations with other women he comes 'back to her for the logical conclusion' that she never refused 'because she had contracted to do it'. On that first night in the bush she anticipated his sexual expectations:

She clenched her hands. She had been away from him for a month. She knew he had been thinking all the afternoon of this hour. She knew that he would not consider the fact that she was tired to death. She knew he would simply feel injured because her vitality was not equal to his own. . . . She gave one hopeless look, like that of a trapped creature, round the mountain, the bush and the river.

Then she went in.[32]

Asia's comments are similarly to the point:

Why don't our parents realise that we children have eyes to see and ears to hear? I slept for years with only a thin wall between my parents and me. Slept, did I say? I sat up for hours shivering, sick and faint. . . . I couldn't understand and I don't understand now how human beings can be so stupid, and so cruel, and make so much unhappiness for each other. Why did mother stand it?[33]

Alice lives in an agonised way. Relationships with Tom Roland and her children (apart from Asia) are obligations rather than pleasures: 'no wandering vibrations of the Zeitgeist had reached her' (in New Zealand boarding houses) and she 'did not see any human relation as fun'.[34] Her emotional release is in playing the piano: 'Alice played to a world of her own, to something in herself that had no other means of expression. She played with delicacy and with passion, with unerring feeling for balance, for light and shade.' But when she finished she 'sat looking helplessly at the keys because she knew she had revealed a capacity for feeling and she wondered why she hated having people know how she felt'.[35] A number of other characters, Asia and Mrs Brayton, an older settler, try to educate her out of these habits of intense privacy and self-punishment. But it is David Bruce who impinges on her by knowing about her in a way that she cannot control.

In a romance plot with a cautious and virtuous heroine the romantic protagonists need to be thrown together in some, at least from her side, involuntary way. The colonial context is good for this with lots of possible adventures and threats to women, such as falls from horses, accidents to husbands, threatening intruders, etc. But Mander's concern with realism produces a quite convincing episode. Alice is pregnant. Her husband is away. She is frightened by a possible intruder. She miscarries. It takes some time for the woman who is usually a midwife to get across country. And David Bruce is, after all, a doctor. He nurses her. Alice's subsequent awareness of the physical intimacies involved in his nursing (she 'passed out' of course) make her more embarrassed by her feelings for him. He reassures her of the ordinariness of his task. Out of this mix, passion and love are allowed to develop, then declared, and negotiated as a special relationship but unconsummated over many years until, in one of the more conventional twists of the romance plot, Alice's husband, Tom Roland, is killed in a horrendous work accident. Coming down the hill on a jigger, Roland swerves to avoid children on the line and falls out.

The last chapter of the novel concerns Alice's anxiety about Asia. One of the fears of the colonial society is that its children will become primitive or sexualised.

All of Alice's own anxieties come to bear on Asia, who first shocks her mother by leaving home and then returns to Point Curtis (the village on the Kaipara where they live) only to become passionately involved with a married man. This scenario echoes all Alice's worst fears. But Allen Ross, a young tourist from Sydney and a prominent figure in the labour movement (Asia has heard him speak in the Sydney Domain), who is holidaying in the area, is portrayed as someone of sufficient integrity and having sufficient reason to break with conventional mores. This part of the plot points up Alice's own situation. There is discussion about divorce and women's freedom. Where Asia can follow her heart, discreetly spend nights with her young friend and plan a life with him, knowing he is trapped in an unhappy marriage, Alice has continued to deny such a possibility. On the other hand Asia's example as a free 'new woman' also educates Alice – she becomes less frightened, more capable of enjoyment, gentler on herself. David Bruce advises no more children and then an operation, presumably a hysterectomy.[36] Alice at forty starts to regain her health – she travels to Rotorua for the services of the best masseur in the country, buys a new and elegant dress (though its colour is brown) and attends theatre and music in Auckland. She also reads H. G. Wells and G. B. Shaw. These activities indicate Alice's new status as the wife of a prominent businessman, and the ways of the newly established middle class in New Zealand, but they are also markers of her self-acceptance and a new broadmindedness.

The story ends with Alice, David, and Asia on the boat bound for Auckland. Alice's new-found independence – finding her voice – will later be expressed by her opening a home for unmarried mothers and in her plans to help single women with children emigrate (to Australia). Asia is embarking on a political career with Allen Ross, and the other daughters in the family are giving up primary school teaching to go to Auckland University.

This novel was written in 1916–17 in New York where, in 1913, Jane Mander had enrolled as the first woman student of journalism at Columbia University. Mander was already in her late thirties when she arrived in America wanting to fulfil her ambition to be a published writer, a desire which she had had to postpone for many years. In New York, as well as excelling as a student, she campaigned for female suffrage and in wartime worked for the Red Cross. Of this period she commented: 'I really love the life as I've loved nothing else', and 'Nothing could describe the adorableness of American women and girls.'[37] Mander had been born in 1877 and raised itinerantly; her family moved frequently because her father was a timber merchant cutting and shipping kauri. She described living in shacks on beaches: 'we moved about the bushes at the rate of about twice a year, living in stores, shanties anywhere there was a roof'.[38] However, despite physical hardship, she seems to have seen herself as privileged by the variety and challenge of this upbringing. She played the piano, worked as a teacher aid, and wrote articles for *The Maoriland Worker* (the labour movement paper before the Labour

Party existed) as well as sending articles to Australia (she later recalled the spurring-on effect of not being accepted by the Sydney *Bulletin).*[39] When her father became a member of parliament for Whangarei he bought a provincial daily newspaper, *The Northern Advocate*, on which she became a subeditor, and after four years, editor. Then she lived for a while in Sydney, where she had connections in government and journalism, before making the trip to New York. For the next twenty years she remained abroad and from 1920 on in London (and briefly Paris) was able to earn a frugal living as a writer and editor.

RESPONSES TO JANE MANDER'S NOVEL

When it was first published *The Story of a New Zealand River* received good reviews overseas but a mixed reaction in New Zealand. As with *The Piano*, there was a certain amount of simple nationalistic enthusiasm. Newspaper reviews commented: 'this is a real novel, written of a real New Zealand'. But there was less enthusiasm for its themes, which were seen as unsuitable for young people. The novelist's public profile was also a problem for the small society. It was embarrassing that the daughter of a much respected member of the New Zealand parliament should write 'sex problem' fiction. Dorothea Turner suggests that locals round the Kaipara read too much significance into the use of actual placenames. However, because the novel was written by the daughter of a member of parliament about a couple who were of the same generation as the author's parents, local readers speculated that the storyline was also true. In the Whangarei public library the novel was on the 'discretionary list' and could be borrowed only by adults who made 'special application'.[40]

This characterising of Mander as a novelist who handled typically New Zealand content better than 'issues' was reinforced with the publication of her next novel, *The Passionate Puritan*. Its picturesque and typically outback action was praised above its themes, a newspaper reviewer singling out a bush-fire passage as 'the kind of thing we really look for in New Zealand fiction'.[41] In the following decades, *The Story of a New Zealand River* was reprinted, first in 1938 and again in the 1960s. It became accepted as having a foundational place in New Zealand literature on the basis of its realism, its use of plain language, its detailed description of the bush, the logging industry, and the way of life of a settler community.

Dorothea Turner's 1972 monograph, *Jane Mander,* in the Twayne's Authors Series reinforced this way of reading.[42] Turner drew attention to traces in the novel of Mander's over-optimism about the progressiveness of New Zealand society (an optimism that her New York friends kept 'burnished').[43] Around 1918 in New York, New Zealand was considered 'a positively exciting country' and one that stood for 'socialism without bloodshed'. And this admiration made Jane Mander, in her own words, a 'university pet'.[44] Turner explained the novel's motivations in terms of this enthusiasm for New Zealand, implying that Mander may have got rather carried away with the progressiveness of ideas about sexual freedom and social change, not realising that what would survive best in the novel would be its handling of local speech, scenery and types. The novel's portrayal of 'typical New Zealanders' was also much valued. Turner focused on this. Tom Roland, a driven and enthusiastic man completely unaware of personal needs or polite conventions, was seen as a portrait of the typical Kiwi male, and Alice appreciated as a demanding but significant kind of foremother:

> Alice is there for our use, with no obligation to enchant or to endear herself; we are committed to her as to a difficult relative. She is a complex of qualities, some dormant, some over-developed, which are so arranged that we are forced through her to question the very nature of virtue, and to question it in ways so relevant to our New Zealand background that we see her as a cultural symbol.[45]

Generally speaking this approach to the novel tended to co-opt its themes into those later preoccupations with realism, puritanism and landscape found in literature from the 1930s on and very much fixed by the time Turner wrote her monograph. Also, although Turner examined Mander's attitudes *vis-à-vis* philosophies and ideas of the period (Nietzsche, Shaw, etc.), she very much took for granted that the novel was the story (needing to be told) of successful settlement and colonial reconciliation. She did not set herself at a distance from the account by considering it a genre piece – that is, as one of a kind amongst many possible narratives of nation.

Graduate students today tend to be very interested in the book but see it in a larger postcolonial perspective, as an example of a genre – the 'settler narrative'. Reading in this way they tend to criticise its use of romance as a kind of controlling mechanism, making the woman over as she should be for this new country. (Perhaps these students do not take the 'problem' of puritanism so seriously; that is, they do not see Alice as desperately needing to be changed.) Students in one graduate class pursued an analogy between how Alice is educated to live in this new land and how the land is broken in, and the kauri felled. They also deliberately read against the grain, showing how the novel uses village people as backdrop and stressing the absence of Maori (except as infrequent picturesque background). There were many Maori living in the Kaipara at this time and two of Mander's siblings married local Maori. But it is interesting that the novel does not include such a plot line. What the students were particularly conscious of is the way the settler narrative incorporates and negotiates colonial values. It is common for novels about nineteenth-century settlement to use a romance plot around rivalry between women who are either suitable or unsuitable for the nation's future – as wives for graziers or settlers. For instance, Katharine Prichard's *Coonardoo* and Jean Devanny's *Cindie*, though written later, are similarly structured.[46]

However, there are other things to find in *The Story of a New Zealand River*. For example, I value it as the imaginative reaching back of the writer to the physical predicaments of her mother and her mother's generation. I see Mander as expressing an understanding of their enforced motherhood and domesticity, physical exhaustion, loneliness, and lack of extended family across the cusp of the century. Dorothea Turner makes very little of this but there is one evocative sentence: 'Jane Mander firmed up her determination to go: her mother moved towards the chronic invalidism of defeat.'[47] It is this sympathy with a mother, and the way that Alice is made to evoke the materiality of a certain period for women, that sets Mander's novel in close relationship with Mansfield's 'Prelude', a reading which I will expand in my next chapter.[48]

JANE CAMPION'S *THE PIANO*

The Piano was the first internationally funded feature to be directed by New Zealand-born but Australian-resident Jane Campion. It is her fourth feature film and though she co-wrote the earlier *Sweetie* with Gerard Lee, this film has been described as marking her 'debut as her own author'.[49] A 'commonsense' précis of the action, confirmed by local viewers, would appear to go something like this: Ada is a Scottish woman who comes to New Zealand to marry a man she has never met. She already has an eight-year-old daughter, Flora, and is assumed to be widowed; the daughter refers inconsistently to romantic visions of her biological father and her mother's previous marriage. Ada is mute – she doesn't talk; the daughter speaks for her and they converse in sign language. Ada and Flora and their boxes are put off (or rather carried ashore by the crew of their boat) on a wild coastline. The boat is going on to Nelson, so this is presumably intended to be some beach at the top of the South Island, perhaps Golden Bay in the north-west, or more towards the Marlborough Sounds. However, as local viewers, very many of us recognise the location and cannot see the setting as anything except the famous Karekare beach on Auckland's west coast. (The film was also shot on locations at Awakino and Matakana.)

For a while mother and daughter are alone on the sands. Then Ada's husband, Stewart, with another European, Baines, and a party of Maori meet them. Stewart is impatient with his new wife's desire to bring her piano. Baines is more uncouth in appearance but ultimately more sympathetic. He is a 'Pakeha-Maori' figure who, unlike Stewart, is part of the Maori community and has a relationship with a local Maori woman. He lives in a simple bare house more like a shack or whare than the cluttered cottage that Stewart offers. Ada is married to Stewart but it is Baines who goes back with her and Flora to the beach so that she can play the piano. And later he has the piano carried up to the village through the bush. Baines is apparently fascinated by the impenetrability of this middle-class British woman and her intimacy with her daughter (epitomised in her silence and their shared sign language) and the way her feelings are best expressed when she touches and plays her piano.

Baines and Stewart are business partners – there are some complications and Baines offers to buy the piano in return for land Stewart wants. He also purchases lessons from Ada in return for allowing her access to the piano. Ada is grim and resentful but has to concur. As big rough Baines watches precise, cool, delicate, beautiful Ada, he makes a crude suggestion – he will sell her back her piano key by key in return for peeps and touches. The exchange becomes even more dangerous when Ada's feelings are awakened by his passion. Baines has the piano returned saying the arrangement is making her 'a whore and him wretched'. Stewart becomes suspicious. He observes their lovemaking through a hole in some floor boards. He locks Ada and Flora up in their house – boarding the doors and windows. Ada tries out her new experience of sensuality on her husband. But she won't let him respond. He is tortured with passion but also ashamed. All hell breaks loose when Ada engraves a formal love message on a piano key ('Dear George, you have my heart, Ada McGrath') and asks Flora to smuggle it out to Baines, but Flora takes it to Stewart. Stewart then cuts off Ada's finger and delivers it to Baines. Meanwhile Baines has recovered the piano key from a local Maori, who has fashioned it into an earring, and had the letters translated by some school children. Flora flees to Baines. Stewart considers raping the feverish Ada but refrains. After some time, in what he considers the only possible solution, Stewart offers Ada to Baines. She and Baines (and Flora) embark on a boat journey out to a new life in Nelson. The piano tips out of the boat and an attempt to rescue it is stopped by Ada, who wants it to go down. She falls (or jumps) overboard as well. When she resurfaces we hear her voice for the first time.

Last scenes are in Nelson where she has a new home with Baines and is giving (more conventional) piano lessons. The last image is of the seabed underwater accompanied by lines (spoken by Ada as a voice-over) from the early nineteenth-century English poet Thomas Hood:

There is silence where hath been no sound
There is a silence where no sound may be
In the cold grave under the deep sea

Like *The Story of a New Zealand River*, *The Piano* is dedicated to the writer's mother ('to Edith') and was written by an émigré New Zealander in her mid life (Campion was thirty-nine when *The Piano* was made, Mander in her early forties when she wrote the novel). Campion acknowledges the significance of writing from outside her country of origin and describes *The Piano* as looking 'like a film made by someone who doesn't live here any more; there's a kind of longing in it'.[50] Her stated intentions for conceiving *The Piano* were a desire to tell a love story from a woman's perspective, to show something new about colonial New Zealand, and to mix the romance genre with realist and unlovely elements.[51]

SIMILARITIES BETWEEN MOVIE AND NOVEL
Anyone familiar with both novel and film will notice similarities. There are common elements of character, situation and setting. As Jane Campion has commented these could be accounted for as 'genre similarities', but there are

also finer points of connection.[52] Some of the common elements are:

1 A beautiful young woman immigrant arrives by water with her young daughter of uncertain paternity and also her piano.
2 She has a marriage of convenience to a local landowner.
3 The bush, sea and river settings.
4 The piano is the woman's most important possession. (Both characters are at some stage piano teachers, both express apparently repressed passion through their playing.)
5 The love triangle. In both cases the 'other' man is more strongly part of the local community than is the husband.
6 The setting of the novel is very similar to the actual film locations (as against its fictional ones). Karekare and the Kaipara are only fifty miles apart on the same coast.
7 Structurally, too, the film develops in much the same way as the novel. The action is resolved by a new marriage with another man and a journey by water to their new home in an urban settlement.
8 There are parallels between particular scenes. For instance David Bruce declares, like Baines, that he cannot sustain an intimacy with a woman married to another man. Like Stewart, Roland finally offers his wife to the other man – the one who is apparently better for her.
9 The word 'impenetrable', used so significantly of Alice, is also used of Ada by Campion in the promotional video. The stress on Alice's silence is intensified in Ada's muteness.
10 The period of settlement and land acquisition in which the film is set (the 1850s–1860s) is twenty to thirty years before that of the novel (from the mid 1880s to early 1900s). However the conditions of life (and landscape) are actually quite similar to the novel's later Kaipara setting because this area north of Auckland was one of the last to be cleared and settled by Europeans.

Campion has denied any relation between the novel and her film. She has stated that she never finished the book ('I never finished it because I really didn't like it that much') and that she disliked the character Alice for being uptight and repressed.[53] Campion and actress Holly Hunter have both stressed in contrast that their creation, Ada, has an amoral attitude to sex – she is a woman without conventional morals, with an 'original kind of sexuality'.[54] Campion has also recorded repeatedly that she started writing the screenplay in 1984, even before the making of her first feature film *Sweetie*, and that the movie had been part of her day-dreaming world since 1984 when she showed a five-page outline to producer Jan Chapman.[55] These statements have had the effect of denying any relationship with 'The River' screenplay and the Mander novel, and by suggesting that Campion began on the idea before the other producers they tend to confirm the originality of her work. Nevertheless, the similarities are such that someone familiar with both novel and film could well speculate that Jane Campion, having read *The Story of A New Zealand River,* and probably the script of 'The River', and though not liking them a great deal, consciously or unconsciously came back to their basic situation and characters as a starting point for her creation.

The aesthetic contrasts of the novel can be paralleled to those of the film. Both create a powerful juxtaposition between the bonneted, cloaked, city-dressed, aloof woman and the rough men, wild coastline, dense bush and mud. Both make use of an extraordinarily beautiful setting which could be guaranteed to be exotic to overseas readers and viewers.[56] But Jane Campion's approach is more modern in developing a more explicitly sexual relationship between the aloof woman and the local man (involving aesthetic and sensual delight in bodies).

The writers who were working on 'The River' apparently saw themselves as having some difficulties with the script. Geoff Chapple explained the problems in terms of the script 'getting' too feminist and therefore losing its potential popular appeal.[57] We know too that there were about nine drafts of the script, though of course this is not an unusually high number for a feature film, but Jane Campion was able to complete hers.[58] In fact, if her script were to be seen as an adaptation it could be seen as paradigmatic, a primer for would-be directors, excelling in concision, symbolism, intensification and dramatisation. Look at how it works: the shy, dignified, often silent Alice – wanting to do things properly, colonised many times over by fear, by the tyranny of her father, by middle-class puritan society in Britain, by her migration and loss of family and connections and by her purchase of respectability in a loveless marriage – becomes mute Ada.

This is an intense way of encapsulating Alice's condition. All the long-discussed and worked-over details which contextualised her feelings and gave psychological, social and material explanations (the cultural codes) for her behaviour in the novel, are summed up in this theatrical trope of muteness. And along with the muteness goes her costume. The tight-buttoned top, the bonnet, the drab colours and the greasy hair all convey Ada's oppression, and her delicacy. They suggest the culture of the country she has come from and what it has done to her. Look at what Holly Hunter says: 'The costumes helped me tremendously: the incongruity of having a woman in a really laced-up corset, huge hoop skirts, petticoat, pantaloons, bodice and chemise trying to gracefully manoeuvre her way through the bush . . . there was an obvious physical fragility and yet strength and stamina.'[59] And Campion: 'I've always loved the sacrificial quality of taking these little women in their completely inappropriate Victorian dresses into this wild remote land and plonking them down.'[60] Alice's lonely predicaments – no-one to confide in, no female support to help her when she has a baby or to manage her young children – are signified in the small figures of Ada and Flora on the wide beach.

Other qualities Alice has in the novel are also narrowly symbolised in the movie. For instance, in the novel Alice expresses her restless passion by playing the piano, but in the film identification of woman and piano is much intensified.

There is a precious, secretive relationship signified by the fact that Ada plays her own music, a kind of inner music, and does not speak. Because of this the action can be developed via the piano. Thus the social realities of isolation and childbirth, which in the novel create incidents that allow intimacy to grow between a standoffish married woman and a local bloke, are in the film all negotiated via the piano. The piano provides a kind of short cut to social, cultural or psychological explanation of the kind the novel favoured. It stands for the woman's difference, her voice, her passion, her attractiveness, and her power, but it is also her vulnerability. Her playing the piano attracts but it also makes her weak. In order to keep the piano, she will do anything; parts of her body that Baines touches buy back parts of her piano. Campion has used the piano to develop modern sexual content in a costume drama which (problematically) rests on an idea of a heroine who is inscrutably unresponsive. Yes, she is unresponsive, but for the piano she will do anything. The piano stands for the body's relation to society and social relations by substituting for a complicated and lengthy storyline about pregnancy and miscarriage. The piano allows the leap from old-fashioned costume drama into modern sex scenes.

The independent-minded daughter who investigates her new environment so thoroughly in the novel is similarly signified. The psychological complexities of Asia are imaged in the wild child (Flora) turning upside down on the sand. The way that Asia explains her mother to others and educates her about their new environment is dramatised in Flora literally speaking for her mother, and communicating with her in a personal sign language. Mother and daughter's identical costumes also reinforce their intense relationship.

When I make these comparisons I simplify for effect, but in broad terms the film seems to contain elements of Mander's novel 'pared back to their cinematography' as a friend phrased it. Like William Wyler's film adaptation of *Wuthering Heights* (1939), *The Piano* and the screenplay 'The River' take in only a first generation whereas the Brontë and Mander novels develop into family sagas with stories of their adult children. This shortening is a strategy that one could argue is sensible in a film adaptation. Another aspect that on the other hand initially seems to differentiate Jane Mander's novel from the movie is period: the movie is set twenty or so years earlier than the novel. However, surprisingly, this makes more for similarities than differences as the action of both takes place in a new settlement where bush is being cleared and first dwellings built – as I mentioned earlier, that part of the North where Mander set her novel was settled late by Europeans. (*The Piano* also created Maori characters but these did not alter the main action as it existed in the novel, as they were in minor and background roles.[61])

What might be seen as simply a Hollywood approach to storytelling, where the emphasis is on heightened dramatic images and conflicts, with much left to the viewer's imagination, can also be seen as a consequence of the attempts at erasure of the novel and the other script. As Sarah Kerr describes it, *The Piano* is a movie which is 'less a story than a situation . . . set up in the first few moments and then turned loose.'[62] Its episodic quality, its reliance on name actors, its lack of clear psychological motivations (Holly Hunter said that she loved the script because it was not expository: 'there are so many whys that go unanswered') and its dependence on exotic settings can all be seen as the signs of something hidden.[63] However, the cryptic, intense style also has its own effect of making the action look ironic and self-conscious. Many of the characters appear like generic types: the Lawrentian Baines, the uptight Pakeha male, the woman who lives through her piano, the wild child, and so on. I'm not alone in observing this. An anti-*Piano* lobby at the time of the Academy awards drew up a list of 'Seven Reasons to Hate *The Piano*', one of which was its 'ironic symbolism'. (Others were 'little girl vomits on beach' and 'too much mud'.)[64]

LOCAL VERSUS INTERNATIONAL RESPONSES TO *THE PIANO*

Local and international responses to *The Piano* and *The Story of a New Zealand River* can be interestingly paralleled. Internationally the movie was very much acclaimed and its representation of Maori and of the landscape were seen as exotic and pleasingly unproblematic. For example, the American Film Commission described the film as catching 'the attention of American travellers' with its use of 'the natural environment as a spectacular backdrop to action, a portrayal of uncomplicated indigenous lifestyles and the interaction and struggle of man with the environment'.[65] Local response was partly guided by the film's international success at Cannes and the Academy awards: 'it's engaging, it's brilliant, it's our own to call a success'.[66] Like *The Story of a New Zealand River*, *The Piano* was welcomed as portraying our country in a way that had never been done before. The landscape, the locations, and the colour were all praised. The mayor of Waitakere City took out a large advertisement to thank Jane Campion for making 'our beach, Karekare, the most famous in the world'.[67]

However, also like the novel, the film provoked less favourable local reactions. It became cultural currency and was frequently alluded to by columnists, comedians and journalists. For example, even a newspaper nature columnist writing about a tramp from Muriwai to Whatipu Beach could not resist the opportunity to make an aside about the movie: 'if you head inland through the pohutukawa grove you will pass the point where the old ladies in *The Piano* took a comfort stop and you may understand why Sam Neill decided to leave the piano where it was.'[68] The power of the local viewer to hit back or jokingly undermine is also illustrated by Raybon Kan's remarks about the filmscript: 'It's still an achievement to be named best screen play when you consider her screen play probably consisted mainly of nothing more scintillating than: "Ada says nothing." Or worse: "Ada plays the piano. She says nothing." Or stage directions like: "the mud is plentiful".'[69]

Local filmgoers interested in issues of representation and gender were disappointed. Few students in an MA film class in 1993 (Auckland University) enjoyed the film. They went to see it 'because of all the publicity' but found it 'silly' and felt that it did not 'do justice to the Maori situation'. Generally speaking these viewers saw the film as traditional romantic bodice-ripper, as out-of-date in its treatment of Maori elements, and as anti-feminist in its 'sex for piano' exchange. New Zealanders overseas (expatriates like the director) seem to have taken the film more seriously,whether in its defence or critically. Expatriate academic John Pocock defended the film against a *New York Review of Books* reviewer who queried the absence of aggression between Maori and Pakeha, in view of the fact that the film is set during the period of land wars.[70] Pocock's defence was made on the basis that it is 'in fact' set in the upper South Island where few Maori were living at this period ('the north-western region of the South Island, in which the action of *The Piano* seems to be laid, was not one in which war occurred').[71]

Another expatriate critic, Lynda Dyson, is in some ways more sceptical. She reads the film as a narrative of 'colonial reconciliation' (which, as I have shown, is one of the elements it has in common with the novel). She suggests that its narrative solution, via Ada's marriage with the Pakeha-Maori Baines, is comparable to a current movement amongst European New Zealanders to 'self-fashion themselves in the ethnic category "pakeha"' in order to 'avoid the connotation of supremacy that the word "white" has acquired'.[72] Dyson is suggesting that the film satisfies New Zealand Europeans' current need for a self-image – 'through the deployment of primitivist inversions "Maoriness" becomes available to fill the absent centre of white identity' in a society where such an identity 'hovers in an uncomfortable space between coloniser and colonised: no longer European but with no real claim on indigeneity either'.[73] Dyson's comments are interesting because they identify an element of the movie that was extremely unconvincing to many local New Zealand viewers. The cultural movement that Dyson is speaking of as a 'reaction to the perceived cultural emptiness which still continues to haunt New Zealand' is, I think, an out-of-date concept. The idea of an empty land and the romanticising of Maori as a trope of race reconciliation are no longer at the centre of New Zealand cultural and political concerns.

However, this was a high cultural representation that did dominate New Zealand in the 1960s when Jane Campion was growing up. The strategies that Dyson is discussing *were* part of the intellectual élite's version of itself, 'the habits of the tribe' as David Bordwell puts it, at that period. This group had long appropriated the term 'Pakeha' to describe itself, but in terms of local New Zealand culture its power to describe and co-opt indigeneity has, in the last two decades, been challenged and thoroughly problematised by Maori identity politics and Maori cultural production (in both literature and film). Therefore, though I would agree with Dyson that the film constructs a romantic vision of race relations still marketable in America and Britain, I would argue that it is *not* one that was taken very seriously by the local audience or by the film's Maori and Pakeha participants (crew, actors, advisers, etc.). This particular group have avoided public criticism of the movie, but appeared to be relieved when public discussion turned away from it to a Maori-directed project, *Once Were Warriors.*[74]

The attitude shown in the representation of Maori in *The Piano* is, I would suggest, significantly closer to that of playwright Bruce Mason and his play *Awatea* (written) in 1964 than it is to current thinking. It was the cultural infrastructure from the 1960s that gave Jane Campion access to Maori advisers. Principal adviser Selwyn Muru had been an old friend of her father, Dick Campion. Dick Campion had directed plays by Muru. However, in spite of Muru and other 'cultural advisers' reworking Campion's original dialogue, the Maori scenes and action remained very much background. The exotic look of the characters is taken from late nineteenth-century photos of Maori, where top hats were worn along with blankets, kete and piupiu.[75] This treatment, as Sarah Kerr comments, makes the Maori characters 'sitting cross-legged in the forest, wearing their top hats [become] perilously close to being backdrop, like the cliffs and waves, contributors to the estrangement the audience is supposed to feel.'[76] The television programme *Marae* also featured an item about the making of *The Piano* in which the Maori participants seemed very uneasy with the style of the movie.[77]

What I have been suggesting, then, is that Jane Campion has brought back from abroad a romantic version of New Zealand culture, landscape and race relations similar to that current during the period when she grew up. The unconscious use of the vocabulary of cultural nationalism (from that period) is evident in the film's preoccupation with landscape and light, as well as its particular way of placing Maori as part of the landscape. The implication of this style is that the land itself creates the people. A lot of the promotional material about the film also emphasises light and landscape. Cinematographer Stuart Dryburgh, for example, suggests that the kind of the lighting they used in the bush scenes is 'natural' and 'honest' to 'the dark place' it is.[78] This essentialist way of speaking, which assumes that the manner of cultural production is driven or determined by the land and the light, was once pervasive in the arts in New Zealand but has since been challenged by books such as Francis Pound's *Frame on the Land.*[79] This tradition, which formerly belonged to the 'high culture' world of visual arts and literature, has (it seems) gradually trickled down into 'middlebrow' areas of the culture such as this film (seen by a vastly larger audience than the one who knew the works of the earlier painters). Such a reading of the film involves placing it in a broad cultural context and focusing on what it shares with other texts rather than focusing on it as a unique masterpiece generated by the original vision of *auteur* Jane Campion.

Other of Campion's descriptions of her film mix up the action of the movie and her own reasons for making it in a similarly essentialist rhetoric. There is a seductive, soft-edged ambiguity operating. For example, in a promotional video, in phrases also recorded in the Academy booklet, she remarks: 'I think that the romantic impulse is in all of us and sometimes we live it for a short time', at the same time describing the movie as 'a Gothic exploration of the romantic impulse' in her own country.[80] This use of the phrase 'romantic impulse' is interesting. Perhaps because of the large amount of publicity that goes with a movie that is an Oscar contender, the publicity anticipates and seeks to control the responses of its audience. In this case those pre-packaged responses mix up the distinction between film and film-maker, and film-maker and audience – they are, it is implied, all in the grip of the same power.

This way of talking about the movie emphasises a range of 'powers' which determine it. There is the power of the 'romantic impulse', the power of the landscape, the power of bodies ('bodyscape'), the power of Maori tradition, and the power of women working together. I suggested earlier that the film and novel employ a similar set of aesthetic contrasts between the civilised (repressed) world and the wild (natural) world. The contrasted naked bodies provide a kind of apotheosis of this old world/new world contrast, her body image coming from Velazquez, his from a primitive work.[81] This rhetoric of naturalness was also used in promotional publications and videos to describe the making of the film. Campion's statements as well as those of the cinematographer, Stuart Dryburgh, tended to blur the difference between the film's intentions and the audience response to it.

This discourse suggests an unmediated relationship between the world and the viewer made possible by the film-maker, as though both were participating in a kind of involuntary romantic experience. For example, the look of the bush (landscape) is described as determining the genre of the movie. And the power of bodies (bodyscape) is seen as acting directly on the audience. This kind of description also flatters the audience by suggesting that the film-maker and viewer are engaging in the same sort of experience. In commenting on the impact of introducing sex scenes into historical drama, Campion says: 'then you get involved in the actual bodyscape of it. The body has certain effects, like a drug almost, certain desires for erotic satisfaction, which are very strong forces too.'[82]

Edward Said comments of French writers in Algeria (Seggelen and Gide) that Algeria became for them 'an exotic locale in which their own spiritual problems [could] be addressed and therapeutically treated'.[83] The era of New Zealand cultural production that we have been discussing is not dissimilar in the way its emotional solutions involve the appropriation of what is considered the simplicity and 'naturalness' of the indigenous people. Estrangement via physical isolation in the wild, and the literary use of the Maori people as background are common in 'serious' New Zealand cultural production from the 1930s to the 1960s. The mood of The Piano is dark, lonely, elegiac – as are these sample quotes from well-known New Zealand poems: [84]

Ask in one life no more
Than that first revelation of earth and sky,
Renewed as now in the place of birth
Where the sea turns and the first roots go down.
   from Charles Brasch, 'Word by Night'

If there had been one bird, if there had been
One gull to circle through the wild salt wind
Or cry above the breaking of the waves,
One footprint or one feather on the sand,
Then the great rocks leaning from the hills
Might have been ruins of great walls.
   from Ruth Dallas, 'Deserted Beach'

October, and a rain-blurred face,
And all the anguish of that bitter place,.
It was a bare sea-battered town,
With its one street leading down
On to a shingly beach. . . .
   from Alistair Campbell, 'At a Fishing Settlement'

Always in these islands, meeting and parting
Shake us, making tremulous the salt-rimmed air;
Divided, many-tongued, the sea is waiting,
Bird and fish visit us and come no more.
Remindingly beside the quays the white
Ships lie smoking; and from their haunted bay
The godwits vanish towards another summer.
Everywhere in light and calm the murmuring
Shadow of departure; distance looks our way;
And none knows where he will lie down at night.
   from Charles Brasch, 'The Islands (ii)'

And there is the hint of the colonisers' reconciliation with the tangata whenua
in the first and last verses of Charles Brasch's 'Forerunners':

Not by us was the unrecorded stillness
Broken, and in their monumental dawn
The rocks, the leaves unveiled;
Those who were before us trod first the soil . . .

But their touch was light; warm in their hearts holding
The land's image, they had no need to impress themselves
Like conquerors, scarring it with vain memorials.
They had no fear of being forgotten.

In the face of our different coming they retreated,
But without panic, not disturbing the imprint
Of their living upon the air, which continued
To speak of them to the rocks and the sombre, guarded lakes.

The earth holds them
As the mountains hold the shadows by day
In their powerful repose, only betrayed by a lingering
Twilight in the hooded ravines.

Behind our quickness, our shallow occupation of the easier
Landscape, their unprotesting memory
Mildly hovers, surrounding us with perspective,
Offering soil for our rootless behaviour.
    from Charles Brasch, 'Forerunners'

And the Gothic is more elaborate in some stanzas from Allen Curnow's 'Spectacular Blossom':

Mock up again, summer, the sooty altars
Between the sweltering tides and the tin gardens
All the colours of the stained bow windows.
Quick, she'll be dead on time, the single
Actress shuffling red petals to this music,
Percussive light! So many suns she harbours
And keeps them jigging, her puppet suns,
All over the dead hot calm, impure
Blood noon tide of the breathless day.

Are the victims always so beautiful.?

to:

An old man's blood spills bright as a girl's
On beaches where the knees of light crash down.
These dying ejaculate their bloom.

Can anyone choose
And call it beauty – The victims
Are always so beautiful.

from Allen Curnow 'Spectacular Blossom.'[85]

There seems to me little new 'history' in the film in terms of an effort to defamiliarise and make new; rather it returns to an earlier generation's way of seeing. Even Auckland's west coast beaches used as locations in the film are associated with important figures of this tradition: Colin McCahon painted at

Muriwai, Karekare is the inspiration of Allen Curnow, and Karl Stead has written about both Karekare and Anawhata. The Waitakere Ranges have since the 1930s been a mecca for the intellectual and artistic community.[86] Perhaps one can see Baines' bare cottage, so unlike the fussy cramped residence of Stewart, as imaged out of Campion's memories of the 1950–60s New Zealand bach which the intellectual middle-class tended to see as a New Zealand icon: loved for its raw simplicity, unpainted wood, corrugated iron and its proximity to beach and bush. It is very interesting in this context to note that the New Zealand Tourist Board did not want to use the film in its publicity because of its 'gloomy Karekare setting'. ('Mr Beatson believes the very people to whom the film appealed would be put off by any attempt to capitalise on it.')[87] It seems that this picture of New Zealand still has high-culture associations. Taking another angle but similarly believing in this picture (and assuming a certain New Zealand audience that agrees with him), John Pocock defends the cosy Nelson-set resolution to *The Piano* because it accords with what he sees as the true narrative of New Zealand as told by its writers:

> . . . to a New Zealander it seems right – not as solution but as the next set of problems. This is a culture in which it has been, probably still is, possible and almost inescapable to move in one step from the primeval to the suburban. Baines and Ada, being survivors uninterested in a *Liebestod* go to the suburbs because, even in 1860, that is where there is to go. We enter the world of novelists Frank Sargeson and Maurice Gee who depict people like this living in suburban houses.[88]

As an endpoint in a tradition rather than a beginning, this film brings to a wider audience an excellent packaging of those themes of dislocation, out-of-placeness, loneliness, emptiness, and anxiety which for so long enclosed the territory of the arts in New Zealand.

GENERAL COMMENTS

Those who do not know history, or do not know it sufficiently well, are condemned to repeat it.

Perhaps because the novel is not openly acknowledged by the film, it cannot be learned from. Thus Jane Campion's film repeats the narrative of colonial reconciliation which is one of the features of the 1920s novel. And it repeats it from a similar émigré distance. The film is therefore not the rethink or reassessment of colonial history (or the re-representation of it) that I was hoping for from this 'art movie': and lest it seem that I was asking the impossible in expecting such sophistication, I should compare *The Piano* with another film, *Desperate Remedies*, released in the same year. This film deliberately undercuts expected representations of colonial history. It is, for instance, filmed entirely inside, using sets, stylised city streets, and cyclorama. Its protagonist is also a European woman but she is not a vulnerable immigrant (the film opens with her meeting a ship from which a desirable young man is disembarking) but a successful business-woman who wants to purchase a suitable husband for her drug addict sister. The fact that her sister is problematically infatuated with a Maori bisexual drug-dealer lover, gives an idea of the film's parodic genre. Whatever one thinks of this style *Desperate Remedies* certainly challenges *The Piano*'s predictable stress on the landscape and its effect on the individual and suggests instead an interest in constructions of psychology and sensuality.

Can we put a rahui (a prohibition/ limitation) on the commercialising of cultural artefacts?

This chapter has offered a reading of *The Piano* that takes in a range of contextual information. It suggests that the significance of the film for New Zealand viewers lies in its absorption of themes long present in the culture, including a novel and a script based on that novel. Campion is thus participating in a common process of popularising what were formerly high-culture representations of New Zealand. Such representations have now become commonplaces which may be 'in harmony with recent perceptions of New Zealand appearing in Sunday supplements around the world', but are not a lot of use to those of us here who want to escape such clichés.[89] This highlights the difference between local and overseas readings of the film (with the general audience tending to show greater enthusiasm than intellectuals). More research would be needed to make these differences more precise. My main point, however, is that the strikingly polarised responses to *The Piano* (ranging from fervent enthusiasm to repugnance) can usefully be related to particular cultural groupings and particular historical developments – that is, once developed in the high culture, a way of reading 'New Zealand' becomes permanently established in the menu of the culture.

It is interesting that enthusiasm for *The Piano* internationally came at a time where there was burgeoning international interest in films made with exotic locations alongside an interest in investing in New Zealand. As a news item from an international agency at the time put it: 'While old empires bust, new economies boom and the concept of free trade takes on a global scale, world cinema is undergoing a tectonic shift of its own'.[90] The article speaks of the 'encroachment of American cinema' on 'local indigenous industries' and 'native talents being co-opted'. This 'cultural-mix-and-match school of film-making' where for instance Australasian directors work with huge overseas investment or in Hollywood, making films very different from what they would have made at home, has its supporters as well as detractors. Consider, for example the adaptation of Isabel Allende's *The House of the Spirits*. This movie is based on a 'novel of politics and passion in Chile', yet has a Danish director and a prestigious international cast. The movie is said to lack 'a single drop of Chilean flavour'. This may not be the objection to *The Piano* which in fact indulges fully in our national preoccupation with landscape. The film *Gorillas In the Mist* increased tourism to Rwanda by 20 per cent the year after it was released. More recently (1999) a Hollywood production filming an adaptation of British writer, Alex Garland's, *The Island* starring Leonardo Di Caprio, has been reprimanded by the Thai government for making landmoving adjustments to its location – a beautiful island national park.

In 1995, not long after *The Piano* was released, Karekare beach residents wanted the 'rahui' already placed on shellfish and driftwood extended to limit visitors to the beach. Even more difficult, however, would be an attempt to control readings. *The Piano* demonstrates the power of international film business (with its huge marketing budgets) to promote a particular film, and to suggest appropriate ways to read it, or appropriate contexts in which to place it (such as Campion-as-*auteur*, or New Zealand as an exotic, cleansing location; or the Gothic romance genre). A complex contextual approach is needed (as this chapter has attempted to show) to 'destabilise' these publicised readings, and to relocate the film within a different perspective. New Zealand culture has always been complex and compromised, constantly under pressure from larger cultures, and frequently unsure of its own perceptions. It can be argued that exceptionally complex forms of criticism, acutely aware of contexts, are needed to understand this situation.

CHAPTER FOUR

•

More Readings of
The Story of a New Zealand River

The screenplay adaptation 'The River' updated the novel *The Story of a New Zealand River* by incorporating 1990s attitudes to the environment, sexuality and race. Made into a film, it would have created a poignant tension between the exhilarating beauty of the settler environment and the extreme loneliness of a young immigrant mother in the remote bush setting, apparently without utilising any of the Gothic elements of *The Piano*. Yet 'The River' does not have the strung-out romantic suspense which has kept readers so enthralled by the novel.

In this chapter a discussion of the screenplay of this unmade movie leads into a new interpretation of the novel, allowing us to read *The Story of a New Zealand River* as an (author) daughter's process of understanding her mother's lonely situation as an estranged settler wife. The novel (I argue) can also be understood, historically, as a performative text enacting in its romance narrative an ideal of New Zealand's future that was envisaged by a specific intellectual and reading community of the time. I use the term 'new historicism' to describe my general approach, indicating as it does the importance of thinking of creative works or 'cultural artifacts' as only one of the many 'interpretive constructions the members of a society apply to their experience';[1] whether such interpretive constructions are in the form of novels, documentaries or parliamentary legislation, they all construct self, marriage, nation in specific ways that may be typical of a period. For this reason we can go far afield, as this chapter does, and find related ideas of nation and settlement in, for example, both a sheep farmer's account of breaking-in his land and Mander's novel – each published in about 1920. Or we may parallel plans for the institutionalisation of rural midwives at the beginning of this century, with the dénouement of the novel. Other intertextual elements, including a discussion of earlier romance fiction, are also shown to be relevant.

'THE RIVER'

'The River,' the filmscript officially based on *The Story of a New Zealand River*, never reached its final form, nor was it put into production. Nevertheless, the script reached an advanced stage of development, so we can gain a clear sense of what it does with the 1920s novel.

'The River' has certain common elements with *The Piano* but it brings to the adaptation some elements typical of New Zealand film. There is a stronger element of 'documentary' realism, and the writers seem more interested in social elements than in the romantic intensities of *The Piano*. It is significant that one of its authors,

Geoff Chapple, is a journalist who has published a life of the New Zealand socialist Rewi Alley and an account of the protests against the 1981 South African Rugby Springbok tour, and that an earlier draft was written by playwright Renée, who also mostly favours a realist mode and use of documentary material in her work.

The screenplay introduces elements of 1990s politics concerned with race and feminism, as well as explicit sex scenes and environmental issues that were not present in the 1920s novel. Also typical of a tradition in New Zealand movies is its reliance on dramatic physical action, particularly a dramatic 'chase' ending to resolve the love story.

The history of 'The River', like that of many film projects, is long and complicated. It began official development in May 1985 when Brigid Ikin and John Maynard purchased the film rights of the novel from Jane Mander's nephew Rangi Cross of Auckland through the literary agent Ray Richards.[2] (The script is titled an 'adaptation', is copyrighted '1990 John Maynard Productions', and runs to 105 pages with 166 scenes.) Brigid Ikin (Hibiscus Films in partnership latterly with John Maynard Productions) initiated the project. Ikin was known for producing works by women writers and working with women directors. She was the producer of Jane Campion's adaptation of Janet Frame's *An Angel at My Table* as well as of Alison Maclean's *Kitchen Sink* (written by Maclean) and *Crush* (written by Maclean and fiction writer Anne Kennedy). In developing 'The River' she consulted widely about the script and also about Jane Mander; there was some idea, early on, of making a documentary on Mander's life as well as a feature film of the novel. In any case the production of the movie as an adaptation would have promoted a public (re)discovery of Mander, as well as of the novel.

Playwright Renée was one of the people initially asked to work on a development.[3] The choice of advisers and writers was in line with Ikin and Maynard's usual preference for people involved with the arts or literature, and typical of their place at the 'high culture end' of the New Zealand film industry. As is usual with script development, there were many debates along the way. Author Geoff Chapple saw himself as being brought in to make the film 'more popular' and less programmatically 'feminist'.[4] The final draft of the script (nine were seen by Victoria University film lecturer Russell Campbell)[5] has four names on its title page: 'Adapted by Debra Daley, Geoff Chapple, Pat Murphy and Helen Hodgman from the novel by Jane Mander *The Story of A New Zealand River*.'[6]

An outline of the screenplay's action and character development shows how it 'adapts' the novel, how it 'reads' and responds to it, and the elements it chooses to foreground, as well as the elements it changes or ignores.[7]

In its storyline the film truncates the action of Mander's novel so that the later episodes of Asia's lovelife are removed but, like the novel, it does traverse some eight to ten years which presumably means that the production would have required the use of two actresses to play the daughter. The screenplay emphasises the importance of locations, and preserves the setting of the Kaipara and the period of the 1880s to the 1890s.

The opening scene, for example, requires pre-dawn shots of the wide calm waters of the Kaipara harbour. A steamer is berthed at the wharf and a piano – a baby grand, on the wharf and half covered by a tarpaulin – has in the misty dawn light the appearance of being airborne between earth and sky.

The script develops its narrative around Tom Roland's business initiatives. His progress from bushfelling to building a sawmill, and from cottage to comfortable villa and family prosperity, is emphasised. Thus the main action is foregrounded against a backdrop of men at work and in the pub, and later local townspeople. Typical scenes are set in the kauri forest, and include the diegetic sounds of ringing axes and sawing. One of the minor, but named, characters is Rangi, an addition in adaptation as there are no named Maori characters in Mander's novel.

This aspect of the screenplay suggests a similarity with the 1993 movie *Desperate Remedies*, directed by writer Peter Wells and Stuart Main. A treatment of the screenplay might have produced a scene not unlike one in *Desperate Remedies,* where workers line up to wash together at a long communal sink. Noise, splashing, camaraderie and rough cleanliness give a picture of male bonding not unlike that of rugby changing sheds.[8] Other new elements include drug problems amongst the workers that connect them with the outcasts of the gumfields.

As in *The Piano*, 'The River' develops the drama of Alice's entry into the wilderness by foregrounding that article of furniture cum musical instrument, the piano. Alice's love for it, and its absurd appearance looming out of the dawn light, on the deck of the punt in the muddy estuary, and sliding along the river between bush-clad slopes, are the focus of these early scenes. Scene 1 also introduces David Bruce, who pulls the tarpaulin off the piano, shaking his head in consternation; while Scene 5 includes emotional exchanges between Alice and David as she demands imperiously that the piano accompany her, and he demurs. Scene 6 highlights the curious disjuncture of the piano with the surroundings of bush and sea when the piano is swung from a hoist silhouetted against the sunrise while Asia hops around underneath and Alice looks on anxiously. The musical instrument is regarded (particularly by Alice's husband and his workers) as an extraordinary accoutrement to bring to such wild territory, and in these scenes mocking laughter is directed at Alice.

The tension between the ocker and sexy relationship that Tom Roland has with publican Rosie and Alice's uptight demeanour is introduced by juxtaposition of Alice and the piano with Rosie and the pub, in an explicit way that is not immediately done in the novel. One location slips into another when Alice's passing punt is witnessed by drinkers on the Hakaru pub verandah. Several scenes are required to develop this juxtaposition. Alice's insistence on avoiding vulgarity and ordinary life by absorbing herself in her piano playing is shown in Scene 7 when she refuses to answer her three-year-old Betty's questions about the bucket available for ablutions on the punt, and instead strikes up the opening notes of Beethoven's *Spring* sonata as they glide along between bushy banks. Stage directions also suggest Alice is intent on imagining the violin accompaniment as she plays.

By Scene 9 Asia and Betty are snuggled up against each other and Alice snoozes in the shade of her piano, sleepily grasping one of its legs while David sneaks glances at her profile – indicating his interest. The next scene is an exterior of the Hakaru pub, and in Scene 12 the two locations come together: drinkers at the pub push up their windows to peer out at the river and toast the punt, waking a dishevelled and embarrassed Alice. The pub crowd then satirise the unlikely group, one mimes a concert pianist, Rosie stares in amazement and Tom Roland arrives to curse the piano and the foolishness of his new bride in bringing it.

The focus on the piano is evident only in the first part of 'The River' script.[9] It is clear that it would have been as effective in 'The River' as it was in *The Piano*. But even in the shared emphasis, one can see there are other important differences – whereas in *The Piano* the musical instrument symbolised the woman's situation and stood in for a (largely unrepresented) naturalistic social dimension, in 'The River' that naturalistic dimension is very much evident. The inscrutable and mask-like quality of Alice's face in the opening scenes described in the screenplay directions is similar to how one would describe the look of Asia/Holly Hunter in the opening scenes of *The Piano*; yet in 'The River' this look and the attachment to the piano are much more clearly motivated. Scenes spell out Alice's terror of the unknown, her narrow notions of propriety and her fear of physical danger, suggesting the social and environmental context we imagine her coming from. This version is consistently grounded in social details, unlike *The Piano* where the woman's muteness makes her so isolated and exotic that she appears to stand quite separate from social context – she is unlike anyone we know except in dreams.

Key passages from the novel are adapted in 'The River' screenplay to signify the special circumstances that Alice will face in her new environment. For instance, the anxiety that Alice feels at her increasing distance from civilisation is shown in the opening sequence as the punt, loaded with her piano, household goods and two children, glides along a river which has fewer and fewer signs of human habitation. And a particularly poignant passage from the book: 'As the punt passed in deep water close beside the bank Alice saw peeping out of the fern on a mound above two small enclosures with rough unpainted crosses falling against the rotting palings', which suggests the possibility of infant or other untimely deaths in this remote area, is replicated in the filmscript when Alice's gaze at the dark bush is interrupted by a glimpse of two recent and rough-looking graves on the riverbank.[10] Similarly all the practical difficulties that Alice will have – living in primitive conditions, dealing with slops and makeshift lavatories, nursing babies, washing outside, and cooking on a wood range – all without any assistance from any servants she was used to, or other women – are introduced into the action early on.

Scenes 20–32, for example, tell the story of the first evening and night in the house on the river. This is a narrative in which Alice's point of view is conveyed by her silence and (presuming a certain camera point of view) the telling evidence of how empty and primitive the house is, which suggests that she is anticipating all the heavy and lonely work ahead of her. These scenes are also particularly well constructed to convey an already triangular exchange of emotion – Tom Roland's gigantic enthusiasm and pride at showing his land and his house to his wife is eagerly picked up by his stepdaughter but is contrasted with Alice's fear of the land and indeed her husband, and also with David Bruce's observant compassion for Alice's predicament – though he is Tom's manager and also enthusiastic about the projects. The raw little cottage, lifted on wooden blocks and approached by high wooden steps and warmly lit by the setting sun, is a vast source of pride to Tom Roland. His words of enthusiasm are matched in a number of scenes by Alice's numb silence; a response that he takes for awed pleasure. Similar responses are evinced to his playful pride in the durable qualities of kauri: in a sitting room scene Alice and children stand silently amongst packing cases and sawdust. The next scene of Tom showing off to Alice his own handiwork –a high, large, wooden bed in a tiny bedroom – is (thankfully for Alice) interrupted by Asia's bursting in to say how she loves her new home.[11]

The following scene is back in the sitting room, still near sunset. Asia's comments that the piano would look well in the room are supported by David Bruce suggesting methods of shifting it up from the punt. Tom, however, changes the subject – they need dinner and he points out to Alice that there are potatoes in the sack waiting to cook.[12]

The next sequence includes shots of Tom busy at carpentry – the kitchen is being lined – and a scene of Alice struggling to get Betty to sleep amidst the hammering builds an atmosphere of tension culminating in six (29–35) late-night scenes. Alice goes outside; she sits on the bank of the river watching the water swirl past in the moonlight, listening to the moreporks and the sound of David Bruce leaving the Rolands' cottage to return to his own, nearby. When Tom calls her she hesitates, and only goes in reluctantly when he calls a second time. The bedroom scene that follows suggests an unpleasant meeting of his passion and her reluctance – a rape-in-marriage scene. The bedroom is lit by a kerosene lamp set on the packing case which Alice uses as a dressing table. She takes time over careful preparations for bed and the brushing of her hair; he drops his clothes on the floor. An atmosphere of tension is suggested as her embarrassment and lack of desire contrast with the romantic setting. Tom, lying on the bed, plays with Alice's hair, promises her pleasure, and then when she protests he stands up to pull her onto the bed. Her unhappy whispers that she is tired are ignored and he proceeds to have sex with her: a suggested last shot is of her face turned away from his, again frozen in expression.[13]

The action of the scenes described above are closely adapted from the novel and they are a filmic attempt to convey something of the dual effect of the novel. As a nationalist text *The Story of a New Zealand River* celebrates the beauty of the landscape and its liberating potential but it also conveys Alice's sense of the possible privations and terrors of life in that new landscape. One might say that the novel's nationalist project attempts to reconcile these two parts by means of a romance narrative. (Although I am speaking here of a different form of nationalism to that which emerged with the *Landfall* generation, which I will discuss in the next chapters.) This duality of the novel is shown in the screenplay as the opposing of points of view of different characters: where Alice sees emptiness, Asia sees fullness. Potential sensuality and freedom is suggested by such features as the sunset falling into a room, the bush, the atmospheric lighting (kerosene lamp) and the fresh simplicity of the little house. But that is not how Alice sees it.

It looks as if 'The River' script is keen to engage the local audience in a tussle of sympathies. A New Zealand audience would be likely to react particularly favourably or emotionally to these icons of settlement – the pioneer cottage, the kauri planks, the bush at night. But at the same time the script shows what this environment might mean for Alice who, as the central character is also likely to engage audience sympathy. For Alice, the man who doesn't understand her, has a parallel in the land that doesn't understand her. And her husband's showing off the house is an intrusion into what she is used to thinking of as a female space – he has created a dwelling which he thinks is a home but she can see is not. His 'home' is comically masculine – some fine raw timber, a sack of potatoes and a good big bed. The audience would be balancing their perception of the beauty of the surroundings against what they perceive as Alice's dread that the exchange she has made (her body and her cooking abilities for a proper name for her daughter and a roof over their heads) will prove a lifetime's ordeal.[14]

So, what will be the outcome of this predicament? These scenes convey very well the anticipation and concern that is expressed in the novel in the semi-narrating voice of David Bruce when he wonders about how Alice will adapt:

> He vividly remembered the morning when he piloted the boss to the kauri forest at Pukekaroro. It had been a case of the blind leading the blind down that winding channel; but in spite of the strandings in the mud and the boss's temper, Bruce had felt the call of the wild, and had accepted the offer to stay. He wondered once, as he saw Alice's face turn towards a gorge in the mountains, if she felt about it all as he had done. He knew that one might well forget the petty facts of life in the midst of that tremendous scenery.[15]

Dorrie Harding, a peripheral character who first appears at the opening of the novel, anticipates the problems ahead for Alice: 'How will she stand it? . . . Tears glistened in Dorrie's eyes. She read into Alice Roland's future things her husband did not think of.'[16] The opening scenes of 'The River' echo Dorrie Harding's presentiments of romance and suffering. By showing the difficulty of this new life for all the characters, these scenes hint at the drama that will arise out of each of their dissatisfactions.

At the end of the bedroom scene the scales are tipped against Alice's adaptation. Her ineffective protests against her husband's insistence on sex when she doesn't want it suggest that instead of learning self-assertion from the new life, she will feel only duty and dislocation. Or is something else possible? In Scene 30 another outcome is hinted at.

Tom and Alice are lying amidst tangled sheets. Alice observes Tom's face as he sleeps. It is placid, and to her uninteresting. Alice's dislocation is posed as a question which isn't answered by this satisfied look. But at that moment a kind of possible answer arrives: diegetic sound of bush and then faint strains of violin music are carried on the night breezes. Alice becomes aware of it. She looks at the window as she recognises the violin accompaniment to the *Spring* sonata she was playing previously. It can only be coming from the next cottage – David Bruce's.[17]

The sound of the violin continues with the next (also night) shots of a swiftly flowing river and then low-angle shots looking up to the tops of bush trees. All this suggests the possibility of Alice being swept away into that nature – by passion perhaps?[18]

This sequence of scenes seems appropriate for the beginning of a romance movie, yet as the screenplay of 'The River' goes on it doesn't centre on that romance. Instead other action is introduced in what I would interpret as contemporary critiques of the novel, and the initial development is disrupted.

One such contemporary critique is of the kauri logging that the sawmill is based round; fairly obvious comments on conservation and ecology turn up in the script. Some of these come directly from the novel but here they are presented as the point of view of the film by being reiterated by characters other than Alice. In Scene 37, a bush scene, Alice in the gloom of huge kauri trees takes off her gloves to touch one of the enormous trunks. Her reach is tentative as if she expects a flesh-feel. In contrast, Tom, approaching through the trees, slaps his hand on a trunk and pronounces on the size and age of the kauri. When Alice protests at the prospect of milling such giants, he jokes that it will be a great challenge.[19]

And in the next scene Tom insists that Alice is being sentimental and that someone has to cut them down if only because timber is cheaper than bricks and the trees will make houses for the poor.[20] Tom's explanation is almost direct from the novel; later in the action, though, when a flood removes all the top soil, one character observes that the felling of the trees is the real reason for this catastrophe. Again this expression of what is an anachronistic attitude is only a detail, but it seems to function as a critique of what the screenplay takes to be the underlying assumptions of the novel – its deeply colonial Anglophile and prudish values, as well as a critique of what the settlers of New Zealand did to the landscape.

A discussion of the ending of 'The River' is also revealing of its rereading of the novel. As I have already pointed out, in 'The River' the storyline is adjusted so that instead of Alice and David waiting and waiting for each other, or living alongside each other in a platonic relationship, they do become lovers and Alice's miscarriage, so important in the novel as an unlikely way to establish intimacy, is of their own baby. This makes the relationship more plausible by our standards today but also less strangely intense. The hero and heroine therefore have to be differently typed. In particular, instead of being noble, David is shown as adjusting to a threesome companionship because it is easier and less demanding. After Tom Roland's death he is wary of Alice, unsure of her feelings. He leaves her alone when she is about to depart the village. Given this scenario it is only a *deus ex machina* that can bring the lovers back together. Mrs Brayton (conveniently still alive) is cast in this role. The last scenes (159–166) unfold very differently from those in the novel. In Scene 159 David is dynamiting a tree-stump, this being a good activity to take his mind off Alice's impending departure from the valley – Tom is dead and the future of Alice and her children is in the city. Mrs Brayton, in a horse and gig, comes to urge him to farewell her. She lambasts him that Alice's uptight morality suits him because it allows him to hang about gloomily owning her but not acting on it. Mrs Brayton's words sting him: 'I love her,' he says. Whereupon Mrs Brayton whisks him into her gig and takes off down to the jetty where Alice's boat – a little steam tug that used to haul logs out of the settlement – is waiting.

This is swashbuckling stuff and suggests that emotional or relationship problems are just waiting to be solved by sudden and decisive action. A series of juxtaposed shots of the steam tug being loaded and the horse and gig careering towards the wharf follow. The steamer toots, Alice, Asia and Betty waiting on deck look anxious, the horse and gig with David clinging to its sides almost overturns, the steamer toots again. More bustling action on deck follows, with shots of the crowd on the jetty and travellers waving. David is still not there. A close-up of Alice shows her sad and looking out from the other side of the tug over the river. (The soundtrack would be very important here as the steamer toots once more and the mill siren goes, drowning out Asia and Betty's excited cries as they spot Mrs Brayton and David.) Alice and David are saved by Mrs Brayton, operating as fate or a fairy godmother, and delighted with her role as charioteer. She has got David there in the nick of time: he leaps on board as the mooring ropes are freed and the tug slips away from the wharf.

In the scene of meeting Alice is taken by surprise as David walks towards her across the deck. He takes her hand and kisses it and then kisses her mouth; her arms go around his neck. As the tug pulls away from the wharf there are more crowd shots, and shots of the family's faces receding as Mrs Brayton waves. Then, from Alice and the others' point of view, Mrs Brayton is a minute figure in the distance. In the last scene (166) the steam tug moves out of shot, round a bend in the river, leaving the glistening water quite still and empty.[21]

Philosopher Paul Ricoeur argues that there are two processes in reading: first, 'distanciation' which is an awareness of the completeness or otherness of a text and then, 'appropriaton'. Appropriation is the process by which readers make a text their own, make it intelligible.[22] This is what is going on in the movement from *The Story of New Zealand River* to 'The River'. The scriptwriters of 'The River' seem aware of those revisions of New Zealand history that I spoke about in my previous chapter and want to incorporate them in order to make the novel intelligible to a contemporary New Zealand audience. Stevan Eldred-Grigg has written about prostitution and drugs in early New Zealand, and drugs are present in the workers' camp (as they are also in *Desperate Remedies*). Similarly, the hotel is a place of sexual licence. Miles Fairburn has suggested that nineteenth-century New Zealand was an atomised society and we can see that atomisation here on the gumfields.[23] In 'The River', nineteenth-century New Zealand history has been demystified, rewritten in a sceptical light.

The filmscript's particular 'appropriation' of the novel implies that it can do better than the limitations of Mander's feminism. It can look questioningly at how the novel depended on the absolute moral guidance of one tall handsome doctor, an Englishman. Within 'The River' this character is critiqued as a 'tin god' and it is not wise restraint but neurotic inaction that marks his character.[24] Thus, the outcome of the novel, Alice and David Bruce getting together, depends on Mrs Brayton when she takes things in hand at the end. Likewise in a series of predictable 1990s changes in attitudes to women, Maori and the environment, 'The River' has the *courage* to represent Maori and powerful women in a way that the novel is frightened of doing. And also, unlike the novel, the filmscript is not prudish – of course there is a physical relationship between Alice and David Bruce that needs to be shown, so the film shows it. And why would the novel make so much of a miscarriage? Of course because (as the script revises) the child was their love child. These changes to the narrative indicate, I think, that this screenplay reads the novel as limited by period assumptions and puts in what it thinks the novel would have really wanted to show if it had fully understood the period it was writing about.

'WHY DID MOTHER STAND IT?'
THE STORY OF A NEW ZEALAND RIVER READ DIFFERENTLY

I would like now to develop a different angle on the novel, reading closely to analyse discourses of choice and sexuality in the novel which can be related to the discursive environment of the 1910s (as an alternative to translating the novel into a 1990s conceptual framework). My approach has connections with the 'new historicism' which attempts to combine discourse analysis of literature with an awareness of history and politics. First of all the fact that the novel was written by a woman of Asia's generation about a woman of Alice's generation can be seen as putting a particular frame on it. It is because of this that I can argue that the novel can better be understood as a daughter of colonial New Zealand addressing her mother's predicament. Mander was a woman in her thirties when she wrote *The Story of a New Zealand River* and as such she was concerned with what effect the constraints experienced by mothers have on their daughters. As a grown daughter, she empathises with the mother's situation. This brings me back to the content I uncovered in 'Prelude', when I read it as the story of an unwilling conception in a settler colony, where white women were expected to reproduce for the sake of the nation – as the story of a period when domesticity and childbearing were of primary importance and also primary anxiety.

This desire to mend a woman's life is mixed with nationalism because the author, in her idealistic state of mind, saw the new country that she came from (but was then living in exile from) as allowing women to become more courageous in both mind and body. Love and passion were the reward for adaptation. As I remarked in the previous chapter, this optimism about social change can be explained partly by Mander's experience in New York. There she found that Americans saw her country as an example of reform and experiment, epitomised by it being the first country to give women the vote. Implied here is the idea that this country could develop a new national type. Dorothea Turner (whose 1972 monograph is still the major critical work on Mander) acknowledges this when she describes Alice as a representative of a possible new type or class, educated by the other characters into a good mix of old and new qualities. Newcomers to the Kaipara, north of Auckland, where Mander grew up, would have been similarly measured by locals in terms of whether or not they passed a test of adaptability, companionableness and manners. Dorothea Turner speaks of the novel as 'continually searching for the cultural essence of a person which will survive transplantation and isolation' and suggests that Mander's 'peculiar upbringing accounted for the analytic precision of her social awareness' – 'people of all types came to join her father's camps and mills, travelling light and often in poor shape; prediction of their potential could be more than a game'.[25] Mander's 'in group', the ones who are capable of adaptation, can also be seen as an answer to the 'what after pioneering' question that Lawrence Jones implies when he quotes a phrase of Mander's from her later novel *The Besieging City*: a '"pioneer and fighting age" demands a strongly developed "masculine element", but for the further growth of civilisation "the artists and the feminine element in the race" must be cultivated.'[26]

However, if sexuality is seen as one of the ways in which power is operated rather than as something in itself, then one can also think of the novel's liberation message as (to use Foucault's terminology) 'the deployment of sexuality' in the service of an idea of nation.[27] Sexuality is deployed as both a problem and a solution: for example, the idea that it is unhealthy not to have enough of it (sex, passion, impulsiveness) is deployed as the problem, and the happy ending to the love story (finding one's sexuality) as a solution – the reward for women changing and adapting to the new country. If this is seen as the strategy that the novel employs, then one must pay close attention to its love story aspect. 'The River' underplays this aspect and instead adjusts issues round women, Maori, and the land. We are looking only at a screenplay here, so it takes an effort to imagine what the filmed version of its ending might achieve, but even so it seems apparent that the writers were aiming at comic action scenes, bouncing on gigs, loading the boat, a last-minute meeting, reconciliation, a fairytale ending and sailing away. This is very different from the quiet, secretive, but explicitly sexual welcome which precedes the sailing away at the end of the novel:

> She ran out onto the verandah, forgetting that someone might see and interpret for himself the reason why she waved her handkerchief. She waved harder than ever when she saw Bruce swing his hat above his head. She would have liked to have gone down to meet them, but she decided that would be too conspicuous. When they reached the landing stage beside the booms she went into the hall. She found she could not be calm now, that anticipation could still raise a ferment in her. But the minute she heard Bruce's voice outside the gate she became still again.
>
> Asia walked off round the garden path, leaving him to enter alone.
>
> It seemed to Alice that his brown eyes held only the old quizzical smile as they met hers, that he came to her with the calm assurance of a husband rather than with the fire of a lover, and the wish half formed in her mind that he would seize her. But she forgot it as he drew her into her own room, that one room in the house in which he had always forced himself to be impersonal.[28]

The house has become the love nest that it was never previously able to be, now complete with a ready-made family and responsibilities:

> Sounds in the hall first arrested their attention.
>
> 'The children home,' he said, raising his face from hers.
>
> 'Don't move. Nobody will come in,' she said.
>
> They sat on till they heard steps outside the door.
>
> 'Mother,' called Asia. 'I'm putting dinner for you and Uncle David in the sitting-room. Now do eat it while it's hot.'
>
> 'Oh, Lord!' groaned Bruce. 'Dinner! We can't even get through a day like this without dinner. And it must be hot too.' He sat up in disgust. 'No use, dear. I've been dreaming of freedom here with you in my arms. But we are not free; we will have to eat dinner every day of our lives.' [29]

The domestic location, the inevitability of Alice and David Bruce getting together and Asia's role in supporting them are all the outcomes of that prudish love that 'The River' has revised. But it means that by losing the obsessive side of the novel, the filmscript 'The River' has lost the power of its outcome. More generally, having lost the love story, 'The River' has lost the central transformative power of the novel, which negotiates a new kind of nationalism via its management of sexuality. To read the novel in this way runs counter to most critical commentaries. Lawrence Jones, in his survey essay on the New Zealand novel, has trouble giving any credibility to the romantic plot line.[30] Likewise early New Zealand critics commented unfavourably on what they saw as the novel's sex-problem aspect (see previous chapter) and Mander's foremost critic, Turner, has insisted that interest in such issues is not a reason for reading the book.[31]

Such readings want to maintain a barrier between the artistic and the sociological. They also suggest that aspects of women's lives and issues raised by and about women – 'the sex problem' aspect – are completely separable from other aspects of society and history. I, on the other hand, would argue that the novel is offering a new way of talking about women's life choices of sex, procreation, termination of pregnancy, etc. It can also be described (in Foucaultian terms) as making a finer definition of how procreative behaviour should be socialised. And perhaps this could be seen as a discourse that was particularly necessary to the colonial society for whom, unlike for example English society, the value placed on the 'Malthusian couple' was in conflict with the imperative to breed new New Zealanders. Looked at in this way, one could argue that the novel uses sexuality to invent the idea of a reproductively and socially well-managed society. Of the period at which the novel is set (the end of the nineteenth century), Foucault comments: 'It can be said that this was the moment when the deployment of sexuality, elaborated in its more complex and intense forms, by and for the privileged classes, spread through the entire social body.'[32]

The novel forms a kind of bridge by which what is already happening – for example contraception, abortion – can be absorbed into an idea of possible choices for all women and for all families, and therefore can become the subject of further medical, social and scientific discussion or research. Its plot line and gaps imply the need for a way of talking which includes women's intimate feelings about desire, fertility, contraception, women's health, etc. And the motivation for writing, implied within the book, is the desire to resolve the opposition between the defeated mother and the daughter leaving for America and Europe. In this, the book has an answer to that 'what after pioneering' question.[33] But, more specifically, the question is inflected from a woman's point of view so that the book looks both back and forward. It attempts to formulate an answer to that question about the future out of its answer to the more specific question that Asia puts about her mother – 'Why did Mother stand it?'

The novel's relationship with Katherine Mansfield's 'Prelude', as I reread it in the previous chapter, becomes clearer. Both texts can be seen as daughters' attempts to renegotiate ways of looking at women's lives in the colonial context. Both writers are exploring a kind of domestic feminism because they see problems involved in being an émigré or exile, perhaps because that has been their own solution. Though it is romantic to be an exile, it has also meant giving up experiences of motherhood and domesticity. And both could be seen as developing new ways for middle-class women to talk about sex, pregnancy, conception, abortion, contraception.

As I suggested in the chapter on 'Prelude', when I quoted from Jean Devanny's autobiography, a new discourse about the physical consequences of sexual choice and contraceptive decisions in and out of marriage was developing at this period. Novels and short stories such as these that appear at first glance to be merely pastorals or romances are also developing this discourse – as much as those temperance and union meetings that historians identify as bringing women together.[34] Such fictions provide middle-class women with new articulations of subjectivity.

In *The Story of a New Zealand River* there are many examples of this developing discourse. There is the hesitant intimacy of conversation that comes about between a man and a woman because of her miscarriage, there is the discussion of pregnancy, there is the recommendation to have an operation (presumably a hysterectomy).[35] Mrs Brayton's response to news of Alice being pregnant is a particularly interesting example, because it indicates a need for a new way of talking about fertility, sex and choice. Alice is consulting Mrs Brayton, seeking advice and comfort after Asia has left home and regretting her own terrible pride in refusing to say goodbye to her daughter. Mrs Brayton comforts her: '"You will get along, my dear," she said gently. "We all do. We all get along somehow. And it is very foolish of us to think we cannot."' But Alice's rejoinder surprises her and her response is a grave one:

> 'Oh, I know; I am not going to die. But, oh God, how I will miss her, and there is another child coming.' Her voice ended harshly.
> It was some seconds before Mrs Brayton could trust herself to speak.
> 'I am sorry to hear that,' she said gravely. She didn't know.
> Mrs Brayton felt this was a case where something ought to be done, though what, she could not have put into words. Then her thoughts turned to helping Alice to face it.[36]

Mrs Brayton's feeling that this was a case where 'something ought to be done, though what, she could not have put into words' suggests the possibilities that there might, in the future, be conversations between women about relationships, sex, choice, contraception, 'family planning'. But at the same time the passage maintains the author's and character's modesty by showing that the old lady 'could not . . . put into words' her thoughts about getting rid of the child, or the foolishness of Alice being pregnant in the first place. The need for dialogue about sex, love, pregnancy, and bodies is also implied in Alice's ruminations on the breakdown of her relationship with Asia:

> But now she saw that she had known only one side of these people, the side that mattered least, the party manner side. She had prided herself that people always behaved in her presence, that they took no liberties with her. She saw now that this meant that no one had ever come to her with a story of sin or shame, that no one had ever come to her with the cry 'Help me' hot upon trembling lips. No one had ever

come to her for the understanding that in desperate moments saves souls from despair.
  She saw that everyone had lied to her and she saw why. She saw that every one had conspired to shield her and she saw why. She saw that because she had shut herself off from life, life had closed its gates to her. And she saw that she did not have to flee from life because life had maimed her, that she should have done as David Bruce had done, that she should have reached out to it, taken it with both hands and used it.[37]

And,

She went over the things that she and Asia had talked about in the last few weeks – the garden, the weather, a summer cover for her bedroom chair, her new clothes, the sunsets, and meaningless gossip about people in Auckland and at the bay.[38]

Clearly Alice needs to be able to talk about intimate aspects of life, thoughts and feelings. If such a discourse would be new for her, it would appear also to be new for the writer who seems herself to be only halfway to using it. Take for example the passage I quoted earlier where Alice and David Bruce get together in her bedroom. The author contrives a modest ambiguity by describing Alice and Bruce's moments alone as their 'sitting' in a 'luxury of silence'. They continue 'sitting' till they hear sounds outside the door whereupon the author betrays the prone position of her characters (presumably on the bed) when David 'sits up' (rather than stands up) at the interruption. Because of this contradiction we cannot quite visualise the intimacy implied here and what is interesting (and amusing) about this is the author's uncertainty.

Throughout her novel, Mander keeps alluding to the possibility of a different way for middle-class women to communicate. This suggestion is made not only of explicit problems in the characters' lives but also as regards the characters interpreting their environment. This is an aspect 'The River' misses when it takes a scene about chopping down the kauri forest and develops it as though it was about the European rape of the country and, metaphorically, patriarchal oppression. It is possible to read more subtly: one can, for example, see the related scene in the novel as being about poor communication between men and women rather than about the unsatisfactory nature of the marriage *per se*. Certainly Alice does see her husband as brutish and unfeeling because of his sheer brute strength – but this perception itself seems part of a self-perpetuating notion of female vulnerability. Let us look at how this scene (in the novel) provides an opportunity for discussion of male and female qualities:

The little party stood tense, their faces turned upwards to the magnificent head of spreading branches stretched into the deep morning blue. There was not a quiver in all the dark mass of foliage, no sign of capitulation to the wanton needs of man. Straight as the course of a falling stone the slaty grey trunk shot up seventy feet without a knot. Nothing could seem more triumphantly secure.
  Suddenly there was a suggestion of a quiver. The sky line wavered.
  'She's coming,' said Roland.

The whole world seemed to lurch, slowly, slowly; then the top branches shook, the great trunk swayed, the foundations cracked. The whole tree gave one gigantic shiver, poised for an instant, suspended, hesitating, and then, realising as it were, the remorselessness of fate, it plunged forward filling the whole visible world, and cracking horribly, till its longest branches caught the ground with a series of tearing, ripping sounds, preliminary to the resounding roar as the massive trunk struck and rebounded and rolled upon the earth.

The air was filled with dust and flying twigs, the whole clearing shook, and from the sides of Pukekaroro the echoes came rolling back. There followed a short extraordinary silence, into which there returned by degrees the familiar sound of the axes and the revolving handles of the jacks.

'There, that's over,' said the boss cheerfully. 'I guess we can have lunch now.'[39]

Tom Roland is casual and triumphant about the felling of the tree. His victory over it is similar to the casual victory of a man who demands sexual compliance from the woman he thinks he owns. The physical power required to fell the tree and the difference in his and her reaction to its falling recalls previous scenes in the novel such as Alice being called inside by Tom on her first night in the wild, and Asia's comments on what she overhears in her parents' bedroom ('I cried, I prayed, I raged. I grew old listening to them.').[40] Alice experiences this association when she weeps for the tree:

He could not understand why Alice had tears in her eyes, or why she looked at him as if he had committed a crime. He set off for the luncheon baskets, swinging his arms and whistling gaily.

And Mrs Brayton expresses it, too:

'There are times when I hate being a woman,' said Mrs Brayton with disgust. 'This is where you and I are nobody.' Folding her heavy tweed skirt under her, she sat down upon a rock. 'This is why men dominate us, my dear,' she waved her hand at the clearing. 'Sheer brute strength.'[41]

So far, so good; one can see why 'The River' makes the analogy it does, but it would be a mistake to take all this awareness of power and physical strength too seriously. The passage could be seen as implying that other kinds of strengths are more important, such as the strength to be a bit frivolous. Notice for instance how Alice is described as taking Mrs Brayton's words 'too seriously':

Alice who had always been a drawing-room woman took her words too seriously. She looked round the clearing at the various evidences of that brute strength, and felt herself trapped into submission by it. Never in her life before had she been face to face with such an exhibition of physical power. It overwhelmed her with a sense of her own helplessness.[42]

Asia reads the event very differently. When the stump is dynamited she 'danced about shrieking with delight'. Alice, dejected, concludes from the incident and Mrs Brayton's words that 'No wonder women have to submit to men' but is corrected by Mrs Brayton: 'Goodness! Don't say that! I've never submitted to them. My dear, you don't know how to manage them. They're more afraid of our tongues than we are of their muscles. Cultivate a tongue.'[43]

This word 'management' and the idea of 'cultivating a tongue' are key terms, used metaphorically in the text, because they imply a way out of the conundrum of 'male power means female oppression', a way of not being intimidated, of bringing men down to ordinary size and of talking about things previously unspoken. Seen in this way, the scene is not to do with conservation or the myth of progress but about the relationship between men and women (particularly in a society that admires physical strength).

New metaphors or semantic connections – the idea of the 'management' of sexual life, and the use of the word 'tongue' for the possibility of talking about intimate subjects (rather than a tongue lashing) will mean that men and women are not opposed but united in planning a life together, including the choice of how many children to have. (Again what I am delineating as new concepts developing in the novel can also be seen as refinements in the strategies by which sexuality is deployed to control and organise society.) The novelty of this idea is more obvious if contrasted with an English nineteenth-century text, *Jane Eyre*. The novels have a lot in common. Both negotiate, via a romance, an ending with an image of a new class alliance, and a new paradigm of family life. And in both cases that family represents the lifestyle of the future. In the Brontë novel we can see, as Terry Eagleton has pointed out, the invention of a new middle-class alliance (allowing a woman's passion for individual freedom to be married with aristocratic confidence). At the end of the novel, in their homely kitchen, Rochester and Jane celebrate a resolution of previously insuperable difference. As Eagleton puts it:

> The point of the novel's ending is to domesticate that [sexual] drive so that it ceases to be minatory while remaining attractive. In the end, the outcast bourgeois achieves more than a humble place at the fireside: she also gains independence vis-a-vis the upper class, and the right to engage in the process of taming it. . . . By the device of an ending, bourgeois initiative and genteel settlement, sober rationality and Romantic passion, spiritual equality and social distinction, the actively affirmative and the patiently deferential self, can be merged into mythical unity.[44]

The endings of both novels mark off a new model of marriage, a dramatically and independently achieved love match rather than a family arranged one. In *Jane Eyre* it is a world in which calling cards and costume balls are discarded for the individual pursuits of walks and horse rides. The desire of the lower classes for a more independent and dynamic existence, the governess's desire, is allowed to be expressed by a love match. By this means the lower class is grafted with the aristocratic class, to make a more powerful hybrid for the future. Likewise, *The Story of a New Zealand River* introduces a paradigm of a new class, celebrates a new kind of colonial family (a rather modern and 'reconstituted' family). It ends with that group together. Alice is united in a passionate new marriage, socially, financially and morally equal with the man she loves. Alice and David Bruce have very different backgrounds but both have painful incidents in them. Before the time frame of the action both have had to leave England. By the end of the novel, they form a new family together, one that is moral in a new sense because it is tolerant of past scandals and allows for the possibility of change. The Rochester/ Jane marriage in *Jane Eyre* merges into a mythical unity and part of its mythic quality is the sense that it will continue. Literally, Jane Rochester has a child. This is not the case with the Alice/ David Bruce union – they are older, she is not fertile (remember her operation) but they already have Asia, who is Alice's biological daughter and spiritually (educationally) David Bruce's. And because Asia does not have a publicly acknowledged paternity, she can be even more powerfully construed as a child of the nation.

In both novels, the struggle of the woman to find a way acceptable to herself to express and act on her passion for the hero is typical of the literature of the female subject in Europe in the nineteenth century. Both novels create a specifically female idea of an ethical subject, where what is important is not that a woman is married, or not, to the man she loves but that she has the independence to be able to say no to that love, before she says yes. As Nancy Armstrong points out, this aspect of *Jane Eyre* is a development from eighteenth-century novels such as Richardson's *Pamela,* where the plot involves Pamela talking her way out of 'the lascivious embrace of an aristocrat' so that 'the narrative of seduction produces female subjectivity as a form of resistance'.[45] Both novels test the love of the woman not only by conventional mores. Hard-won individual struggle is required. Obvious solutions are no good. For example, the excuse of a mad wife is not enough for Jane to 'yield' to Rochester. And though when she returns to Thornfield Jane is legally able to marry Rochester, because Bertha is dead, she has actually returned in ignorance of this fact, motivated instead by her new sense of independence and romantic conviction (complemented perhaps by her new financial independence).

Eagleton says of this notion of choice and atomisation: 'what distinguishes *Jane Eyre* . . . is that the primordial moment of embracing one's lonely destiny is neither muffled, displaced, nor efficiently dispatched.' He adds that this is an important example of the development of 'a language of the modern self' where the individual can be understood as able to be made out of nothing and not determined by social conditions.[46]

In *The Story of a New Zealand River* Alice's failure to choose her first relationship is not at stake; the novel is interested in how her passion for David Bruce can be accommodated (or how to domesticate her desire). Alice's passion, like Jane's in *Jane Eyre*, is eventually sanctioned by personal change and (fortuitously) by financial independence, and, as in the 1840s novel, it takes an awfully long time.

However, though *The Story of a New Zealand River* can be compared to *Jane Eyre* as a development in the literature of the female subject, the later novel is fundamentally different, in that it places a frame around this story of individual development. This frame is formed by a kind of addendum which is the account of Asia's ideas and personal solutions. It shows up the first part of the narrative. It suggests that the deprivation, moral struggle, and submission to an unwelcome husband that Alice endures (in order to become a subject) should not be allowed, even in fiction, to take a whole lifetime. And it says this by means of focusing on the materiality of colonial and married life which was mostly outside the scope of *Jane Eyre*. It is as if the focus of the narrative gets closer; in *Jane Eyre* it is on courtship and marriage choice, but Mander's novel goes inside the family, to explore intimate matters of personal morality, individual choice, problems of marital love. Specifically we are shown the repercussions on a daughter of her mother's unhappy marriage to her stepfather. Such issues, while occurring in earlier romantic fiction, were not its central concern.

From this perspective the novel can be seen to alter, modernise and colonialise its *Jane Eyre*-like narrative of personal struggle and personal education. First it associates unruliness and passion in both men and women (which in *Jane Eyre* was marked by Bertha) with the wild environment. And second, it adds to the discourse of moral choice ideas of how to manage a life in terms of sex and fertility, thus introducing a vocabulary of sociobiology (which partly undermines the very idea of the subject that the fictional tradition had previously developed).

Mander's position as a colonial woman makes for this re-vision of the 1840s novel; imperialism necessitates new deployments of power and of sexuality. She is attending to the need for a way of speaking about female bodies, female health and fertility: questions prompted by the isolation in which colonial families lived, the narrrowing down of life around the nuclear family, and the population imperatives of colonial society. In *Jane Eyre* Bertha has been read mostly as 'a projection of Jane's sexually tormented subconsciousness'.[47] Nancy Armstrong also sees her as an example of 'the monstrous female' and explains this type, common to nineteenth-century fiction, as 'a site where political resistance was gendered and neutralised', that is, as the turning of 'political information into a language of the modern self'.[48] Mander's novel is written in a context where the romantic novel no longer needs to delineate 'acceptable behaviour' by contrasting it with aberrant sexuality – for example, the terrifyingly-out-of-control woman. That has been done and is the history of the later novel. *The Story of A New Zealand River* is more a modification of a form, and if seen as a discourse that achieves social control by praise and blame, it is a fine-tuning of judgements about gender and generations. Armstrong would suggest that the limits of normalcy allowed in such a novel, as against say the Brontës' novels, have narrowed, and unruly elements have been locked out. The only echoes of wildness in the novel are to do with landscape and weather. The action is able to be about choice and subjectivity: to let the mind wander is to sink socially and materially, while 'to train the mind' to ignore misery, as Asia proposes, is the way of the future.[49]

The other addendum to the *Jane Eyre* paradigm is the development of a vocabulary, or at least the awareness of the need for a vocabulary, to describe the body and sex in this new environment. I am thinking here of the word 'management' which is used throughout the book in many different contexts to suggest the individual taking responsibility for the physical and emotional aspects of her life, particularly in marriage relationships. In one sense it is a coy euphemism but in another sense it is pervasive enough to function symbolically.

When one finds a writer using a single word over and over again as if it is a shorthand, one can become suspicious. The 'hermeneutics of suspicion' is an amusing catch-phrase to describe post-structuralist attention to the interested nature of any discourse, where claims to truth and objectivity are constantly undermined by not being entirely conscious or disinterested.[50] Deconstruction can transform our reading of a text by its relentless pursuit of metaphors. Paul Ricoeur has a slightly different strategy. He suggests that an unusual metaphor can be a way into a new 'reality', drawing attention to how categories are defined or how differently they could be defined. Instead of dissolving a structure he sees something new opening up. Jane Mander's use of the word 'management' has this quality of standing for many things. In the space of two chapters there are many examples. It is used of Alice: 'Asia's success at managing people, and particularly Roland, brought home to her her own continued failure in this direction' (p. 161). While Asia comments: 'I've managed her husband for her' (p. 168). And Mrs Brayton remarks to Asia: 'Well, if you can manage it as well as he does' (p. 169). Later: 'Mrs Brayton stood still, a few unmanageable tears straggling down her cheeks' (p. 173).

The reverberation that 'management' has in the passage I quoted earlier, about the felling of the kauri, evokes a sense of female sexual autonomy. It suggests that Alice learning to manage her husband involves not being overpowered by his desires, and making sure that he doesn't dominate. David Bruce describes it as Alice being able to 'resist' Tom Roland's 'pressure', and advises her not only that she doesn't have 'to produce his slippers in two seconds when he demands', but also that 'The whole house doesn't have to hold its breath when he comes in.' (p. 148).

In his 1972 essay on 'Word, Polysemy, Metaphor', Paul Ricoeur suggests that it is by means of metaphor, especially new or unusual metaphors, that we come to change our categories of reality because 'metaphor has the extraordinary power of redescribing reality.'[51] If one's sense of what human life is is bound up intimately with one's ideas of its possibilities, then the idea of planning reproduction, whether by choosing or refusing sexual activity or by accurately producing or inhibiting fertility, changes ideas about female existence in particular. British novelist Angela Carter describes the changing association of the female body with childbearing in this way:

We are living in a period where this alteration of significance is under debate in a variety of ways. Techniques of contraception and surgically safe abortion have given women the choice to be sexually active yet intentionally infertile for more of their lives than was possible at any time in history until now. This phenomenon is most apparent in those industrialised countries where the social position of women has been a subject of dissension since the late eighteenth century and the beginning of the industrial revolution; indeed the introduction of contraception is part of the change in the position of women over the last two centuries. But all this speculation does not seem to have lessened the shock of the psychic impact of the division between the female body and the fact of child-bearing. It ought to seem self-evident that this body need not necessarily bear children but the trace-effects of several millennia during which the fact was not self-evident at all, since it was continually obscured by enforced pregnancies, have clothed the female body almost impenetrably with a kind of mystification, that removes it almost from real or physiological fact.[52]

The desire to remove this mystification of the female can perhaps be seen in Mander's use of the plain ungendered term 'manage'. The implication is that the lessons Alice learnt in the not-so-good marriage are to be used in the good one. She is to learn how to enjoy life, how to take charge, how to be informal; how not to be intimidated by men, or class, or vulgarity; how to want sex or to say no to it, how to be unashamed.

FROM FEMALE SUBJECTIVITY TO THE SURROUNDING CULTURE

This new discourse can also be seen as in some respects typical of a settler society on the cusp between colonial and postcolonial. The term 'management' used of an individual's life suggests an analogous picture of a well-managed and balanced 'new society' in which certain informalities of behaviour and taste are to be cultivated, and English formalities discarded. In the novel all kinds of conventions are included in this picture – the design of gardens, houses, styles of entertainment and the upbringing of children. Even the informal and hybrid character of interior design is emphasised: not slavish conformity to overseas fashion but a mixture of the imported and the indigenous. This ideal kind of colonial house should show in an unpretentious way that its occupants are as familiar with bush lore as they are with figures from antiquity or the works of, for example, Voltaire. This is how it is when visitor Allen Ross wakes up in the Rolands' house. First he is bemused, he does not know where he is: the wallpaper is in different tones 'grey, with a frieze in pastel shades of blue and rose' and 'Daphne never fled from Apollo on the pub wall. Of that he was certain.' Then he is delighted: 'over the top of an old silver bowl of glorious roses that stood beside his bed he could see the head and shoulders of a small "Venus de Milo" and parts of brass candlesticks and bronze ornaments on a high mahogany bureau. It all seemed so unreal that he had to open his eyes upon it several times to be sure that it was really there beside that lonely river.'[53] For Allen Ross it is delightful to see old culture recycled at a lonely end of the world and adapted in a practical way that seems to epitomise the best of colonial society.

Mrs Brayton is also keen on such hybridity – the '"Winged Victory" of Samothrace' is taken from her house to the Rolands' presumably after her death. The surprise Alice first felt on seeing this unlikely object in Mrs Brayton's drawing room is replicated in Ross's waking in one of the bedrooms of Alice's own house some fifteen years later. Alice has followed the older woman's example in the decoration of her house. The need to produce an environment that is simple, adaptable, but also aesthetically enjoyable is part of Mrs Brayton's plan. She advises Alice, who complains of having no vases for the flowers picked from her garden: 'You have bath-tins and buckets. . . . Use them.' This makes Alice smile 'into a cluster of tea roses'.[54] One can see how these are the kind of feminine and artistic qualities that Mander wanted to develop after the pioneering period, and it is important those qualities and tastes are not fussy or exclusive.

Ways of bringing up children are also different in the new society; children still need to be guided but with a different notion of appropriateness. When Alice instructs Asia to take off her boots when going indoors, Mrs Brayton adds: 'You can take them right off, my dear, and keep them off till you go . . . I love children in their bare feet.'[55]

Mrs Brayton's garden celebrates the same kind of mix, where 'Trees from England, trees from semi-tropical islands, and trees from the native forest grew . . . side by side.' They are listed evocatively: 'There were creamy magnolias, pink and salmon lasiandras, sweet laburnum, banana palms, white trailing clematis, the scarlet [sic] kowhai and bowers of tree ferns.'[56]

Styles of dress are also modified by new circumstances: when Alice and Asia visit Mrs Brayton they find that instead of the 'fairy tale dress' worn the week before she is wearing 'an old and grimy Holland dress, short to immodesty' and for gardening 'her little hands were lost in thick leather gloves'.[57]

Entertaining too needs to be done differently. Asia's instinctive way of welcoming Mrs Brayton when her mother is asleep is the right one. Asia is proud of what she has – simple though it is. When she puts the violets into water she epitomises (albeit a little parodically) the way the new colonial housewife should be able to behave: 'She went to the cupboard and selected a plain white enamel basin. She loosened the flowers and arranged the leaves around them. Then she buried her face in them for a minute, and sniffed energetically. Finally she placed the basin carefully in the middle of the bare, kauri slab table.'[58] The scene where Alice at her kitchen table chats with her husband's foreman about his forthcoming marriage epitomises the easy and unpretentious communication that is the mark of the best in New Zealand society.[59]

This emphasis on hybridity and adaptation can be compared to a contemporary work of non-fiction *Tutira* or *The Story of A New Zealand Sheep Station*, first published in 1921. Like Jane Mander, W. Herbert Guthrie-Smith (farmer, naturalist, and amateur anthropologist) sees himself as writing at a moment 'after pioneering';

his preface begins: 'so vast and so rapid have been the alterations that have occurred in New Zealand during the last forty years'. His aim is to explain the changes which have emerged in the 'physical surface of the countryside [and] . . . the whole outlook with regard to agriculture, stock-raising and land-tenure'.[60] Like Mander in her description of trees and gardens, 'every subject has been treated deliberately from a local point of view'.[61] Also like Mander, Guthrie-Smith is concerned with management, particularly the appropriate management of sheep on Tutira sheep station – the dangers to them from crossing rivers in punts, drinking sea water, eating tutu, suffering lameness or falling in to pits. New methods have to be used in these difficult circumstances. ('The decency of high-class shepherding was impossible in such broken lands.')[62] The price of experience is purchased hard: 'it had yet to be bought by lives of sheep and money of pioneers – to paraphrase Kipling, by the bones of the sheep of Tutira, Tutira has been made.' And as is also shown in *The Story of a New Zealand Sheep Station* the breed of the import influences the difficulty of adaptation:

> Conditions were not ameliorated by the nature of the breed of sheep then run in Hawke's Bay. They were merino and there is something maddening to the merino in the sight of his fellows escaping to fancied freedom. There were in early times numerous stretches of narrow marsh, firm enough to bear the weight of the foremost dozen or score of sheep, yet insufficiently sound to withstand the puddling and poaching of hundreds of hoofs. The leaders of the mob would safely traverse such a barrier. It would then become a quaking slough, the original line of traffic marked by bogged animals. The wallowings of the wretched sheep in their mud baths. . . . Where hundreds had crossed dozens remained – their carcasses sinking into the morass or remaining half submerged.[63]

Consider the story of Alice alongside this: not only do the graves of her babies (and babies and children of others) literally mark the settlement, but also, for her type of person, adaptation is particularly difficult as it is for some breeds of sheep. And for each single sheep that gets through the bog there are many left behind. This tendency to discuss New Zealand in terms of sociobiology, whether writing about sheep or people, is interesting. As in the novel, the nationalism in Guthrie-Smith's account consists of celebration of adaptation and hybridity, even though (humorously) he is just as likely to write about the fear of contamination involved in the drama of settlement. His piece on weeds is a case in point:

> A friend visits you who elsewhere has unthinkingly pulled up a low-growing Chenopode or other thousand-headed undesirable . . . . a single seed has lodged itself under his right-thumb nail; in your garden he dusts a gritty tally to ascertain a name. The deed is done. The single seed has detached itself. It germinates.[64]

Guthrie-Smith's history also includes 'the stocking of the run with man' and 'the early failure of acclimatisation of *homo sapiens* on Tutira before his ultimate acclimatisation'. And like Mander, he has an audience in mind:

Every man has his idiosyncrasy: it has been that of the writer for half a lifetime to note small things; it has interested him. Perhaps therefore there may be found, if not a hundred, then haply ten righteous men to share that interest – to read, mark, learn, and inwardly to digest the subcutaneous erosion of a countryside, the ancient way of the Maori, the fortunes of pioneer man and the beast, the acclimatisation of alien flora and fauna, the disappearance of the squatter, the rise of the bold yeoman in his stead.[65]

This description of an audience would also be an accurate one of the audience for *Forerunners*, a magazine published in Hawke's Bay (Havelock North and Napier) just before and just after the First World War. Guthrie-Smith's work was included in the magazine as were works (poems and essays) by Blanche Baughan, Elsdon Best and a number of women who had written for *White Ribbon*, the suffrage magazine. Articles and illustrations showed the work of the architect James Chapman Taylor, who was engaged in designing the 'right house' for the New Zealander.

All of this suggests that Mander's novel would have appealed to this audience and that at this period (1910–20) there was a synthesis (or sense of synthesis) amongst a small group of people whose ideas about the environment and social behaviour, housing, relations between the sexes, farming, and Maori culture all rolled into a kind of nationalist vision of the future, very much built round the land and domesticity.

It is not easy for a late twentieth-century reader to recognise the significance of this domestic type of feminism, value it, or acknowledge it as such. Mander is a feminist as she is a nationalist in terms of the 1910s and 1920s. To acknowledge this moment helps us to understand what happened after. It is interesting that there was an attempt at synthesis of nationalist and feminist ideas before the cultural nationalism of the 1930s which (as I will show in the next chapters on Robin Hyde) was predominantly masculinist and engaged in defining true New Zealand culture against cultural conservatism and mass culture, both of which were identified as female.

I have one last example which may also help to place Mander's novel in this specific nationalist and feminist context. It is an account of the system of midwifery in late nineteenth-century and early twentieth-century New Zealand by a midwife and critic of the current medical system, Joan Donley.[66] Donley particularly identifies the period in which Mander was last in New Zealand as a time when it looked as if there would be a handover of the local, practical knowledge of uncertificated midwives (who had worked in rural areas) to the city hospitals. She describes how these uncertificated, trained on-the-job midwives supported women in successful childbirth right through the nineteenth century and how this tradition was institutionalised around 1904 into the St Helen's hospitals, which aimed to help poor women have healthy well-attended natural births. However, as she explains, this transfer of knowledge ran counter to another push for increasing medicalisation of childbirth, emphasising the role of doctors, obstetric nurses, hospitals specialising in obstetrics and gynaecology, medical student training and use of drugs. Thus the anticipated integration of the successful, rural, women-based system into the newly urban society did not happen. Donley may be idealising the early period but her description fits in with the pattern, which Mander elaborates in this novel, of the best ways developed in the country – manners, morals and economies – being taken to the city. Mander's later fiction, particularly *Allen Adair*, and her journalism express dismay at the failure of New Zealand society to develop in this way, and at the contrary tendency for city attitudes to 'infect' the country.[67]

•

All three texts discussed in these two chapters, novel, screenplay and film tell the story of an individual assuming that 'our liberation is in the balance' and that sex will make us free.[68] But this means something different for each. I have shown how the film and the screenplay read the novel. In contrast, my own 'reading' has been 'new historicist', in that I have tried to show how important it is to acknowledge the social and reproductive context of society from 1890–1920 in order to understand the idea of managing marriage and nation which I find in the novel. This is as distinct from a 1990s understanding of women, which both *The Piano* and 'The River', in their very different ways, cast back onto the novel.

•

CHAPTER FIVE

Robin Hyde:
From Incoherence to Immersion

My chapters on the relationships between *The Piano*, 'The River' and *The Story of a New Zealand River* introduced contemporary ideas about the rewriting of history. These next two chapters will explore similar concerns from a different angle. These chapters are about the work of Robin Hyde (1906–39), poet, journalist, novelist and critic, who wrote in the late 1920s and 1930s. Thus, clearly the writing is not contemporary, but what is current is the debate over the significance of her work. There has been more fluidity in the reading of Hyde's work and in the corresponding assessment of her importance as a writer than there has been of Mander or even Mansfield.

Many of the reading issues that have emerged in previous chapters are important here: for instance, changing emphases in literature and society encourage certain thematic concerns and certain qualities of writing to be foregrounded while others are relegated to the background or no longer noticed. Hyde's reception has been dramatically marked by just this kind of shift of 'dominants'.[1] Other relevant issues are the role that biography plays in informing how we read a text and the tendency of feminist identity politics to cause a swing from marginalisation to adulation – from one extreme to another – in the reception of a woman writer. Once again I am attempting to arrive at an overview of ways of reading this writer that at least does justice to the complexity with which students of the mid 1990s were able to approach her.

Paul Ricoeur has described processes of reading by which readers in their search for coherence, 'feeling themselves to be on an equal footing with the work, come to believe in it so completely they lose themselves in it'. But on the other hand if 'the search for coherence fails, . . . what is foreign remains foreign, and the reader remains on the doorstep of the work'.[2] One could say that the work of Robin Hyde has been read in both these ways. For example, Allen Curnow, who established an influential attitude to Hyde's work in his introduction to the *Penguin Book of New Zealand Verse* (1960), is 'on the doorstep' of her work, while another poet and critic Michele Leggott, who has used Hyde's lines in her own poems as well as writing about her critically, is 'immersed'. It would be possible to see both positions as overemphases or stages in a debate, but no less significant because of that. One group of readers, mostly male and mostly from the 1940s and 1950s, have a mixed reaction to Robin Hyde's writing and ultimately push it away, while another group of readers, mostly women and mostly reading in the 1980s and 1990s, become 'immersed'.

I am using the term 'reading' rather broadly in this chapter to refer to the overall interpretation of an author's work which includes critical judgement, the perception of a writer's strengths and weaknesses, and the creation of a sense of the author as person (the person who stands 'behind the work'). It is normal for a critic to be consciously or subconsciously extrapolating these aspects as he or she reads, in addition to the basic cognitive processes involved in reading. As in the previous chapters, I will sketch out contrasting interpretations and then, in another reading, attempt to encompass them in a more sociological explanation. In the entirety of my discussion I am attempting to enact the kind of reading processes Ricoeur describes. What I am looking for is not a balance between extremes (which is never achievable) but a sense of the way that in reading one plays with one's distance from the text – so that the illusion (of its coherence and one's complete knowledge of it) is by turns 'irresistible' and 'untenable'.[3]

Robin Hyde, writer, has had a number of manifestations: she was well-known as a poet and journalist in the 1920s and early 1930s, and increasingly by the mid 1930s as a novelist and critic and even political commentator. However, after her early death by suicide just before the outbreak of war in 1939, she was seen as a less significant figure. It seems that not only was her reputation naturally enough eclipsed by the contemporaries who outlived her but also that she was relegated into a certain mould as a minor (or major-minor) figure in the national tradition. Feminist-based critical attention in the 1980s and 1990s has valued and categorised Hyde's work very differently, but because the ways in which she has been constructed have not gone through a critical sorting process she is still a problematic figure to discuss, particularly as this sense of unclear boundaries and contradictions is associated with her as an historical persona as well as with her work.

ROBIN HYDE READ WITH DISTANCE AND DETACHMENT

Hyde was born Iris Wilkinson but from 1927 on, for her poetry and major prose works, she mostly assumed the name Robin Hyde – the same name she had given her baby son who died at birth in Sydney in 1926. In her lifetime she published three volumes of poetry: *The Desolate Star* (1929), *The Conquerors* (1935), and *Persephone in Winter* (1937); and, between 1935 and 1938, five novels: *Passport to Hell* (1935), *Check to Your King* (1936), *Wednesday's Children* (1937), *Nor the Years Condemn* (1938) and *The Godwits Fly* (1938). A collection of her journalism, *Journalese*, was published in 1934 and *Dragon Rampant*, an account of her travels in China during the Sino-Japanese War, in 1939. *Houses by the Sea*, a posthumous collection of poems, was published in 1952 with an introduction by poet Gloria Rawlinson, a friend of Hyde's who had informal possession of the Hyde papers until Hyde's son Derek Challis came of age.[4] In 1970 *The Godwits Fly* was issued in a revised edition, also with a Rawlinson introductory essay. An edition of *Selected Poems*, edited by Lydia Wevers, was published in 1984.[5]

Broadly speaking, these are all the works on the evidence of which the distanced view of Hyde was fashioned. A certain idea, or one might say myth, of the writer is associated with this view, which was formulated by Allen Curnow initially in his 1945 *Caxton Book of New Zealand Verse*, where he described Hyde as having talents 'above the commonplace' but being too conscious of herself as an '*ingénue*'. She was too much drawn into a 'habit of sentimental posturing' common to the period to be a significant poet.[6] Curnow's assessment was somewhat modified in the 1960 *Penguin Book of New Zealand Verse*, because by this time the later poems were available, but the basic conception of the writer remained: 'Her writing was near hysteria, more often than not, and she was incurably exhibitionistic: any moment we are likely to get the awful archness of her lines on Katherine Mansfield: 'our little Darkness, in the shadow sleeping,/Among the strangers you could better trust. . . .'[7] However, Curnow also had a more positive story to tell about what he considered the best of her poems and how they came to be written.

In this formulation Robin Hyde was seen as being preoccupied with finding 'a home in this world'.[8] As in the popular characterisation of Janet Frame, she was seen as an emotional, intense and sensitive writer who needed to find a secure sense of her own worth, a place, a home, and perhaps a likeminded community, in order to produce her best writing.[9] Because of her fragility she was pictured as the victim of a hypocritical and conventional society who condemned her for being different but also absolved her because she was sentimental enough to satisfy their idea of an artist. Allen Curnow puts it in this way: 'New Zealand had concentrated all its forces to confound one who had neither the will nor the opportunity to escape early, as Katherine Mansfield did.' His argument is that Hyde struggled to free her work from habits of sentimentality and posturing and that she did this by 'incessant writing and incessant change'. Again:

> Robin Hyde knew her subject well, when she wrote in one of her last poems,
>
> But where to turn? Feathered in what delusion
> Sing the fierce swan-song . . . ?[10]

He seems to imply (among other things) that the 'subject' she knows well is her own capacity for illusion (or 'delusion').

In this account her best poems were produced under the stress of speaking about dislocation, and only attained clarity once she had lived outside New Zealand and came to understand the importance of the relationship between self and country. For instance, in the long lines and free forms of another late poem, 'What Is It Makes the Stranger', she expresses her own 'pilgrimage of self-discovery'[11] via a conversation between 'Ear', 'Mouth' and 'Heart' in a land of 'black curled roofs, curled like wide horns . . . on a highway so ancient as China's':

> Remember this, of an unknown woman who passed,
> But who stood first high on the darkening roof garden looking down.
> My way behind me tattered away in wind,
> Before me, was spelt with strange letters.[12]

Curnow's conclusion is that she saw her own life and country in a new perspective in these poems 'of her China pilgrimage'.[13] In 'Deserted Village' similarly 'she made a precarious peace by art between the inner and outer worlds whose quarrels allowed her so little peace in her life'.[14]

A presumption here is that the central problem for a New Zealand poet is her relationship to her country, and that it is the creation of a system of symbols forged in the struggle to belong that makes for a successful art. Curnow speaks of poetry in spatial or cartographic terms: 'The best of our verse is marked or moulded everywhere by peculiar pressures – pressures arising from the isolation of the country, its physical character and its history.'[15] But Hyde can only half fit this formula. Her restlessness and infatuation with the idea of 'poesy' and 'faery' distracted her from the role of local poet. Her early poems were full of Arthurian images of castles, steeds, mead, woods, knights and maidens. Curnow considered this vocabulary of the world of the imagination a hackneyed Victorian one. Even in her later verse, there were poeticisms (of style and image) which a reader of Curnow's group would have found distracting or lacking in 'energy'. An example of this can be found in a stanza from 'The Wanderer', the opening poem of the posthumous volume *Houses by the Sea*:

> Yet I learned the all that this surly land could teach –
> Aye, though it broke my youth like a wave on its shore.
> What if I hungered at night for my native speech,
> For the gleams of a rainbow lore?

The theme is the poet's relationship to her country but someone reading from Curnow's perspective would find 'Aye' and 'rainbow' and 'lore' intrusive. In the same poem Hyde expresses a theme of exclusion, a Byronesque search to belong to the life of her country:

> Such were the seaways, I come in a mean disguise
> Back to a world that seems but a wraith of the foam,
> Back to the laughter of alien lips and eyes –
> Where shall my heart find home?

Curnow might again have approved of the theme but the intensity of her question about belonging is still resolved by a kind of magical Walter de la Mare litany which has its origins in an enervated tradition:

> Sings the bird of the woods, there is comfort yet,
> Music, beauty, the tender truths of a friend.
> How if he lie? I shall turn to the west, and forget.
> Ship-wrack and sea-voice chanting, these also must end.[16]

Similarly a poem such as 'The Dusky Hills' is inspired by the landscape but it is awkward in its treatment of the local when it rhymes 'manuka' with 'far', or uses an archaism such as 'drouth':

Write that I died of vanities,
Fire gone to embers in my brain –
But with a single dusky glance
The hills have builded me again.
And of blue cloud, of poignant small
Wraith blossom on the manuka,
Anew are woven those gestures grave
That pilgrims take, for going far.
The hills have given me quiet breasts,
Young streams for ease in time of drouth,
And a star's sweet astonishment
Kindness, to lay against my mouth.[17]

This is the kind of short poem that was seen as tripping easily off Hyde's tongue and pen as if her facility were a liability. The theme of this poem is familiar – strength coming from the hills as in the biblical psalm – and her poem could therefore be seen as conventional in its ideas as well as its language. A certain picture of the artist goes with this critical evaluation: Hyde is (it seems) a prolific writer with a prodigious memory. As her friend and fellow poet Gloria Rawlinson recalled: 'she knew by heart and could recite many plays of Shakespeare, Milton's "Paradise Lost", long passages from Chaucer and Spenser and carried in her head a huge anthology of world poetry'.[18] But, her storehouse of quotations was often inaccurate – as we can see in examples in her letters and novels – and in Allen Curnow's opinion, she was guilty of a 'passionate crush on poetry' which was the 'worst enemy' of her verse.[19]

A similar view of Hyde was carried over into the standard assessment of her fiction. That sense of urgency to find 'a home in this world' was also seen as driving her to attempt numerous ambitious fictional projects, projects which latterly drew on her discovery of her own country as a possible solution. Her novels *Passport to Hell* and *Nor the Years Condemn* (both woven around the life of Starkie, a returned soldier of 'complex racial heritage') attempted an explanation of the New Zealand psyche by reconstructing the shifting panorama of national life in the early decades of this century – 'the New Zealand that exchanged the uncouth simplicity of pre-1914 years for Cairo and Flanders, that came back to the riotous interlude of "boom and bust", that knew the years of the depression, the excitement of the 1935 election and the shadow of another war'.[20]

Allen Curnow's diagnosis of Hyde's generation was that it tended to be neither truly here nor there, at a difficult adolescent stage between settler and national consciousness, and therefore producing a 'sickly second-growth of verse' overly influenced by English writing and given to making naive, overenthusiastic assertions of New Zealandness.[21] The related opinion of Hyde's novels would be Eric McCormick's comments on the outmoded prose conventions and stereotyped characters that she used in *Wednesday's Children*. This novel, according to McCormick, was a 'venture' into the 'hazards of whimsical romance' albeit set in the suburbs of Auckland and on an island in the Hauraki Gulf. He described a Darcy-like English gentleman, an eccentric old uncle, and colourful (Maori and Latin) figures as a set of 'stock characters' in a narrative that was 'further weakened by the unrestrained exercise of personal fantasy'.[22]

However, Hyde's conventional habits in both prose and poetry were understood as falling away when in the last years of her life, and following a 'breakdown both mental and physical' she discovered her own country.[23] Curnow and McCormick agree in relating her breakthrough to this discovery which they see in her last volume of poems, *Houses by the Sea,* and her semi-autobiographical novel, *The Godwits Fly.* According to McCormick, *The Godwits Fly* successfully added to her ambitious and sometimes sentimental interest in nation and character 'the familiar territory of her own experience, the middle-class home of "Houses by the Sea."'[24] In this novel she recalled the minutiae of her childhood life and the economic instability that played havoc with middle-class aspirations after the First World War. She locates a central dissatisfaction in the 'godwit' predicament of the title. The godwits symbolise, in Hyde's words, 'our youth, our best, our intelligent, our brave and beautiful [the New Zealanders who] must make the long migration, under a compulsion they can hardly understand; or else be dissatisfied all their lives long'.[25] But, as Eric McCormick commented, although 'the theme is not worked out to a point of resolution in this novel . . . an article written in the course of Robin Hyde's own long migration makes it clear that she had reached a stage of equilibrium between paralysing subjection to the prestige of England and strident nationalism'.[26] Gloria Rawlinson put it this way:

> Earlier influences were cast off as her vigorous and observant mind, with so much of its own to say, strove to translate into poetry her 'young knowledge' of New Zealand.[27]

Other critical comments have tended to reinforce this picture of Hyde's development. The sequence of poems, 'Houses by the Sea', written in her Milford bach during 1937, was also revised and developed alongside *The Godwits Fly* and it was seen to be directly involved with her literary transformation, particularly because she took the manuscript on board ship with her when she left New Zealand for England.[28] Gloria Rawlinson describes: 'it became a part of her personal luggage in the next two years, read over, revised and collected in many strange places'[29] as (in Allen Curnow's words) by 'incessant writing, incessant change, she fought to free her vision from its literary swathings'.[30] McCormick similarly claimed that under the pressure of distance and perhaps owing 'some of its poignant intensity to the effects of absence', Hyde created something extremely rare in New Zealand writing, a sequence that suggests 'the sense of tradition' and continuity with an earlier writer, Katherine Mansfield.'[31] In McCormick's summary:

> The work opens appropriately with a group of poems, 'The Beaches', set in the hot

endless summer of adult retrospection; thence it moves, in 'The Houses', to the more confined surroundings of suburbia, and passes to its conclusion in 'The People'. Skilfully combining narrative verse with lyric, thus effecting great transitions in tempo and theme, the poet recreates the small complex world of her youth – the background of sea and hill and sky, the physical sensations, the emotional discoveries, the moments of terror and precocious intuition. . . . In reading the sequence, one is constantly reminded of Katherine Mansfield's stories. It is not a matter of derivation but of related approach by two writers to rather similar material, so that 'The Beaches' carries with it undertones of 'At the Bay', 'The Houses' subtle suggestions of *Prelude*, 'The People' faint echoes of 'New Dresses'. The effect is one of multiple associations, common enough in an older civilization, extremely rare in New Zealand; there is the sense of a literary tradition – only incipient, as yet limited and precarious, but still a tradition.[32]

This reading of Hyde values her for the local associations she develops in her later work, when she explores personal childhood experience in that 'hot endless summer of retrospection'. However, this positive view was undercut by the critic and poet James K. Baxter. Baxter found her discourse very limited because she dealt uneasily with the explicit aspects of her own material. He saw personal timidity and outworn feminine conventions of gentility getting in the way of the national and personal project which he regarded as needing more earthy openness, more sensuality. His position was close to that expounded by Curnow:

[New Zealand] writers . . . were strangled by a bad tradition. The Georgian dilemma had its roots in the structure of New Zealand society: in the great pressure towards conformity which prevented poets, and novelists also, from exercising a free and critical insight. They were quite literally afraid of what they might find themselves writing: and the demand by every newspaper reviewer for an optimistic sentimental tone prevented them from following up their own best work.[33]

Like Curnow he believed that Hyde, 'whose failures were as significant as her successes', was aware of a problem, such as 'the lack of sensuous directness particularly in her own early verse, and tried continually to remedy it'. But he added: 'If we compare R. A. K. Mason's similar poem 'The Lesser Stars' . . . we see clearly that the failure is not wholly a matter of tradition or lack of tradition (Mason's poem is an equally formal and traditional gesture) but stems from a basic timidity, an uncertainty of the reality of her theme.'[34]

Her symbols are predominantly narcissist, the beleaguered castle, the mirror, the shield; and the focus of her clearest and most direct poetry in *Houses by the Sea* indicates the source of her conflict:

Close under here, I watched two lovers once,
Which should have been a sin from what you say . . .
It wasn't long before they came; a fool
Could see they had to kiss; but your pet dunce
Didn't quite know men count on more than that . . .
. . . and when they'd gone, I went

Down to the hollow place where they had been,
Trickling bed through fingers. But I never meant
To tell the rest or you what I had seen . . .[35]

Baxter quotes selectively to emphasise the embarrassment he sees Hyde as expressing: 'She feels that she is dealing with forbidden material and the gesture is partly one of apology for writing at all.' This is, he suggests, inappropriate because 'the poem derives its strength from the direct sexual implications'.[36] Baxter has firm views on explicitness – the right way to write about 'erotic adventure'. The implication is that Hyde is essentially Victorian in her attitudes and morality, and therefore produces slightly squeamish work, whereas with a little more courage and virility she could have broken out of her narcissism.

•

This reading of Robin Hyde – one which emphasises the unevenness of her work – has been sketched out with reference to the commentaries of Allen Curnow, Eric McCormick, Gloria Rawlinson and James K. Baxter; but their reading of Hyde has been reinforced by a wider critical community of writers and readers, mostly male and mostly associated with literary nationalism – what Nick Perry has called the 'developing data base of an officially sanctioned and institutionalised aesthetic'.[37] Thus subsequent readers came to know Hyde's poetry by certain late poems, her fiction by *The Godwits Fly*, and her journalism not at all.[38]

Once again we see a discourse of value (about what is modern or what is good writing) affiliated with a nationalist discourse. This has been done in several ways. In terms of the theme, the debate about New Zealand identity is valorised. It seems that there is a prescription that the writer needs to be obsessed with New Zealand to be driven to write well or to break through to a kind of truthfulness. 'Strident nationalism', as McCormick described what he saw as a tendency of Hyde's, is to be avoided.[39] Strident or sentimental nationalism was seen as a characteristic of a previous generation of writers, and as different from a 'true' struggle for identity. For the new generation the idea of nation was creative because it was seen as a problem rather than a solution, so that restlessness combined with the struggle to express local and personal experience put a pressure on the individual that caused the kind of transformation that makes for good poetry. The argument (as Curnow formulated it and many others accepted it) was that cultural 'backwardness' in New Zealand was a consequence of nineteenth-century settlement: 'The nineteenth-century colonists achieved their migration bodily, but not in spirit.' And the 'shock of so distant a migration' caused poets and readers to huddle for shelter within literary and social conventions which created a protective wall between themselves and reality – 'the recoil of imagination from realities'.[40] This wall needed to be vigorously, even violently, shattered by the best of the New Zealand poets (such as those Allen Curnow identified).

Of course the claim to have got rid of conventions is always made by those who are busy constructing new (albeit they might claim more 'natural') conventions.[41] The approved style, defined in opposition to the previous generation, was 'hard' a metaphor borrowed from the international movement of modernism (for example, from Pound's 'hard' and 'soft' categories).[42] Adjectives or images that did not have the approved texture were despised.

IMMERSION

By the 1950s Hyde was understood to be a minor, or at best a 'major-minor' figure.[43] It was generally accepted that she had produced quality work but that it was uneven and expressed concerns that were increasingly out-of-date in both a literary and a social sense. However, in the 1980s and 1990s editors, publishers, academics and critics wanting to tell a different story have been responsible for new editions of her work, publications of manuscript material, a collection of her journalism, accounts of her life and new critical assessments. Why did a new perspective emerge at this time? The impulse seems to have risen primarily because of a new feminist consciousness; but there was also an increased interest in her papers and manuscripts, and in her life, which was facilitated by a common sense of purpose between three people – her son Derek Challis, academic researcher Patrick Sandbrook, and film maker Tony Isaac.[44] Her 'restoration' has had a huge, continuing impact on readers and scholarship because there was, in fact, a great wealth and variety of material to uncover.[45]

The new print publications were *A Home in this World: An Autobiographical Fragment* (1984), and *Disputed Ground: Robin Hyde, Journalist* (1991). Four prose works were brought back into print with new introductions: *Dragon Rampant* (1984), *Passport to Hell* (1986), *Nor the Years Condemn* (1986) and *Wednesday's Children* (1989).[46] A *Selected Poems* came out in 1984 and in 1993 *The Godwits Fly* was reissued with a new cover to match the feminist representation of Hyde's work.[47] In addition to these books Patrick Sandbrook's bibliographical essay in the *Journal of New Zealand Literature* (1986) described her unpublished work as well as her diaries.[48] An official biography promised by Gloria Rawlinson since the 1960s did not appear,[49] but an essay in *Disputed Ground* revealed, as did other critical work, more about the writer's life. A number of doctoral theses also add to the body of work that has made up this rereading of Robin Hyde.[50] In addition a theatre production *The Flight of the Godwit*, a solo show written and performed by Bridget Armstrong, was first presented in 1982, while *Iris*, a telefeature biography, was screened in 1984.

The feminist rereading foregrounds different aspects and values different content. Instead of seeing Hyde as a victim of 'booksy vulgarity' and 'guided by impulses she barely understood', she was seen as sharp and self-aware, highly conscious of the problems of being a woman and a writer. A useful example was

Hyde's epigrammatic statement about women writers made in an article in *The Press* in 1937:

> A woman writer's life is certain to make her neurotic. Unless she's so massively thick of hide that it's impossible to be any good at all. In that case she wouldn't have the acute perceptions which go to make a really fine book.[51]

This sample of Hyde's ability to analyse (and self-analyse) was used to preface the introduction to the 1986 edition of *Nor the Years Condemn.*[52] In this passage Hyde had gone on to suggest that the brittle overwrought quality for which women's writing was often criticised could in itself be valued because that brittle quality was relevant to the woman writer's difficult situation. This statement, challenging as it does an objective criterion of literary value, is just the kind of interpretive gesture that a feminist critic might want to make on Hyde's behalf. Since Hyde herself was making the analysis here, she could herself be claimed as a feminist.

The writer who had been thought of as impulsively out of control, an '*ingénue*', was now seen differently. Bunkle, Matthews and Hardy pointed out that 'the emphasis on mental anguish in the interpretation of Hyde's work *has* often obscured the vigorous, perspicacious woman determined to relate to the world and to "see" even its worst problems'.[53] She was now able to be acknowledged as a working woman; a woman who had no family advantages; who attended secondary school only with the help of a scholarship; who was a journalist (a cadet reporter) from the age of seventeen and parliamentary reporter at eighteen; and who always supported herself and also struggled to support her child. She was valued as physically and mentally courageous – she battled poverty and ill health, she had the courage to travel into China as a war correspondent, and as a woman who spoke out on issues that were not fashionable in the 1930s, such as the subdivision of Maori land at Orakei in Auckland. These are the points emphasised in the Introduction to the 1986 edition of *Nor the Years Condemn*. It is a profile which is reinforced in the essays accompanying the collection of Hyde's journalism, *Disputed Ground*, in 1991. What Gloria Rawlinson had to half apologise for – 'She was a champion of causes, mostly lost ones, and wrote for the unemployed, the Abyssinians, the Orakei Maoris, and the loyalists in Spain' – could now be applauded as foresighted and her outspokenness could be endorsed as a role model for New Zealand women.[54]

In his doctoral thesis on *The Godwits Fly* ('Robin Hyde: A Writer at Work') Patrick Sandbrook similarly viewed Hyde as a highly self-aware poet and novelist:

> Her critical statements on the nature and function of art, her letters, notebooks, drafts of novels and the novels themselves are examined [in this thesis] in order to establish that Hyde was a careful and deliberate as well as a gifted writer.[55]

He saw his approach as correcting previous assumptions:

> . . . in the past she has often been regarded less as a creative writer than a journalist

who simply recorded experience as it flowed past her, unable to exert any more control over the form or the style of her work than was dictated by the conventional expectations of feature writing or popular fiction.[56]

Opening up the personal context of Robin Hyde's life by uncovering manuscript material, letters and writing from other contexts has led to a number of positive images of the writer as well as her work. Sandbrook stresses her interest in theories of writing and technique. Phillida Bunkle, Gillian Boddy and Jacqueline Matthews admire her advocacy of Maori and women's issues, while Linda Hardy and Phillida Bunkle suggest that she was a shrewd critic of the 'empty-land aesthetic of her male writing contemporaries'.[57] The assumption that Hyde's literature is compromised by its Georgian (premodernist) elements has been challenged in doctoral theses by Susan Ash and Elizabeth Thomas. They suggest that the literary debates of the time cannot be characterised simply as 'modern' versus 'traditional' modes.[58]

Hyde's reassessment began with the recovery of her eventful biography. In 1982 Derek Challis wrote the introduction to his mother's previously unpublished autobiographical fragment, *A Home in this World*.[59] Challis was eight years old when Hyde died in England, and is in possession of most of her unpublished manuscripts and letters.[60] His account of her life mirrors the difficulty his mother had in telling her own story. He circles around his subject, not moving linearly but coming back to one period several times. Speaking of himself in the third person, he writes:

> In Wellington the child was put in a nursing home while Robin Hyde searched for work and tried desperately, by correspondence, to persuade the child's father to make some contribution to his upkeep. She found no suitable work and eventually visited Hawkes Bay with the child where she stayed briefly with her closest and lifelong friend. Although she found happiness in the open company of her son, passing him off to neighbours as the child of a 'dead sister' the visit was not a success and within a short time, after arranging board for the child in Palmerston North, she returned to Wellington to continue search for employment.[61]

And

> The pressure of constant deadlines, poor health, the conflict between the insatiable need of the magazine for material and her own needs as a poet for time for more serious writing, despair about her own circumstances, and deep concern about the welfare of her child led to the inevitable breakdown.[62]

His introduction seeks to reposition a woman whose personal quests were ahead of their time and subversive because she saw love as existing outside the conventional possibilities acknowledged by the society she lived in. Subsequently Challis wrote a biographical introduction to the reprint of *Dragon Rampant*, appeared in *Iris*, a telefeature about Hyde's life, and became an ongoing advocate for his mother's work.[63]

In 1991 a collection of Hyde's journalism appeared, accompanied by two lengthy essays – one about her life, the other about her journalism. The circumstances of her life were seen as throwing a new light on her texts and much information about the contexts of her writing emerged. Hyde, like other women of her times, proved to have had a number of difficult, even tragic, events in her life that were not easily spoken about. There was an injury to her leg, a hospitalisation and a subsequent drug addiction, the death of a young man who was tremendously important to her – an idealised lover, a hidden pregnancy and death of a baby, and the birth and fostering out of a second child. With this new information all sorts of connections could be made with her novels and poems, highlighting their depth and seriousness. Take, for example, Hyde's article on 'The Problem of the Unmarried Mother' written in response to the issuing of the findings of a government commission on abortion:

> And the others who did not resort to abortion, criminal or otherwise – is there any means of investigating their number and position at the present time? Where did they have their children – in hospitals with proper care, or in isolation and misery? How many of them lived, and how many died? Where are their children – how many in institutions, or in the smaller, though legally registered, baby homes with which every city in New Zealand is studded? How many of them had to pass their private lives through the courts, before establishing even a question of their right to maintenance of their children at the rate of 15/- a week?[64]

Hyde herself was, twice over, an unmarried mother, giving birth to her first son, Robin Hyde, in 1926 in a hospital in Sydney – he was born dead or died at birth – and a second son, Derek, who was born in Picton in 1930. (She was spending her pregnancy in the Sounds, in hiding, hoping to keep her condition a secret from family and friends and so as not to lose her position on the *Wanganui Chronicle*.)[65] Her interest in this issue of the welfare of the unmarried mother was clearly neither purely academic nor only philanthropic.

The notion of Hyde hiding personal secrets or socially unacceptable material in her texts has led to a closer investigation of what Michele Leggott calls the 'coding' of her writing. Thus in the poem sequence 'Houses by the Sea' Leggott observes 'folded into it, by enigma and double coding, the narratives of emergent female sexuality', carefully placed. What Baxter saw as timidity was (for a woman of that time and place) a shrewd and necessary strategy of understatement and allusion. For instance, in the lines from 'The Beaches':

> What is that quickens the blood?
> Smell of the sun-soaked, salt white wood.
> What is the tameless thing?
> Gull's shafted wing.
> What is it that lads deserve?
> White boat's arrowy glimpsing curve.[66]

Leggott sees rather than 'just longing for a lost world', sexual implications. 'It is,' she states, 'a searching meditation on emergent female sexuality, all done by riddle and enigma, all double coded. . . . Transfer the feminine boat onto the female body it stands in for, and you've got the beginning of Hyde's code.'[67] The stanza goes on:

> What is silk to my foot?
> Tide on the turn when spongy trees uproot.
> What makes the sweethearts quarrel?
> Third mouth, pink as coral.
> What shall a maiden do,
> Stay true or be untrue?

But Leggott suggests that there is subversive hidden material:

> 'What makes the sweethearts quarrel? / Third mouth, pink as coral'. The interloper who separates sweethearts is third point of a triangle. But the third mouth, 'pink as coral', the one that causes trouble is also unmistakably sexual. And there it is, the vulva image sitting in a poem written in 1937, masked for propriety in a culture that refused to countenance talk of the body. . . . Hyde hides what androcratic society will not countenance: sexuality celebrated and inscribed by a woman.[68]

The irises in Hyde's poems provide us with a similar play of Hyde-and-seek. The rainbow is the sign of Iris who, in Greek mythology, connects heaven and earth, and thus Iris Wilkinson can be seen as simply elaborating the clue of her given name.[69] Leggott also developed this connection in her own sequence of poems 'Blue Irises'. For example, in 'Poem 16' she recycles lines from Hyde's poems and a letter but also connects the lives of women poets (herself and Hyde) and their babies:

> Coming home like a derelict Egyptian, changing
> worlds, a baby delivered in a jacaranda mist *just*
> *like mine* The trees are quiet now, the baby grown
> and sorrow gone from the place it lay down in
> long before I was born What are we going to do
> about that moon in the ngaio tree beating
> like a fontanelle? Can we go on reading the summer
> constellations that do not pretend to be literature?
> Cicadas Avacadoes But where's that frightening dog
> sorrow? *Lord butterfly on lord hibiscus spray*
> are we through crying and the heart's big conversation
> with pain? Two sons, two sons and a crowning
> isn't a light word any more than a light kiss
> resembles a dark one Which you are[70]

This idea of Hyde allowing a life story to be subtly revealed in her writing puts a different value on other poems. 'Isabel's Baby', a poem for a young mother and infant, hints of Hyde's own experience as a young woman of twenty giving birth to a baby in Sydney, alone – and burying that baby, whom she named Robin Hyde, days after its birth:

> Isabel's baby, Isabel's baby
> Didn't cry much but wouldn't be fed;
> She had a dark and delicate head
> Curled wax fingers, like any daughter
> Long dark lashes she had; between
> Birds flew out of an orchard green,
> Flew from her eyes like hidden water.[71]

'Isabel's Baby' was a poem written as part of a longer work, 'De Thierry's Progress'. Isabel was the daughter of De Thierry, an actual historical figure who is also the subject of her novel *Check to Your King* – he was a nineteenth-century settler, a prominent figure in the North living amongst Maori. The poem is delivered as in the voice of another woman watching Isabel, marking her progress, pondering the baby's future and its mother's fears, and at points addressing the small children around her:

> Run away, little boys, run away!
> Run away Abigail, stout commanding
> Fox-red-saxe-blue-little-girl-standing,
> Standing staring at Isabel's baby,
> Run away, bowl your hoop of day!
> Maybe you'll frighten Isabel's baby,
> Maybe you'll steal its doll; ah, maybe
> Isabel's baby can win like you
> Cherry-red pegtops, mug so blue.
> Sky and fishing boats aren't so blue.
> Whisper and tiptoe, shout and run,
> Fat brown children who grasp the sun,
> Here must Isabel watch and pray
> (Long dark lashes and orchards green),
> Quiet people who pace all day,
> Plotting to steal her little dark baby.

The poem goes on to describe the oppositions of health and physical fragility – where some 'win' and some do not. Isabel's muslin dress hides 'her small and shrunken breast' and she 'Sees how the bold ones stay alive'. Though she tries 'to match them, trying to think / How to make her baby drink' the end of the poem tells us that the baby has died:

> (Isabel's baby, I'm told its dead).
> Star falls and moth falls, a fire in your hair –
> But the India muslin trails wet, my dear.
> Earth that was thirsty has ceased to care.

A feminist reader might consider this poem's narrative in the light of the fact that it was written by a young woman who had the experience of her own baby dying and who had been been deprived of much of the care of another. She had to lodge the second child, Derek, secretly in a home while she went back to her parents' house where her mother commented: 'You look about thirty. Fat and coarse. I can hardly believe you're my daughter.'[72] Consider then Hyde's imaginative return to the situation of Isabel, a pioneer woman – amongst strangers with a sickly baby – who feels herself besieged by healthy nature (vivid colours and energetic children) and her baby conquered by the principle of the survival of the fittest.

This approach to reading Hyde, with its stress on the personal, produces interesting reversals. Take for example the poem 'Dusky Hills' which (as we saw earlier) can easily be read as belonging to a diluted sentimental Victorian tradition, an outdated aesthetic. Nothing to move one. But a reader attuned to Hyde's 'coding' can see a strong female image in the last stanza:

> The hills have given me quiet breasts
> Young streams for ease in time of drouth,
> And a star's sweet astonishment
> Kindness, to lay against my mouth.[73]

Conventional landscape imagery is reversed; instead of the figure in the poem being refreshed by the dusky hills, her own quiet breasts are able to give 'young streams' of milk 'for ease in time of drouth': she is herself a source of comfort. The lines evoke the image of a baby's head, gently tucked in against its mother and receiving its mother's kiss, as well as a baby's mouth tucked over her nipple.[74] In these terms the images are unconventional and intense.

The new approach to Hyde has also challenged a common historical assumption that only those writers who published with the Curnow group could be taken seriously. Those who were published in the anthologies of Charles Marris and Quentin Pope or in newspapers deserved the scorn they received from writers such as Denis Glover. Hyde was represented in the Caxton collections, and later the Caxton anthology, but she also published work in a number of other contexts.[75] For instance she also sent 'Isabel's Baby' to the editor Charles Marris for inclusion in his *Best Poems* 1937, anthologies which were derided by Curnow in the *Penguin* introduction: 'she had written little to lift her above the ruck of best poems contributors'.[76] Pope's anthology, *Kowhai Gold,* was similarly reviled for its sentimental, animal and baby poems and its 'hobbyist' contributors.[77] Such literary judgements tend to suggest that what is regarded as female content or themes, writing about babies for instance, is necessarily tasteless.

In the collection of unpublished poetry that Hyde left there were many baby poems (poems about her babies) as well as a manuscript of poems for children intended to be combined with some of Gloria Rawlinson's and made into a collection under the title 'Paper Moon'.[78] Today the publication of such poetry, by a man or a woman, would not be viewed as a liability or a lapse of seriousness. Similarly Curnow's judgement of the *Auckland Observer* as 'a shabby weekly which has since died unlamented' has come under question. The journal did publish some interesting articles, including some shrewd criticisms (by Hyde) of Curnow and Glover's brand of nationalist writing. It also included Hyde's questioning articles on, for example, the abortion issue and the land dispute at Orakei.[79]

All of the associated writers are liable to be seen differently when one writer in a circle is re-read. Thus Gloria Rawlinson, a younger woman and friend who herself had great success as a 'girl-poetess' and was responsible for collecting Hyde's poems together to be published posthumously as *Houses by the Sea,* can now be seen not as a protégée pathetically struggling to keep the older woman's reputation alive, but as a significant poet in her own right, as well as a scholar of Hyde's work, an editor and perhaps in the future as a major contributor to the joint biography presently being finished by Derek Challis. Boddy and Matthews' biographical essay in *Disputed Ground* reports that Rawlinson's negotiation with Caxton Press over the publication of *Houses by the Sea* was 'difficult and protracted'.[80] It was only after Denis Glover left the press that it went ahead. In that introduction Rawlinson explained what she saw as the importance of Hyde's work. While Rawlinson accepted the received nationalist model of the writer, she also devoted a lot of space to the relationship between Hyde's life and her work and the circumstances of its production. In order to evoke Hyde's particular struggles, she quoted a number of her last letters in full. However, while Rawlinson knew (as only Hyde's closest friends did) about her children, she held back from mentioning them in her introduction. Instead she prefaced it with a quote from Hyde herself: 'Family history should be terse if mentioned at all; the glitter in it is so brief – sunlight on a broken sword; after that the long years that the locust ought to have eaten, unless dullness is the locust'. The social and critical sensitivities and values of the period made it unwise to dwell on 'family history'. Today, however, the quotation could be seen as a reference to an important absence.

The circumstances of our own period have made it no longer a problem to acknowledge children born to an unmarried mother, but literary etiquette is still unclear, questions of taste and appropriateness in the use of biographical information are still debated. An academic constraint fell on Patrick Sandbrook in 1986 when he was encouraged to remove a substantial amount of biographical information on Hyde from his thesis on the grounds that this was irrelevant to his literary argument – which was that she was a more conscious writer than had hitherto been acknowledged. Despite this, the most compelling parts of Sandbrook's thesis still rest on the relationship of Hyde's life to her writing, so his work can be usefully grouped with the feminist readings.

Sandbrook compared two drafts of the semi-autobiographical novel *The Godwits Fly*, bringing to light personal material when he showed how difficult Hyde found the redrafting from its first version, written as a therapeutic account to be read by her doctor (Tothill) at Avondale Hospital. He uncovers the development of this first version of *The Godwits Fly.* In it, Hyde was developing Eliza's trip to Sydney as a journey to get away from a boyfriend with no mention of a pregnancy. Then, in an aside in the draft, she reflected at length on 'how difficult it is to tell the truth' and went on, in a radical change of direction, to include the story of the stillbirth of Eliza's baby.[81] It seems (as Sandbrook comments) that Hyde was 'unable to continue with the fiction in a form so radically removed from the autobiographical fact'.[82] In a diary entry written at the same time Hyde elaborated her feelings about truthfulness:

> Strange how difficult it is . . . to tell the truth. I don't think now, that the cause of that is any sort of shame. . . . Not shame. But an old, deep pain, that says, 'Let me lie in peace.' Why trouble with truths, then? Only to prove something. . . . That life is a long strange highway, and that its last resting place is not what we have been taught.[83]

From this, and a number of other examples, Sandbrook makes the inference that Hyde's work was of its highest quality when it was also therapeutic. In other words, telling the truth was a breakthrough both aesthetically and personally. He concurs with Hyde that the sensitive individual suffers from the malaise of the society as a whole. Her 'breakdown' is really the sign of the hypocrisy of the society. In a sense the artist is the sane person who goes forward from her sickness (a kind of therapeutic trauma) to be 'supernormal' and to write the truth about her experiences.[84]

Understood in this way Hyde's view of the artist's role is similar to that which Sylvia Plath proposes in a letter to her mother:

> Don't talk to me about the world needing cheerful stuff! What the person out of Belsen – physical or psychological – wants is nobody saying the birdies still go tweet-tweet, but the full knowledge that somebody else has been there and knows the *worst.* Just what it is like. It is much more help for me, for example, to know that people are divorced or go through hell, than to hear about happy marriages. Let the *Ladies' Home Journal* blither about those.[85]

Patrick Sandbrook quotes an article of Hyde's on mental health in New Zealand, where the problems of adolescence tend to be 'locked up': 'blaming the parents, shutting the parents away from the child, is not enough. The parents were sufferers too. A whole code needs revision and enlarging.'[86] In such passages Sandbrook sees Hyde attributing 'the cause of individual suffering to a malignant social code, in this case identified primarily with restrictive sexual mores'.[87] This suggests that her subtle coding of sexual and personal details in her writing is based on an awareness that society cannot handle such material directly. With this in mind we can see a new way of reading 'Beaches IV', making 'the gesture of apology' – which Baxter denigrated – a thoughtful part of what Hyde wants to communicate. The poem reads in full:

> Close under here, I watched two lovers once,

Which should have been a sin, from what you say:
I'd come to look for prawns, small pale-green ghosts,
Sea-coloured bodies tickling round the pool.
But tide was out then; so I strolled away
And climbed the dunes, to lie here warm, face down,
Watching the swimmers by the jetty-posts
And wrinkling like the bright blue wrinkling bay,
It wasn't long before they came; a fool
Could see they had to kiss; but your pet dunce
Didn't quite know men count on more than that;
And so they just lay, patterning the sand.
   And they
Were pale thin people, not often clear of town;
Elastic snapped, when he jerked off her hat;
I heard her arguing, 'Dick, my frock!' But he
Thought she was bread
I wished her legs were brown,
And mostly, then, stared at the dawdling sea,
Hoping Perry would row me some day in his boat.

Not all the time; and when they'd gone, I went
Down to the hollow place where they had been,
Trickling bed through fingers. But I never meant
To tell the rest, or you, what I had seen;
Though that night when I came in late for tea,
I hoped you'd see the sandgrains on my coat.

This poem can then be seen as drawing attention to the writer's embarrassment as a problem in a particular social context. The simple and important act of communication between mother and daughter could not be made on this occasion, and presumably could not be made on many such occasions. The theme of mother-daughter communication (and its difficulties in a patriarchal culture) has received considerable attention in feminist studies. In this case it could be argued that 'the rest of you' gives the poem a broader reference than simply her mother, though she would be the person most likely to notice the state of the coat.[88] Even so, the poem is clearly more complex in its depiction of a child's experience within a puritanical society than Baxter's criticisms acknowledge. Baxter's poems are often similar to Hyde's in their combination of landscape and sexual images. Her images of sexual parts and bodies – that 'third mouth pink as coral', or her sexual associations with sailing, are no less evocative than Baxter's. And her writing is free of that ancient horror of women as witches and hags that colours Baxter's poetry.[89] Both poets see life-denial in prudery and gentility, but Hyde has a different analysis which is alert to the problems of a macho culture in which a man sees a woman simply as 'bread'.

Feminist reading has related the somewhat patronising view of Hyde to a general male uneasiness about female culture and sexuality. Curnow's phrase 'an exhibitionism verging on hysteria' was matched by the emerging Caxton group. A. R. D. Fairburn saw her as belonging to the 'menstrual school of women poets'.[90] Charles Brasch's autobiography *Indirections* contains an anecdote in which Brasch recounts a suicide attempt by Hyde after what he implies was his rejection of her sexual advances. He describes: 'she suddenly turned to me for closer comfort and reassurance. But physically she repelled me; I could not respond more than in friendship. Feeling slighted and rejected, she went upstairs, lay down, and swallowed half a bottle of her sleeping draught – all that was left of it.'[91] What is interesting here is not the truth or falsity of the episode but Brasch's implicit assumption that the reader shares his sense of repulsion at the incident – an assumption made slightly more uncomfortable by his being inexplicit about the fact that he was generally not attracted into intimate relationships with women. This amongst many other squeamish comments has provided the basis for a feminist conclusion that 'Hyde was fighting a number of interconnected battles, most of them deriving from a generalised, historical antipathy to women, behind which lay determinable fears of female sexuality.' This also explains the 'series of flank attacks by her literary male contemporaries'.[92]

Discovering that Hyde was well aware of these 'flank attacks' against her by the new nationalists also allows the feminist reader to see parodies of their sexist attitudes in her work. For example, there are the portraits of enthusiastic, idealistic but selfish young men in *The Godwits Fly* and *Nor the Years Condemn*. Perhaps there is also parody in the contrasts drawn within 'Journey from New Zealand', which has been seen as a quintessential nationalist poem. Instead of reading it only in terms of the effects of the depression and restrictive social mores, we can also relate it to gender representation:

> Your crude country, hard as an unbroken shell . . .
> She was hard to love, and took strength, like a virgin.
> Sometimes, in money or dust, the little farms ebbed away,
> Dripping between disconsolate fingers like blood
> Of that harsh girl, who would never love you.[93]

A feminist reading can extrapolate the suggestive 'your' (rather than 'our') as an image of the new nationalist poetry that portrays male suffering as arising from the intransigence of the land ('who took strength like a virgin') and women ('that harsh girl who would never love you.') It seems reasonable to suggest that Hyde was well aware of the gender implications when she created a 'virgin' land, and would have done so with irony.

Today's feminist readers see an element of absurd posturing in the male nationalist poets with their angst-ridden images of a harsh landscape. They prefer the imagery of community that used to be distrusted as domestic – the sense of ordinariness seen (in the following lines of this poem) in evocative urban closeups: [94]

But in the cities (old days!)
We could live better, warm and safe as the sparrows,
Twittering through the evening like young sparrows.
Ours was a city, like any city,
But with more, perhaps, of sea and cloud, not long loved.
November tar, ripening, blackened our sandals.
Our cities had doorways, too many shut.
Morning and evening, facing the rampant crimson brutes of the light,
Nobody had the beautiful strength to decree:
'Leave your doors open morning and evening –
Leave your gates wide to the stranger.'
So ours was a city, like any city, but fair.
At seven (still light), the children snuggled down
Like rabbits. The rest sat on in the lamplight,
Sat still or spoke words by their failures.

INCOHERENCE VERSUS IMMERSION

These conflicting accounts of Hyde's work can be explained by putting the
readings in their historical and social context. If the qualified view of Hyde can
be situated socially among nationalist men (mostly) of the 1940s and 1950s, then
the more enthusiastic view can be situated (mostly but not only) among feminist
women of the 1980s and 1990s. This newer style of reading arose in response to
international feminist consciousness, when feminism acted on (and was in some
cases formulated through) the study of literature. From this perspective Hyde
was seen as an example of the masculinist erasure (or at least under-reading) of
an important woman writer.

This rereading of Hyde was, like the cultural nationalist view, associated with
a particular group or coterie. This group comprised of women publishers and
Broadsheet Magazine contributors, including prominent individuals such as Wendy
Harrex and Phillida Bunkle. Publisher Wendy Harrex laid much of the groundwork
for Hyde's return to prominence – commissioning introductions to new editions
of three works, while Phillida Bunkle was a joint editor of the reprint of *Nor the
Years Condemn*, contributed to the highly critical review of *Iris* in *Broadsheet
Magazine*, and with Harrex initiated the project to publish Robin Hyde's journalism
and the lengthy essays on her life and work in *Disputed Ground*.[95] The same
group was also, in the mid to late eighties, having an impact in social and political
contexts. Phillida Bunkle is better known as co-author, with Sandra Coney, of a
magazine article 'An Unfortunate Experiment' which, at a time contemporaneous
with the Hyde resurrection, challenged institutionalised use of women in medical
experiments at National Women's Hospital in Auckland.[96] The public inquiry
that followed Bunkle and Coney's article had a far-reaching effect on research in
New Zealand universities as well as on the medical establishment. One imagines
that Hyde would have approved of this kind of investigative journalism aiming to
remove the repressive silence around issues of women's health. A later aspect of

Hyde's reassessment belongs to a more postmodernist moment. Michele Leggott, for example, first read Hyde as a university teacher, and grew so interested in her poetry that she incorporated lines and echoes from Hyde in her own series 'Blue Irises', only later coming to write on her in a more academic context.[97] This quotation and pastiche of Hyde's work also suggests that ownership of language is not as important as communality, and that relating closely to a writer involves a potentially ongoing process of recycling and incorporation.

Thus one could say that challenges to the literary representation of women have been associated with other more direct challenges to professional, academic and artistic establishments. The effect of feminism on a 'high culture' associated with cultural nationalist ideas was to challenge the assumption that national identity should override other categories of analysis such as gender identity. The feminist re-evaluation has not gone unquestioned. Typical is the prickly attitude shown by a newspaper reviewer, Stephen Danby, who challenged the enthusiastic feminist angle of the editors of *Nor The Years Condemn*, describing the novel as confused and almost proto-fascist. However, in his review of *Passport to Hell,* which had no such feminist heralding, Danby was moved to comment that 'if Robin Hyde hadn't existed it would have been necessary to invent her', because 'today's women have a need for spiritual ancestors'.[98]

However, although I would disagree with some of the assessment that Danby develops about these novels, I think that we need to acknowledge his uneasiness about a possible over-reaction. It is, as he infers, a need of the time, and as if Hyde has been read *all one way,* and now she is to be read *all another.* If Curnow and his group, taken up as they were with nationalist concerns, felt unable to bring her work into their world – and so viewed her in a detached and critical way – then the feminist reader is immersed inside Hyde's world, repeating her words, touching her clothes, eager to identify with all her stories about life as a mother, critic, activist, and as a besieged woman. The 'involved' feminist view reveals a wealth of ways in which female experience constructs the work but it tends to categorise the past in terms of the present. It has the effect of reinforcing gender oppositions by not exploring their historically specific aspects. Clearly Hyde is extremely valuable to feminist critics – for Bunkle, she defines the difficulty of being politically active and a woman, and for Leggott the difficulty of being a prominent poet and a woman. But can such an emphasis do justice to other factors such as class, race, or the difference of generational experience?

In the next chapter I shall explore an alternative reading in which 'the personal' and 'the national' are integrated in a different way and with a different sense of the reader's relation to the text.

•

CHAPTER SIX

Robin Hyde:
A Political Reading

I found myself under a sort of compulsion to try and relate the lives of people I knew to the panorama of history. *John Dos Passos*[1]

This chapter starts out with the question of how readers should position themselves to see meaning and unity in Robin Hyde's later works, 1936–39. These works seem problematic both because they are so diverse and because they are such a departure from her earlier production. Familiar readings include attempts to see her as a nationalist or as a feminist. This chapter is an attempt to develop a different kind of political reading. It retains aspects of previous readings but takes a different approach to reconstructing the 1930s political/historical contexts, both national and international. Like previous feminist readings, it focuses on Hyde's construction of herself as a female intellectual and her interest in the representation of women but when it discusses gender it tries to do so with specific reference to the 1930s political context. In this way it tries to transcend the familiar debate between feminist and nationalist readers, and the limitations of the way in which Robin Hyde had been 'restored' by recent critics.

I can indicate the limitations of the way Robin Hyde has been 'restored' by discussing an anecdote told by New Zealand/Australian novelist Ruth Park in her 1993 autobiography *Fence Around the Cuckoo*. During the depression, because of financial circumstances, Park was forced to leave school to live with her parents in a 'backblocks' area of the King Country:

> Life is never speedy enough for the young, especially the despairing young. I did read the living-room walls, standing on a chair, hunting for consecutive pages. These came from very old copies of the *New Zealand Observer*, and the text was solid Robin Hyde, whose style became so familiar to me I believe I could even now recognise it anywhere. How I envied her, secure in her job, praised as a poet, with a beautiful future. But in fact at the time she was overworked, ill-paid as all women journalists were, worried about her child, always in pain from a diseased bone, and planning suicide.
>
> A year or so later, too shy to speak, I was to pass her in a newspaper office, unfortunate Robin, a lame, worn-looking woman, pale and ill nourished, with lank light brown hair. It must have been just before she left for China, a journey that led to her early death.[2]

Could this example of a shift in understanding about Robin Hyde's life have come about without her 'restoration'? Ruth Park has clearly read Derek Challis's description of his mother's plight in the introduction to *A Home in this World* as well as Hyde's own description in that work. The update is significant because it is only latterly that the circumstances of Hyde's life were seen to be important to understanding her work. However, the outcome is not very satisfactory – the way that Ruth Park opposes her once naive assumptions about the successful journalist, to the painful reality, seems to me to be not only patronising but also unhistorical. Park's double-take is matched by what has happened in Hyde's feminist rereading, which – because of the interest in Hyde's suppression as writer and woman – risks a sense of special pleading. It also gives a tragic tone to the work that may have other possible aspects. A more detailed reconstruction of the 1920s and 1930s may suggest that this was not so much a tragic individual situation as part of social life, especially women's life, at this period. Park hints at this period context with her phrase 'as all women journalists were' but her focus is on the 'unfortunate Robin'.

Another example is helpful here. An MA student who, like Hyde, had experienced the death of a baby, presented a seminar in which she put manuscript material from Hyde's 'Autobiography' (manuscript MSS 412 held in the Auckland Public Library) alongside the veiled account of losing a baby in *The Godwits Fly.* She then suggested that a number of Hyde's poems are also about this heartrending experience, particularly the experience of never being able to hold the dead child.[3] She finished the seminar with a reference to a claim in MacD. P. Jackson's survey essay on New Zealand poetry in the *Oxford History of New Zealand Literature* that '. . . no New Zealand poet would have thought of writing a poem about being pregnant and losing the child', a claim which seemed to ignore Hyde's poems on that very theme.[4] In showing a critic's blindness to the existence of certain subjects in literature this student was linking her example with the feminist argument that female writers and female experience had been suppressed by male critics. But Jackson's claim could be debated in other ways. For instance he ignores the significance of radical attempts during the 1920s and 1930s to relate literature to the lives of ordinary people. This was an international trend which also touched New Zealand. Perhaps the interpretation we make of Hyde's writing should not focus exclusively on gender but acknowledge the radical democratic spirit in her writing.

Even Patrick Sandbrook's thesis, *A Writer at Work*, which uncovers subtle interconnections between Hyde's unpublished letters and autobiographies and her novel *The Godwits Fly,* still uses an old-fashioned literary critical mode. Thus Robin Hyde is identified as a gifted individual struggling within a narrowminded society, rather than a writer whose choice of material, preoccupations and genre tendencies were shaped by her context, as much as she herself shaped these elements. I cite these examples not to criticise individual critics but to draw attention to the way readings have changed their emphases in recent years. Obviously other types of reading (including more heavily theorised and less personal types) are also current, but it is the tragic and heroic modes that have attracted most attention; and indeed without them it is likely that the Hyde revival would not have had so much impact. My point here, however, is the familiar tendency for revivals to oversimplify their topic by adopting an adversarial approach. What kind of reading can transcend the dialectic thus produced?

It is no longer necessary to argue for the importance of Hyde's work, but one does need to look more closely at the writing in its original social and political context. This is, however, not a simple matter: a complex historical view is needed. We cannot turn to some neutral history to make a recontextualisation. The post-Second World War picture of the 1930s and 1940s as a time of cultural birth is a story that has been told not only by novelists and poets but also by historians, so that we also need to recover the period from their mythmaking. Nationalist historians, like feminist historians, are naturally driven by their particular values and priorities. For instance, historian Bill Oliver in *The Oxford History of New Zealand* celebrates this time of cultural birth when 'a magazine, an orchestra and a small [literary] fund' came into being.[5] But even in his acknowledgements of the role of women in this enterprise he seems unconsciously grudging, as when he describes a group of women painters as 'eminent among the more modest participants in the revolution of the 1940s' but as 'cautious painters, attaining an authentic personal vision within a narrow compass'. And again, though he admits that they did transcend the limitations of being 'beneficiaries of that colonial-genteel tradition that made it acceptable . . . for middle class girls to occupy themselves with paint', he also stresses that they did not 'break new ground'.[6] What Oliver's comments lack is an interest in distinguishing between the traditional 'amateur' and 'hobbyist' status of women artists and their actual production. His narrative is so much concerned with national discovery that other subtle forms of innovation are overlooked.

Fortunately in the last five years the historical view has been enlarged. Other works by Robin Hyde have been republished and studies such as Rachel Barrowman's *A Popular Vision: The Arts and the Left in New Zealand 1930–1950* and a range of essays on women in the 1930s have looked at issues such as unemployment and contraception, and allowed us to develop other angles on the period.[7]

To further our political reading let us start with a consideration of Hyde's approaches in 1936–38 when she wrote her last two novels, *The Godwits Fly* (1938) and *Nor the Years Condemn* (1938). These both treat the post-war and depression periods – *Godwits* ends with the tramping feet of unemployed men, circa 1928, and *Nor the Years Condemn* finishes with the Labour election in 1935. Both are distinctly pleas for the underdog, the poverty-stricken, the one who has no expectations of life. This theme was not Hyde's alone. What we think of as the most significant poems and stories of the 1930s speak to it too: for instance, Allen Curnow's 'House and Land', Denis Glover's 'Magpies', and Frank Sargeson's 'Piece of Yellow Soap'. Clearly there was a strong political streak in nationalist writing. Discovering one's own country should not be thought of as a purely nationalist discovery but also as a complex political one. Hyde herself seemed to be in no doubt, in 1937, that the best writing should comment on society. She argues for Katherine Mansfield as a sociological and political writer, too seldom appreciated as such: 'New Zealand hasn't achieved any writers whose writings have an exceptional political or sociological value – except Katherine Mansfield, and nobody ever seems to notice that aspect of her genius.' Hyde saw her most importantly as making 'a picture of the structure of society'.[8] She also reproved Denis Glover for a posturing gloominess that was, she thought, obligatory for the 'strictly-modern school' and fostered from a romanticised idea of waiting for revolution ('the necessary economic uprising') but which she implies has little relationship with real international tragedies, 'the bloody duels in Spain, or in Abyssinia, [which] bear witness to the insecurity of the present'.[9]

Patrick Sandbrook has argued for the deliberate choices Hyde made as a writer. He also stresses her sense of 'democracy' with her readers. I would want to go further and suggest that the method of her last novels and poems – which includes stylistic innovation, experiments with montage, and the inclusion of documentary material – can be seen as belonging to a widely shared impulse to convey the new character of the time by breaking down boundaries between fiction and documentary. In this way one can argue that Hyde was in fact very like many of her Australian and American contemporaries who had a new conception of the novel, not so much as an expression of individual genius but as a text which captured history as a spotlight which flashes for a moment on an individual and an environment, a 'record' of her time. Some local critics have described Hyde's last novels as using two modes, the visionary (or utopian) as well as the social realist, but again the wider international context of politically identified writing gives us a way of seeing Hyde's utopian monologues as part of the whole text – the novelist's attempt to paste intellectual discourse into her collage of the period, an impulse typical of a new genre of radical writing.[10] The monologues in *Nor the Years Condemn*, for example, can be seen as Hyde's attempt to explore the current problems of the thinker and writer in a time of social unrest.

An Australian cultural critic, David Carter, in an essay titled 'Documenting Society', describes radical fiction from the 1930 to the 1950s as breaking down the distinctions between 'fact' and fiction by opening up the novel to 'a new social reality – at once individual and historical'.[11] Detailed descriptions of work and workplaces, broken narratives, extracts from personal journals or newspapers, radio dialogues and popular songs, and utopian passages all occur in a novel typical of the time (he is describing Alan Marshall's *How Beautiful are Thy Feet*). By looking at such writing as a collage, he argues, we are discovering not its naturalism so much as its modernity.

Nor the Years Condemn elides fact and fiction because the protagonist, Starkie, is based on a real person whom Hyde knew and interviewed. Likewise within the novel there is a brief mention of a young woman journalist who, it is implied, could be associated with the author of the novel. While the characters Bede Collins and Macnamara could possibly be associated with 'real people' they can also be seen as the author's way of formulating the relations between the intellectual and society. For instance, one could go through the narrative and find plenty of connections between Hyde and the character of Bede. Bede is an experienced woman in terms of relations with men but also a woman alone, and one who wants to minister to her country – as Hyde the journalist and novelist did. Bede is a nurse not squeamish of physical suffering and squalor – she, like Hyde, has been through some of the worst of experiences and can look at suffering open-eyed. There is an even more specific connection in that the protagonist in Hyde's supposedly autobiographical account of drug addiction, *A Night of Hell*, is also called Bede. And Bede in both novel and essay lives in a tiny bach lighted at night only by candles. The connections between texts and life are myriad. Readers and critics are endlessly fascinated by them.[12] Yet questions remain about these representations that are not answered by recourse to 'fact' or biography. Instead perhaps we should think about both autobiography and fiction as contemplations (necessary to the period) on the role of the female outsider or intellectual, and a consideration of the difficulty of being political and middle class. And perhaps middle class and poverty-stricken. The example below follows the character (Bede) rescuing a baby hedgehog:

> She left the saucer outside, went in, and read the *Communist Manifesto*, with six prefaces by Engels. It convinced and depressed her. The Communists – Brigadier, *vous avez raison;* but what the devil were they going to do with people like herself, riddled with good intentions and emotions, like old ships riddled with rats? Oh, well: she supposed they might sink her for a breakwater somewhere, and anyhow, the individual was not proving so important. Certainly she liked the Communists much better than their opposite extreme.[13]

The passage ends with a return to Bede's anxiety about the hedgehog. When she found its saucer empty 'she regretted not having been able to keep the baby'. The placement of Bede's monologue alongside the animal rescue (and the human resonances of 'baby') reinforces her predicament as having the problems of specifically a female thinker and intellectual: one who has the impulse to mother and comfort but who at the same time wants to see the world in larger perspective. I am suggesting, therefore, that a connection between a real and the fictional character should not be seen as simply hiding the 'secret story' of the author but rather as opening up both character and author to history as positively as possible, so that both can be seen not as merely 'representing subjectivity' but as 'sites where social forces and ideologies play out their effects'.[14]

Another character from *Nor the Years Condemn*, Macnamara, could also be discussed in terms of the author's biography. Like Hyde, Macnamara journeyed from one end of the country to the other.[15] And he could also be seen as based on one of, or a composite of, a new idealistic, questioning group of young men – thinkers, artists and politicians whom Hyde describes in an essay on New Zealand writers: 'its [the depression's] stimulating effect on the thought and culture of rebellious young minds, in a silent country which at last learned to be articulate, was probably worth all the hardship involved'.[16] She is probably thinking of figures such as John A. Lee, Joe Heinan, John Beaglehole, Eric McCormick – figures who seemed capable of putting into action the sense of spiritual and material urgency that the depression stirred up. (Even in 1936 they were starting to work on a centennial publication that would put New Zealand on the map as a cultural entity. They were the kind of thinkers who went on after the war to institutionalise the arts in magazines, funds, galleries, museums and education programmes.[17])

Yet again, rather than getting caught in the anecdotal, perhaps we should see the invention of Macnamara as a way of including a utopian discourse in the book. Macnamara is looking for the right model for the future; his travel parallels Starkie's, but Starkie has been programmed with outmoded ideas which means that his solutions always go awry. Macnamara ministers to others; he solves and salves moments of rancour. He rescues a 'Homie' in a small-town pub and takes him back to the house that he lives in. The setting is the Ureweras, the township is Wairoa. This early settler's house has the 'right' relationship to the country in which it is built: Macnamara is able to appreciate its history, which the 'Homie' also glimpses for the first time. On the walls are maps of New Zealand, which allow the two men to familiarise themselves with the country, its landforms, its produce:

> The flickering lamplight revealed a house of old steady dignity, which, despite its emptiness and its corridors fit for ghosts, pleased the Homie better than anything else he had seen since coming to New Zealand. Two big maps, one of the North Island, one of the South, with little Stewart Island tacked on down under, showed up on one of the bare walls, which was of unpainted, unvarnished wood, the solid and honest tree. The roof was very high, and the stove, which Macnamara lighted to make coffee, as rusty as it was immense. In the corner stood a harmonium.[18]

Macnamara advises the settler to also familiarise himself with methods of farming and to gradually make a decision on his own land purchase: 'You see the maps? In your spare time I'd like you to study them back, front and round the corner. They've got products marked in, and a good many other things.'[19] Macnamara is an image of the astute, informed, compassionate citizen whose forward thinking will overcome the problems associated with the returned soldiers (from the First World War) and the depression. How he lives combines the right mix of nonmaterialistic elegance and consciousness of history that should become a model for the nation, just as his generous handling of the blokes in the pub should become a model for the relations between people. His gentle gesture of covering Starkie with a coat later in the story, when Starkie is reduced to a night in a 'shelter', also recalls Hyde's picture of John, the father in *The Godwits Fly* – a similarly socially committed character, who tiptoes in at night to cover his daughter with his overcoat.

Yet Macnamara's portrayal is not only an obviously nationalist construction, it is also an internationalist one. The question of how a writer should contribute to a society (and a world) felt to be in crisis was an international one. This question was also important to other local writers. In her section of the introduction to *Nor the Years Condemn*, 'Hyde's Masquerade', Linda Hardy says of Hyde's approach: 'Unlike Mulgan, or the early Sargeson, Hyde is not merely content to imply the limitation of the gruff pragmatic masculine voice. Instead she makes these other voices [of Bede Collins and Macnamara] carry the metaphors of utopian desire.'[20] The comment is convincing, yet it is important to stress what Hardy is assuming here: that all three of these writers were working in different ways on the same problem of how the bourgeois intellectual can relate to society – how he or she can engage a receptive audience for their work, how to be loyal to the working class, and also how to promote and lead changes in society. Critics have spent so much time debating nationalism in literature that they have not noted all the ways in which it connects up with international trends and debates – such as the debate about the future, or not, of socialism, or the practice of new kinds of social organisation. Rachel Barrowman's book has been a welcome exception.[21]

David Carter is an Australian working in the area of cultural studies, whereas Nick Perry is a New Zealand sociologist whose book, *The Dominion of Signs*, brings together essays on popular culture and literature; both are interested in innovations in writing styles in the 1930s and 1940s. They explain these in terms of language and literary conventions being outstripped by societal change and conventional meanings being destabilised, but they articulate this very differently.[22] David Carter puts his stress on the international changes: 'For many writers the historical sequence of depression, fascism and war meant a profound disturbance in their sense of social relations. Society becomes not just an arena for the play of individual motives but of momentous historical forces, of class divisions and "mass villains, mass victims . . . an awakened mass consciousness."' (Carter takes these last phrases from M. Barnard Eldershaw's *Tomorrow and Tomorrow*.)

> This notion of crisis was itself symptomatic of a crisis in liberal humanism whose traditional terms seemed inadequate to comprehend such massive social change. Mass social forms and ideologies seemed to threaten human nature as a source of value and continuity. For a number of writers this ideological crisis produced a serious involvement with communism . . . or with socialist and populist ideas, often in nationalism.[23]

Carter's point is that 'in order to engage with this new social reality – at once individual and historical – works of fiction are forced into *formal experiment*.'.[24] Nick Perry, on the other hand, attributes the fracture in meaning mostly to cultural dislocation caused by displacement. The social dilemma of the provincial was the problem of sounding too smart and patronising for New Zealand audiences or too 'down home' for English ones. Bill Pearson described it as an uneasy choice between sycophancy (writing in a 'nervous tie-straightening' way for the English market) or overconfidence ('attitudinising' in 'bad habits' picked up from local 'journalism').[25] Perry sees Sargeson as an example of a writer who found a solution to the problem:

> His early writing offered a model solution to the social dilemma of a provincial intelligentsia. Here was a frugal, austere prose, responsive to the idioms of ordinary New Zealand speech, in which the locals might recognise themselves. And yet for the bookish it was manifestly literature rather than reportage; it was made not recorded.
>
> Accomplishing such apparent simplicity depended upon technical sophistication; for literary insiders such stories worked through resonance, through indirection, through a predisposition to read against the text. . . . He offered a celebration of the local and the ordinary couched in a technically demanding form. [26]

A particularly useful aspect of Perry's work is his interest in showing how Sargeson's formal idiosyncrasies once made sense to a particular reading community. I am trying to do something similar for Hyde. However, the nationalist reading community Perry describes went on to dominate our high culture. Hyde's internationalism and interest in gender politics came (for a time) to seem *passé*. But even with the help of feminism it is not easy for us to return to being the kind of reading community that made sense of Hyde – the mood of the period after the 1935 labour election was eclipsed by war, and then by postwar nationalism, the post-war baby boom, and the 1950s cult of the family, not to mention the consolidation of nationalism in the arts.

David Carter's internationalist approach (which he uses to re-evaluate the significance of certain overlooked Australian prose writers of the thirties and forties) is more useful in some respects than a nationalist approach to explain Hyde's style. Robin Hyde's poetic, or at least her discussions of what she sought to do in her writing, is better understood in these larger international terms of wanting strategically to elide the division between documentary (including autobiography) and fiction in order to make a record of her time in which the concept of the individual, and humanism, were no longer sufficient. Of her autobiography (which became the draft for *The Godwits Fly*) she wrote that it '. . . is not a novel but a sort of sliding picture of the days . . . I know indeed that it is not clever, it was not intended to be so: but it is utterly sincere and true, not just my halting truth but the truth of all the faces, tormented and inarticulate and quelled by life, that slid past.'[27] History as history of the individual is too selfish. Given the mass of experience and suffering in the world all the writer can do is to get the truth of the detail. Later, perhaps, it can be seen in context:

> Now I think if I could get exactly the special sort of water that flows under the Days Bay wharf, everything would be quite clear and complete, and there would be no need to write, because somehow it is I, and I am it. It was a water colourless at the edges, too protected for foam, except when on very grey days it was a burnished steel mirror for the skies —[28]

Instead of seeing this passage as an attempt to capture essences, or as telling us about the psychology of a gifted writer, I think one can argue that it is one way of expressing the radical impulse of the period, to find a way to record the precise shape and texture of life as she knew it, particularly life lived differently than ever before. This is not to forget that collage and imagist methods were also used by writers central to the nationalist tradition (such as A. R. D. Fairburn in 'Dominion'). But Hyde's particular use is best understood by relating her to overseas writers with a strongly political – or what at the time was sometimes described as journalistic – emphasis. John Dos Passos, whose trilogy *USA* was published between 1930 and 1937, was also obsessed with the idea of capturing the present through documentary details. Dos Passos described his work as creating characters whom he then put down in 'a snarl of human events'[29] and his own writing impulse as a compulsion to see detail in a larger perspective:

> I found myself under a sort of compulsion to try and relate the lives of people I knew to the panorama of history. The method was experimental. As I worked I used occasionally to reassure myself with the thought that at least some of the characters and scenes and feelings I put down might prove useful for the record.[30]

Dos Passos and Hyde both wanted a new way of showing an individual living in the world, and at the same time of questioning the boundaries of self and world. They were interested, not so much in subjectivity for its own sake, but in sites where social ideologies and forces were busy playing out their effects. In the service of this I have already suggested Hyde blurs documentary, journalism and fiction so that her novels and poems spill out undefinably into the tide of 'history'.

There are also specific techniques that Hyde uses that are illuminated by comparison with the strategies of John Dos Passos. (The comparison is illuminating without implying a direct influence – since such techniques were 'in the air' in the period.) Both favour what one might consider a pictorial or tableau method by moving from a close-up to a 'wide-angle' view. In *USA* this technique is drawn attention to in a section entitled 'The Camera's Eye'. In *The Godwits Fly* such changes of perspective occur from moment to moment:

> Then, Augusta said, 'Man, woman and child; man woman and child.' She said it standing in the silent street, with the four-leaved clovers pinned to her fuzzy astrakhan stole, and the old houses dazed with peace and the coming of sunset, behind their hedges of bright plumbago and the tumult of hydrangeas.[31]

In another example, the fragment of a conversation between daughter, husband, and wife is juxtaposed with a distant perspective, making clear that there are other stories to be told and different ways of looking at the world:

> John got the parts of a *History of Mankind*, which ran in small print and coloured plates through a weekly magazine. Carl Withers sold them to him for sixpence, and bought them back for a penny. Some of them upset him dreadfully. He came rushing in and slammed the door, his hair standing up on end, his thin face flaming:

'Look at that. That's your capitalist system. That's what they do to men. Look at that, I tell you.'

Augusta looked. 'It happened two thousand nine hundred years ago,' she said tonelessly.

'They're all the same. Capitalists – murderers. Look, Eliza, that's what your mother wants me to put into parliament. That's what she votes for herself.'

'Must you defile the eyes of your own children?'

'Let them see what the world is. Look, Eliza!'

Eliza looks, and sees a picture of some slaves flayed alive by an Emperor. They lie huddled, not unlike the raw pink rabbits that have to be soaked overnight in the sink before they can be stewed. The Emperor stands over them with his whip, looking rather like Daddy in a temper.

'Yes, Daddy.'

John fires off his parting shot.

'That's your Imperialism. That's your *God* for you.' Augusta, hard tears forcing themselves between her eyelids, continues to pare very thin rings from the potatoes.

Two people, solitaries, dreamers, winning out of their first environment, find a dog chain twisting their ankles together. Still they fight for their escape; one lonely, shy, suffering under a sense of social injustice, for escape into the steaming companionship, the labouring but powerful flanks of mankind: the other fights for what blood and tradition have taught her, fields of bluebells ringing all on the one exquisitely lengthened note, courage, craftsmanship, the order which for her has existed only in a dream, so that she cannot know if its grey stone pile be crumbling today. They are young when it begins; their words, like their veins, are hot and full of passion. They share a double bed, and have children. One day an ageing man looks round and finds himself wrestling with an ageing woman, her face seamed with tears.[32]

The suggestion that this juxtaposition of immediate and broad perspectives (in time and space) helps to describe an inexplicable urban world, and a world in crisis, is reinforced by the fact that the characters are engaged in their own kind of struggle to understand their place in history: their attempts at perspective open their minds to other lives and other stories, to the whole social field so complex and difficult to sum up in abstraction.

John's book shows him that wage slavery is simply a continuation of an older history of exploitation and tyranny, while Eliza has a flash of perception about John because the picture of the emperor looks like 'Daddy in a temper', putting the children presumably in the place of those 'raw pink rabbits'. The father sees class tyranny, the daughter, tyranny of father over children, and possibly one sex over the other. The image of pink rabbits soaking overnight also reminds Eliza of Augusta's attempt to nourish their family in times of poverty. The final 'Two people, solitaries, dreamers' is a kind of time-lapse narrative seen by the older woman narrator (implied, though not present, the older Eliza). The two figures fight over their ideological positions in a dialogue similar to that Hyde uses in her long poem 'Husband and Wife' which was written in 1936. The passage brilliantly juxtaposes these different perspectives, these different social truths.

In a scene from his play *The Garbage Man* (1926), Dos Passos uses a similar extreme long shot to show an individual being caught in meaningless constraints. Because these lines belong to an absurd character, 'the Telescope Man', who sells 'ten cent squints at the moon' on Union Square, it is suggested that the world is continually being reframed in new metaphors, whether grandiose or trivial:

> Every day they're tied tighter in ticker ribbon till they can't move, till they don't have time to look at the moon. . . . And time slips through among the garbage cans in the canyon streets. Time is a great snake through gray streets, wearing away angles of stone cornices, wearing ornaments off marblefaced sepulchres. . . . Time is a grey ash dropping from the souls of fat men in swivel chairs. . . . Time has his undertaking establishment on every block.[33]

This freedom to shift point of view (reminiscent of the film medium) is very characteristic of Dos Passos. Hyde, too, used this method of juxtaposition of views to suggest different relationships of power. The passage below from *The Godwits Fly* uses this method ironically to make what today we would call a postcolonial commentary on various narratives of nation.

> Mr Bellew, the headmaster of their school, loved trees, and tried to fight the emptiness of the raw clay around his brick building by getting the children to dig their own little garden-plots, where they could grow anything from potatoes to sweetpeas. Gradually he weaned them to trees and shrubs, and gave them long lectures about the duty of preserving their heritage of native bush – which they never saw, as it lay miles away over the hills. His favourite day in the year was Arbor Day, when he always managed to conjure up a Member of Parliament, like a whiskery watch-chained rabbit out of Mr Bellew's top hat. The Parliamentarian, having cleared his throat and rasped away at the children for twenty minutes, would scratch the ground with a trowel until the hole was deep enough for a sad-coloured, skinny little native tree to be planted. It didn't matter if he stuck it in lop-sided, because Mr Bellew would make the big boys replant it when he had gone.
>   Rear view of black trousers bending over: then the Parliamentarian came up to blow, and the Top Girls, Standard Six, of whom Carly was smallest and shyest, trebled:
> > 'Bird of my na-tive land, beau-tiful stranger,
> > Perched in the kauri tree, free from all danger.'
> Bird-of-my-native-land was supposed to be the tui, but none of the children had ever seen one, or a kauri tree either. Sparrows hopped everywhere, living as the Lord provided, on spilled crumbs and dust and chaff leaking from the nose-bags of patient old reddy-brown horses, who stood stamping and shuffling their feet. And there were thrushes, if you had a coprosma hedge with fat little orange berries to tempt them. The Hannays had, and used the berries for sovereigns when they played Shops.[34]

The struggle to make sense of lives ('normal life in the twentieth century is a blasphemous and obscene travesty of what was meant for humans', she wrote to a friend, John Schroder)[35] is evident in other narrative strategies in these late novels. Different perspectives are multiplied by the pasting in of types of people, types of behaviour and types of conversation. For instance in *The Godwits Fly*:

> A special Day's Bay voice, hard and authoritative like a chunk of brown wood, shouts from the lower deck, 'Stand away from that rope. Stand clear, now, stand clear of that ro-o-ope'.[36]

Another feature of this narrative style is the excess of detail. Many descriptions do not advance the narrative, but document the physical and social environment:

> The men's dressing-shed is much bigger than the women's, and of stone, not tin. Under the women's roof, the room divides into wet-floored sandy cubicles, in most of which there are cobwebs.[37]

> Dancing on a whale washed up at Lyall Bay. Hundreds of children were taken to see it and they danced up and down. Underfoot was nothing but slippery black, gashed with the yellow clay from their boots. 'Now I am dancing on a whale.'[38]

> Auckland is further ahead with the Copper Trail, than Wellington, and that is a disgrace for Wellington. The Copper Trail a huge snake of pennies, has to cover the whole length of the North Island. Then it will be spent on comforts for the wounded soldiers and sailors. The children do not realise that its length will only be measured on the map; they see actual pennies laid end to end, shining through bush and ti-tree, over stubborn hills, and Wellington's disgrace sticks in their throat.[39]

Within the novel there are some explicit references to memories as filmic shots:

> A last shot, the old picture show everyone called the Fleahouse. Simone was sitting near the front, her short-sighted eyes peering up at some film negroes.

And this 'shot' is placed alongside the narrator's real-time picture of her friend:

> At the top of the Gardens, the quiet manuka place where sunlight stroked the seamed old face of the world, she was so much more Simone: a girl in a green and golden shellcase, deciding that women are inevitably licked, and that somehow, magically, she wouldn't be.

and also alongside the glance of some passing schoolchildren:

> Their faces, upturned, saw also the grown-ups, the two fantastically dressed creatures with silk stockings and hats, lying side by side in the brown grass. [40]

Typical advertisements of the period are also reproduced, pasted in:

> Do you know that serious diseases can result from this simple neglect? Communicate Dr Smith, Box 19937. Men – do you want women to look at you in the street? In ten days I increased my chest measurement. . . .[41]

The excess in these details draws attention to itself as more than is strictly necessary to advance the narrative, and also suggests that the narrative is not clearly separate from the 'real' world outside the novel. Conceptually it challenges any idea of fiction as a single perspective; it hints to the reader that fiction can choose the events it foregrounds or backgrounds. The effect is to suggest that this author has selected details with an awareness of the difficulty of interpreting the world. Overconfidence (even of the importance of the individual) would be dangerous when so much of life has been altered by war and depression, and now the possibility of more war. Another passage describes the contemporary relations between men and women as epitomised in the scene at a cafe, Gamble and Creeds, on a wet working day where 'everyone ate hurriedly in a good smell of coffee and a bad one of stinking rubber-lined mackintoshes'. Once again it emphasises the juxtaposition of different perspectives:

> Choleric little faces, they had; queer, bonded race, so helpless and yet so powerful. Women, a minority, sat alone, reading books propped up against the drip-nosed nickel teapots. It was interesting to watch them come in. They always looked about for a table where there was nobody, crossed the whole length of the room to find one – as if a ghost occupied the seat opposite. They were all business girls. Many kept sentimental trysts with themselves, pinning bunches of daphne or heavy-fragrant brown boronia on their costumes. The men fraternized, talking shop. Flying particles of it came over – stock exchange, politics, smut, all on a harder, crisper plane than the feminine talk though you could spot a goodly percentage of bores. It wasn't that the men weren't ignorant, but they had the courage of their gutturals. It was evident at once that they had a life apart from the women. The women – they had the toy boxes called their homes, the rag dolls called their babies; or the business ones had a room ('the flat'), with a pink lampshade. . . . The value of men to women was plain in everything they did; even among these close-faced women, who watched unobtrusively as a cat watches. The value of women to men was debatable. If women weren't there, Eliza had a feeling the men would continue to talk shop for about ten years before they noticed anything. Then presumably they would want some fresh tea . . . or to reproduce their kind. Unless they had killed one another off in their wars. . . .
>
> Eliza wanted none of it. Only the rafters of the pinewoods over her head, and Timothy, his sandshoes slipping on the warm russet needles, his eyes full of little prickles of light.[42]

This emphasis on the gap between men's and women's lives is again part of the flavour of the period. The picture of men's contempt for women and general lack of interest only interrupted by the occasional compulsion to sex for intimacy or comfort is similar to the picture drawn in *Nor the Years Condemn*:

> It was no good: bright light, thick dark, the gulf between men and women existed and widened, and after their first shiverings they got used to it, and decided they hated one another. The girls said they were content with their jobs, and took expensive beauty treatments. The men lounged together, telling stories, pretending a vague homosexual philosophy, toying with an equally vague day of love and wrath, when, banded together, chesty but very forgiving once they had satisfied their dignity, they would put the women back in their place. And the faces of both would have been exceedingly funny, if their mouths had not become so drawn, especially the mouths of the girls. For the girls were more untrained, and consequently more easily bewildered.[43]

A schism between the sexes is also evoked in other writing of the period, for example Frank Sargeson's marriage portraits, and particularly his portrait of Bill in 'That Summer'. Bill, like Starkie, feels an obligation to be married; both men think that is what women want – so they had better want it, too. Their actual feelings are momentary, fleeting. In the above passage Eliza, the young woman writer, is keen to disassociate herself from this kind of stand-off between the sexes. She focuses particularly on the pathetic aspect of the women, their need for men who don't need them, their sentimental trysts with themselves. These are humiliating role models. Hyde illustrates her own very different take on what should be the relations between men and women in a number of ways – by showing that a woman such as Eliza can be different, can enjoy talking shop, can have a career, can enjoy camaraderie and adventure, can want sex not marriage, and, in interesting contrast to later feminism, can want a baby not an abortion.

So far I have suggested that the mixture of perspectivism and collage of 'facts', political rhetoric and utopian images found in Hyde's last novels (and one could argue last poems as well) is best understood politically as well as 'sociologically'. As David Carter suggests:

> The forms of documentary developed in the 1930s were not simply modes of recording contemporary experience. Style and subject-matter were politically motivated as writers attempted to represent forcefully, in literary discourse, facts and attitudes which they believed literature had conventionally excluded or falsified.[44]

This 'expanded form of fiction' was a reaction to a crisis in social relations, which itself was provoked by war, depression, the rise of fascism and the failures of socialism.[45] But how was this crisis in social relations manifested? In more specific terms Carter talks about 'crisis in the family' and as one example suggests that the story 'of an abortion' appears typically in a novel of the period 'representing the contemporary crisis in social relations'.[46] A critic summing up John Dos Passos's *Manhattan Transfer* (1925) makes a similar point: 'It created a montage of events that did not coalesce into cause and effect patterns implying traditional moral standards, and many of these events – the ones dealing with abortion, homosexuality and some types of violence – were rare in modern fiction.'[47]

This seems relevant to a study of Hyde. Does abortion signify differently for the woman writer? Or does she use it in the same way as her male contemporaries – to represent that crisis in social relations, a loss of values and despair in the society? What I would suggest is that the specifics of the crisis in meaning taking place in New Zealand society, after the First World War and in the Depression, was very much expressed in terms of anxiety about gender roles and relations between the sexes, and in fear about women ceasing to want families and children – and that this is one of the main ways in which international events (war, boom and bust) impacted on New Zealand society.

To understand Hyde's engagements with the concerns of the thirties, in her autobiography and her last novels and poems, one has to be thinking about her negotiation not only of the role of the intellectual in a changing world, but also her negotiation on behalf of those like herself: she was equally a woman, a journalist and an unmarried mother. It is for this reason that Hyde's last novels, one with a female protagonist and the other with a male, include juxtapositions of male and female perspectives, expectations and misunderstandings; in short, men's and women's ideas about each other and sexual difference. Thus the New Zealand crisis mentality which despaired about relationships between men and women, feared race demise (both Maori and European) and hated abortion could be seen as very much part of an international moment and not simply as the inheritance of a misogynist pioneer society. It is the contention of Mary Louise Roberts (in her *Civilisation Without Sexes: Reconstructing Gender in Postwar France)* that at this period 'thinking about women (and thus about sexual difference) was a way of thinking about the war and the new social and economic realities that had ensued'.[48] Roberts is suggesting that very often the discourse produced by 'thinking about women' was in contradiction with what was actually happening in the social and economic sphere. I would see Hyde as both recording some contradictory aspects of this 'thinking about women' and also as participating in it, bound up necessarily with what were the contemporary ways of thinking about the future. Hyde offers a 'gem' of popular discourse about women in *Nor the Years Condemn*, when a man blames women for unemployment:

> What did the women want, taking our jobs in the first place? That's what started the slump, didn't it? If the girls were made to go back home, where they belong, half the men wouldn't be out of a job, so the girls could get married, and she needn't have taken that lysol. It was the suffragettes started it.[49]

This conversation takes place during a relief squad's discovery of the body of a young woman. Another man suggests the dead woman has probably taken the lysol because she lost her job. He points out to his comrades that there is 'no relief work for women' (nor was there an unemployment benefit for them, though working women of course paid taxes). The same man speculates: '. . . then some josser with a necktie tells 'em he's got a job waiting if they give him a treat first, and after that they wake up and find there's a kid on the way and no job either, so there's everything against them. Plenty more taking the long jump before the slump's over.'[50]

Mary Roberts argues that French women after the First World War

> were perceived as responsible for a crisis in the birth-rate which statistically speaking, did not in fact exist until the 1920s; and increasing the birth-rate was itself [as it was in New Zealand] quite anachronistically viewed as a means of restoring France to full economic and military strength. . . . Women as mothers validated the soldier's experience first by miming, as metaphor and in female terms, the sacrifices of their menfolk. . . . It was only when women became mothers that the veterans could regain a sense of their own manhood: relations between the sexes were thus the imaginary sphere in which the effects of the war could be worked through and resolved.[51]

It is the tensions between new realities and old assumptions that Hyde captures in these two last novels. (*The Godwits Fly* uses a female *bildungsroman* method while *Nor the Years Condemn* is a picaresque narrative largely constructed out of Starkie's episodes and failures with women.) These novels show that thinking about changes in society was often articulated as a discourse about women. Life was not improving, and the opportunities for children's education (particularly female children's) that had seemed to be opening up before the First World War were effectively blocked. Likewise, many men were unable to earn enough to support their wives and many women had part-time or under-the-table work.[52] At the same time women in official employment paid taxes, but could not claim any unemployment relief for themselves or their families if they lost their jobs. Orphanages were full and families were reluctant to take in illegitimate grandchildren. Fostering was common but secretive. Contraception and legal abortion were hardly available but there were many illegal abortions and the rate of death from septic abortion was very high. The birthrate for Europeans was the lowest it had ever been. Maori health was in crisis. Yet the rhetoric of the family and motherhood prevailed. The Labour government in 1935, when laying the foundations of the welfare state, was legislating for 'a family with three children which no longer existed'.[53] The idea of the family was protected: at the time Hyde's son, Derek, was born in 1930, homes for unmarried mothers were still often called 'Magdalen' homes – a name that carried all those biblical overtones of fallen, sinful women.[54]

It was this kind of contradiction in society's own view (or construction) of itself that caused individual men, women, and children to search to articulate their experience, which often involved suffering. If in the larger perspective it was hard to believe in humanism and values based on the individual because the scale of war and fascism dwarfed them, then this contradiction in the family and in society was the 'close-up' reason for doubt. This could be seen as a determining factor in the hostility to official and conventional discourse that we find in 'the New Zealand school' (Glover, Curnow, Fairburn,etc), in the editorial approach of *Tomorrow* magazine and in John A. Lee's novels. In Hyde's work we see a similar hostility manifested towards the directiveness of the radio – 'the big radio voice' – Rotary members, ANZAC puffery, picturesque versions of New Zealand life and the complacency of those who accepted conventional rhetoric.[55] Clearly the cultural innovations of the period were fuelled by strong social motives, not by narrowly personal or aesthetic ambitions.

Robin Hyde's poem 'Husband and Wife' is a case in point.[56] This long poem is a dialogue between 'HE' and 'SHE' that suggests an ongoing or long-term debate. It appears to borrow its form from the dialogue poems of Robert Frost, and was written in 1936, published in *The Caxton Miscellany* in 1937 and collected in *Houses by the Sea* in 1952. It is a poem little commented on, and never anthologised, perhaps because it is so involved with debates of the period and needs contextual explanation.[57] In May 1936 Hyde was writing to John A. Lee on the subject of political commitment in writing and writing style. In response to Lee's suggestion that she use themes that have 'the hot news value of 1936', and write about local struggles of working lives (the 'axe in the woods and the crane on the wharf') she demurred that she found it hard to write of 'the vanquished' in her poetry, and then went on to describe her own experience of living in Redfern, Sydney in 1926 (when pregnant with her son, Robin):

> Rainer Maria Rilke wrote a line about the slums, which for some obscure reason I am never able to forget:
> 'Children and cherry trees are always ailing . . .'
> I've seen that place, with the jamtins and the tomcats in the back yard: moreover lived in it – in Redfern, in Sydney – But there was always some pull <u>away</u> from people – to books, to enormous old trees, to staring at clouds and admiring wild duck and brown youngsters as tidy as horses, to being alone. I don't think it's snobbishness. More likely, sort of diffidence – and continual over-stressing of the importance of individuals who never mattered a tinker's damn – [symbol 'therefore'] all I have done is been a lonely sort of apparition (as far as poetry is concerned), with no sense of community in it – But I *feel* a sense of community sometimes, only not as you'd approve it: more as if the old derelicts with their shabby stories untold, and the children drinking like sparrows at a bubble-fountain and the dead also, tucked away in Grafton cemetery, *belonged* to me – [58]

In her next letter she speaks of the conflict between desiring (or needing) social change and the possibility of making a comfortable niche for oneself in society: 'enduring all the aches of this rotten system and yet being socially in tune with it'. She goes on to ascribe love for the old prosperous pleasurable life as a 'gentle sort of mist' that 'can soften rough edges' and acknowledges that 'women do love like that, a good deal'. There is an internal conflict indicated in her letters as if she feels the era when life can be understood in terms of the individual is over (and needs to be for the sake of the future) but she does not want that to be so. (Yet, there is also an interesting ambivalence in her attitude to Lee's mentoring.) In the poem, as in the letters, this conflict is enacted in a gendered political discussion about the importance of the individual versus society. The husband and wife's exchange can be understood as 'a domestic', one of those rows that comes from irritation with the familiar responses of a spouse to familiar stresses, the sort of argument that could potentially lead to physical violence. Their debate is about how best to respond to their own predicament. It is implied that their situation involves financial, emotional, and personal entrapment. Their row is an outcry about that oppression. How to live? 'HE' is a political intellectual who feels it his duty to think constantly about the political problems, and suffering of the day. 'SHE' sympathises with his politics but also wants some personal happiness. The possible choices are complicated by jealousy and tenderness. When his wife goes out walking, the husband is jealous of what he sees as her escape into nature. But is his conception of thinking and feeling for 'man' necessarily more 'real'? He wants to be made to feel alive by pain. She wants the healing of a leaf. Where is the right course? Where is reality? And how to distinguish it from didactic or melodramatic versions of 'Reality' (with a capital 'R')?

The poem opens:

HE: 'You've been with spring. Your eyes are full of it.'
SHE: 'Hush and lie still. I'll be with you as soon
     As I've got off my coat and combed my hair.'

He mocks her carefree manner:

But I tell you, she's the paramour of spring
She's got that lying quiet around her mouth,
She comes here, and her fingers crackle green.
I lie abed, while slowly she unsheathes
The body that was mated with a wind,
And scent of spring stuff forces through the keyhole,
She comes in reeking bracken, rank with gorse.
If I peered over her shoulder in the mirror
I wouldn't see a woman, but a tree,

The wife responds by reminding him that she has the power to heal his anxiety:

'If I let down my hair, it hides your face,
Covers my shoulders and the piece of world
That's gone dark blue between the slats of blinds.
Now we lie in the woods, John, lie in darkness.
Why do we wrestle, hurt each other so?
I only crossed the road.'

But he will not give up his jealous rant. He wouldn't, he says, 'thwart her slight vagrant liberties' if it wasn't that she had that 'cursed trick . . . of sinking/ Into the last look of a far-stretched landscape':

'Printing your gaze on rocks that won't forget you –
I hear them leaping down the quarry-face
Rattling clean and blue, now while we're lying
My face on yours. I see the yellow cliffs
Clear in the sun, where moonlight ought to be.
I've heard the green wheat sighing while you sleep
Out of your bones. Don't tell me you're no leman;
One night no doubt you'll come home caught with child,
Still with that borrowed radiance in your eyes,
Because a cloud rode silver on a hilltop.
If that's not treachery, tell me what?'

When it becomes clear he is accusing her of committing a kind of symbolic adultery with nature, and being disloyal to a socialist struggle, she protests:

SHE: 'But John,
     If you didn't make me cry, you'd make me laugh
     Because we lie and hurt each other so.

> Listen: we needed milk. Surely that's human?
> One pint of milk. I ran across to get it.
> And then it's true, I'd been indoors all day,
> The house was like an oven –'

He responds:

> 'That's how we live.
> That's how the poor live, if they've any honour,
> Sweating and sick and faithful, in an oven.'

She understands his argument but defends herself: 'I didn't look/ at the old gardens, I know how you dislike them, And I shut my ears to the rosepipes sprinkling rain.' For him, to admire the houses and gardens of 'the comfortable ones' is to be co-opted, 'safely as a rat in cheese', by the status quo – and therefore unable to protest or change things:

> I tell you, when a Red thinks for himself
> Thinks of a higher screw, a softer bed,
> A whiter breast, a roof that doesn't leak,
> They've got him safely as a rat in cheese.
> But when he thinks for men, he's dangerous.

Yet throughout the dialogue, as the husband curses his wife's 'treachery', her disappearance into another 'softer' world, he describes that world so carefully that one is reminded of R. A. K. Mason's 'Footnote to John ii, 4' in which the son describes, gradually, tenderly, the rotten overprotective way in which his mother used to tuck him up at night. If 'Footnote to John ii, 4' is about a struggle to be able to accept love, so is 'Husband and Wife'. There is jealousy and pain as well as a sense of failure here: this is male authority without any power except to command suffering and to suffer – because suffering is the only dignified course. She acknowledges the predicament; though perhaps in a way that might irritate him: 'God meant us to be very baffled now.' And she also understands his tenderness when she uses his description in the last lines of their dialogue: 'You say my hair/ is osier leaves. See how its shadow spreads/ Across the farthest star, and covers us.'

Amongst left-wing intellectuals of the period the exchange would have been a familiar one about political commitment versus faith in natural beauty, art, love or aesthetics. In the letter to John A. Lee, Hyde suggests that this is as an argument she frequently has with herself. She describes a 'pull' away from needy people 'to books' or 'enormous old trees'.[59] It is a pull that she feels guilty about as escapism, 'a continual over-stressing of the importance of individuals who never mattered a tinker's damn' – but at the same time she sees it as 'a gentle sort of mist' that can 'soften rough edges'. The poem dramatises this interior dialogue as a debate between a man and a woman. It shows the relations between the sexes under strain even amongst political allies. Perhaps, using Mary Louise Roberts' model, it suggests that an examination of what are thought of as women's tastes or sensibilities is a way of thinking about the future – that because we cannot know the future, we come to it, at any one time, via our obsessions. Hyde's poem tackles the future in a dialogue about how men and women should behave. The dialogue takes place between two characters carefully placed in a material and social context. We as readers measure what they say against their circumstances. For instance, the man's work takes him outside the house. Is the wife, then, meant to live all day not only physically inside the 'hot little house' but also mentally burning with anger for other oppressed people? The wilderness is just across the road, it is somewhere to go when you get some milk. It's an escape more effective for her than the contemptuous victory he imagines: 'One day fat fools will call this cottage charming/ And hold an auction for our chamber pot'.

Most critics have played down Robin Hyde's socialism. Sandbrook argues that she championed D'Arcy Cresswell's idea of 'a spiritual renaissance' as opposed to 'a firmer and juster materialism.'[60] Other critics have contrasted her description of her involvement in the protest march that turned into riots in the main streets of Auckland in 1932 ('I being more than a little pro-Bolshie was with the crowd in Karangahape Road') with her sceptical remark in her autobiography that she rejects 'the dictatorship of the commissariat in favour of 'Shelley's "Masque of Anarchy."'[61] These critics of course have an accepted tradition of thinking on their side – political commitment equals didacticism, equals poor writing. On the other hand, one can see these different positions dramatised in Hyde's later work (in this poem and in the novels) as ongoing dialogues in which the possibility of a just movement against injustice is complicated – but not necessarily abandoned – by showing characters and their gender positions. Her radicalism can also be observed in her impulse to 'get the bigger picture', to document all discourses of her period. And she documents the arguments marshalled by men and women against each other, not to say simply that ideologies are wrong, but that human beings reach for them as a response to social pressures and injustices.

Hyde's collage or montage technique puts her alongside other radical writers in an international context.[62] If one must look explicitly at intentions here, there is corroborating evidence of Hyde valuing multiplicity and dialogue in her comment about the popularity of Social Credit being a manifestation of New Zealand 'awakening to internationalism' in response to the Depression: 'A sudden access of thought on the world's tangled problems must necessarily lead to mistakes, fallacies, petty Waterloos . . . but it should lead further.'[63] Hyde's interest in different voices and ideas is an interest in multiplicities of opinion as broadly representing the world, documented in order to understand it better. Hyde was herself involved in various political groups, including Douglas Social Credit, and interested in the ideas and activities of friends who were communists.[64]

This may be a more powerful way of reading this later work than a purely feminist account. For instance I do not, as Michele Leggott does, see the wife's words at the end of the 'Husband and Wife' as a solution, but rather as part of the ongoing debate.[65] In *Dragon Rampant* Hyde comments: 'Anyhow I have small use for the female principle segregated from life. It could help and it won't; it knows nothing, except to be pitiable and bear children. For the rest it is all talk.'[66] 'Husband and Wife' puts both sides of the bafflement – the (self-denied) male desire for tenderness and the (denied) frustration inherent in the female immersion in nature. His insistence on brutal reality, and hers on healing nature, add up to a painful conundrum of failed communication.

Contemporary problems faced by women were well illustrated by a government Committee of Inquiry into Abortion that took place in 1936–37. The debate round this inquiry revealed contradictory discourses. Historian Barbara Brookes, in an essay on 'Reproductive Rights: The Debate Over Birth Control and Abortion in the 1930s',[67] focuses on the inability of the committee to acknowledge the principal problem they were faced with, the extraordinarily high maternal mortality from illegal abortion, where 60 per cent of abortions became septic and caused death. Women's groups spoke favourably of contraception as an alternative to abortion. Mrs Elsie Freeman (better known as Elsie Locke) explained the economic necessities leading to abortion and argued for access to birth control to allow spacing of children.[68] However the committee felt these proposals were condoning immoral behaviour and lack of control, as were proposals for legalised abortions. The committee was, as Barbara Brookes points out, preoccupied with other issues:

> The Committee's concern with the declining population was so absorbing that at one point they had to be reminded that the topic under investigation was abortion and not the national birth rate. Their interest reflected the wider discussion taking place in the popular press. Explanations for reduced fertility ranged from the familiar complaints of economic insecurity and women's preoccupation with 'preservation of the female figure and youthful charm [and] social life without juvenile ties', to more sinister causes such as a new disease of womankind:'a deadly psychological disorder called anthropophobia – hatred of mankind – hatred of life'. Articles and pamphlets explored the possible consequences of under population.[69]

Interestingly enough, Hyde in *Woman Today* contributed to this very debate and also commented on the hypocrisy of the committee in refusing to acknowledge the need of unmarried women for help with either contraception or their children. Brookes regards the most insightful appraisal of the report as the one published in *Tomorrow* Magazine which, she comments, 'correctly divined that the Committee had failed to recognise the true nature of the situation [and] suggested that it was more realistic to investigate the safety of legalised abortion.'[70]

But Hyde takes a slightly different tack. Her approach perhaps shows how thinking about women was, in the thirties, a way of thinking about the future. Her interest in combining socialism and feminism has a particular applicability to the way she may have constructed the story of her own life. In discussing the inquiry, she assumed the importance of the unmarried mother – her essay was titled 'Less Happy Parenthood: The Problem of the Unmarried Mother'. First she drew attention to the hypocrisy and contradictoriness of the committee's report:

> What the committee's report cites as cause 3 of resort to abortion is pregnancy amongst the unmarried. It adds, 'For dealing with the problem of the unmarried mother, the committee considers that the attack must be along the lines of more careful education of the young in matters of sex, prohibition of the advertisement and sale of contraceptives and a more tolerant attitude on the part of society towards these girls and their children. A little further on, one finds: 'Contraception may be considered under three headings – one, the practice of contraception extra-maritally, which only needs to be mentioned to be deprecated.'
>
> I would be very interested in knowing the mental attitude of others, both men and women, to the above. It seems to me that a few more facts and figures would be advisable before deciding where and what to deprecate.[71]

She went on to explore the difficulties faced by a single woman with a baby: the problems with accommodation, the potential isolation and misery. She made the point that even if the baby was healthy, there were more problems of economic survival, including the unpleasantness of any court dispute to get money from the father: 'Even if she is one of the lucky ones who gets and keeps a job', there was still the social punishment. She might be thick-skinned for herself and manage to support the child, but 'it is not easy to become indifferent' to the thought of her child being ostracised 'at school, and in after life'.[72]

Hyde ended her assertion with a plea for the unmarried mother: 'Then decide whether some alleviation of their circumstances is not necessary, unless you are going to leave them three choices – contraceptives, abortion, life-long insecurity.'[73] To women in the 1990s who tend to think of contraception as a right, and abortion as an unfortunate necessity, her way of grouping these three choices as all second-best alternatives to having a child with support seems very odd. But I think it is a particularly revealing comment – calling attention to the importance of different issues for women in the thirties. There has not been a simple continuity (or even a progressive advance) in women's lives from then to now. Because of the depression of the 1930s and Hyde's own experience of both wage-earning and poverty, as well as of supporting a child, it seems that her primary concern was the economic inequality faced by women, where later feminists have stressed 'reproductive choice', often particularly choice *not* to have a child. It also seems as if she shared the common belief of her time that abortion was a sign of general social failure. A useful way of summing up her kind of 1930s feminism, as compared to the feminisms of earlier and later women, would be to say that for Hyde a woman needed not only the wherewithal to have 'a room of her own' (to think and write) but also the wherewithal to have (and to be able to take care of) a baby of her own.

Let us look at it this way: Hyde as an 'intellectual', as I have designated her, lived inside (not outside) the social contexts and discourses of her period. Her sense of the emotional sterility of marriage relationships, her criticism of the hiding of information about sex, her anxiety about the increasing loneliness and isolation of urban society, and her sense of urgency that unless some change took place individuals would despair and lose their desire to live, were all attitudes that were important in the period. What was different from mainstream or official culture was Hyde's idea of the future – one aspect of which seems to have been this concept of social equity for women, particularly women with children. The society, the media, and the legislators were anxious about the falling birthrate, and about race despair, and Hyde's sense of hope for the future also favoured fertility but it depended explicitly on an ideal of a woman being able to support the baby she conceived, as if she was presciently looking forward to the era of the Domestic Purposes Benefit. Her feminism was different from that of Jane Mander, for example. Mander envisaged a future epitomised by the character Asia, a young woman who chooses to have a sexual relationship with the man she loves, though for reasons beyond her control she cannot marry him. Asia's choice is possible because (it is implied) she knows about contraception. A child is not an important part of Mander's proposition. Robin Hyde, on the other hand, envisaged a maternal future, a future in which a woman would have the financial independence to refuse marriage or to manage without it and keep her baby, either supported by the state or employed so she can raise a child on her own.

It is a question of emphasis, Hyde seems to be saying; what is freedom to have sex, without the freedom to love and sustain (literally) the consequence? This is an attitude (or imagination of the future) which Hyde elaborates in specific comments about herself in *A Home in this World* as well as in her portrait of Wednesday in *Wednesday's Children*. It is also very much present in the way she chooses to arrange the material in *The Godwits Fly*.

The wrong direction of modern society is signified by a man's refusal of his unborn child, whether by washing his hands of the problem or by his friendly offer to procure an abortion. Hyde's negative judgement of the society which allows the casual offer of money for an abortion as an acceptable social interaction is as strong as that of John Dos Passos in the third book of *USA*. Mary West in *The Big Money* (like *Wednesday's Children* published in 1937) is a journalist. Her choice of an abortion is a sign of her weariness with unsatisfactory relationships. Her lover is a university lecturer who champions the working class ('it wasn't until she actually saw him come into the lecture hall that she remembered that he was the nice skinny redfaced lecturer who talked about how it was the working class that would keep the country out of war at Vassar that winter.')[74] Although she had been in love with another man she has reluctantly accepted the lecturer's advances – she needed the companionship. But when she falls pregnant and he offers the name of a doctor to perform an abortion, she feels cynical and disappointed:

At last Mary wrote George a special delivery letter asking him what to do. Next evening she got a reply. George was broken hearted, but he enclosed the address of a doctor. Mary gave the letter to Ada to read. 'What a lovely letter. I don't blame him at all. He sounds like a fine sensitive beautiful nature.' 'I hate him,' said Mary, driving her nails into the palms of her hands. 'I hate him.'[75]

There is a parallel quotation to be found in *A Home in this World* where Hyde reports the reaction of the father of her child to the news of her pregnancy: 'Lonnie's first comment (by letter) was, "Do you think you could find your share of £20?" The £20 was for an abortion. Well, I thought, you can't say we haven't got sex equality all right. I wrote back and said I didn't want that.'[76] Shown here – as in *USA* – is pain at the insensitive modern solutions that a man will easily reach for in a time of crisis. Implied also, is anger about naive conceptions of sex equality when nothing about the conditions of men and women are symmetrical: when the choice to have a child is seen as the woman's, yet the danger of an abortion is also all hers.

Hyde, however, was well aware that in a time of economic recession a pregnancy suggested alarming financial responsibilities to a man – and Lonnie was already supporting a wife and family. ('Married women, unmarried women with babies . . . money-spiders,' she also writes in *A Home in this World*.[77]) Yet in both *The Godwits Fly*, and pivotally in *Wednesday's Children*, there are scenes where a man's true character is tested in his reaction to news of his lover's pregnancy. In *The Godwits Fly* a chapter opens like this:

'You don't want to marry me, do you?'
'I came here with a perfectly open mind.'
'But you don't want to. Well you haven't got to. Listen. I'm going away to Sydney. Nobody need know. I haven't told. I've got my passage money but not much else. I'm afraid you'll have to help.'
'Of course I'll help. But what about the baby?'
'You'll have to marry me if it lives – if I live. Somehow I don't think I will.'
'Don't talk like that.'
'Do you mind promising – if that happens.'
'Of course I promise.'[78]

In *Wednesday's Children* one passage indicates that all of Wednesday's lovers have failed this 'test', but the victory for Wednesday is that she hasn't had to be dependent on their disappointing responses:

It was difficult, none the less, to realise that Michael had left her. Wednesday had a clear picture of him, the back of his neck, brown joined to white at the collar of his shirt. She heard herself saying to him, in a slightly raised voice: 'Michael I am going to have a baby.' For the fraction of a second, the razor hung suspended, flashing as Wednesday's oar flashed now when she raised it out of the sleek dark water against the moon. Then it came down, sword of Damocles. She knew Michael wasn't going to pass the test. . . .

Knowing that meant knowing exactly what he would say and do in the next few minutes. First his face, handsome, reckless face, would go like an obstinate pudding. Only a woman knows. She has put in the right ingredients, the oven is perfect, the mixing a work of art, the recipe handed down carefully from one grandmother to another. The pudding remains obstinate. 'I won't,' it thinks, looks and feels. Only that, and nothing more. It selects its destiny, which is refusing to do the thing you meant. It is a type, ageless. It always (metamorphosed into Michael's face) says exactly the same thing. . . .

'Hell . . . very softly. Then: 'You're sure?'

Later: 'But how can you be sure?'

Later again: 'Well, you'd better see a doctor, and make quite sure. I don't see how ...

Later again: 'Hell ...'

Then a little whistle, hurt, miserable, which says plainly: 'Oh, gosh, women.'[79]

The sign of a man who genuinely wants a changed relationship between men and women *and* a better society seems to be the (freely felt) desire to father a child. 'What use are you to me if you aren't free,' Wednesday comments to herself of Michael's sullen reaction. The experience of fatherhood is what Timothy in *The Godwits Fly* actively desires. But he is a rare exception: a woman cannot rely on finding such a man. For her the just society of the future will be one which allows a single woman the freedom to have love affairs and sustain the consequences, by allowing her to work and care for her child. This aspect of Hyde's understanding of sex relations is reinforced by this passage of *Dragon Rampant:*

Paul said something funny, but true, one night. He said, wrestling with a collar and stud: 'Oh, well, I guess most women are permanently shellshocked.'

I guess we are. But I don't think for a moment men quite understand what it implies, what it might lead up to, without any premeditation or sociological homework. Just tearing a world up like a piece of dirty paper, setting a match to it, and saying, 'There: now I hope you like it, as it's been a long time you've kept on asking for it.'[80]

What is she getting at? Again I think she is referring to the difference between the idea of freedom for women and the reality; or, in other words, to the lies and evasions implied in the idea of sex equality in an unequal society. She is also commenting on the idea of equality as it is experienced at a time of economic recession; she acknowledges that change in socialised behaviour is difficult and painful, even when desired.

British novelist Angela Carter once remarked in an interview that she became 'mildly irritated when people, as they sometimes do, ask about the mythic quality of work I've written lately'. Instead she stresses: 'I believe all myths are products of the human mind and reflect only aspects of material human practice. I'm in the demythologising business.'[81] It is possible, as I believe other readings do, to make a similar mistake about Robin Hyde's work. Because, for example, in *The Godwits Fly* she assembles a montage of women suffering, and women criticised, this does not mean that she is showing the dignity and significance of suffering. Instead I see her as documenting aspects of the period, which are products of its material conditions, juxtaposed with Eliza's dissatisfaction, in order to suggest other possibilities. The way the ghoulish expectation of suffering had been constructed as part of the female character needed to be counteracted, more so because Hyde had to battle that expectation in her own life, and in her representation of that life. The association of women and suffering was so dominant in her period that it was particularly important to find a way of acknowledging and overcoming it.

For us to understand Hyde's narratives only for their pathos is to reduce their significance. In the 1930s both the international economic questions and the feminist questions had a place and she examines their interaction as she portrays the way women took the brunt of the recession. There is, for instance, Ritehei's story in *Nor the Years Condemn*. Ritehei has no food and too many children, and wants an abortion, which will probably kill her but only more quickly than the pregnancy – which actually does so. This is the story of a woman who takes the weight of the economic depression on her own body. And added to that weight is the weight of racist oppression which wears down her spirit as effectively as hunger and babies wear down her body. Starkie is against getting the abortionist – letting 'the killer in'. Ritehei argues with him. How is it different from the killing he had done as a soldier? 'You did plenty killing at war,' she reminds him.[82] The implication is that she is right; there is no difference. But neither is that a justification. Both killings are signs of a dehumanised futureless society. Later, when Ritehei is dying in childbirth, Starkie thinks: 'After all I ought to a had the killer in. It was better that than this.'[83]

In *The Godwits Fly* two chapters sit alongside each other contrasting male and female formative experiences. The hospital that Eliza is admitted to when she hurts her leg is a place of female suffering, whereas the hydro workers' village that Timothy goes to is (it seems) a place of freedom and discovery. The women in hospital are maimed as a result of thoughtless male behaviour and they blame themselves for the result. In the ward there is 'a light, bantering curiosity, a sense of being linked together as girls at a school are linked, and endless gossip'. The gossip is about what other women have done to bring suffering upon themselves:

> ' . . . They're keeping all her things apart, cups and everything. Do you know what that means? She's got a disease, and they've brought her in here to have the baby took away. I had two operations for that myself but mine was different, it was because I had T.B. A shame, I call it, putting her in with decent married women and young single girls.'
>
> Dark faces, dark sullen faces, their silence remembered for ever. Nobody spoke to the girl in the flannel nightshirt, one of us might have done . . . And the little sparrow gossips. 'Two years since I had me radium in, and now the doctor says I've got to be opened again. Life's a business isn't it?'
>
> Kathleen with the tawny lion's mane around her white cameo of a face, her eyes grey, her mouth lovely. 'Appendicitis – not her. Don't you have anything to do with her, my dear, she's no better than a street-woman. I'm warning you because you're a young single girl. She's been in here before, she has.' But Kathleen sat on the side of

Eliza's bed and talked. Once she was a waitress; there was a baby, and now she was here. 'Just appendicitis,' she said, shaking back the lion's mane.[84]

It is clear in the context of the novel that how these women are described, and describe others, is questioned. Eliza, even though she is 'a young single girl', is not there as the consequence of an abortion; she is able to comment on what she perceives as this compulsory suffering. Her enlisting of culture in the service of understanding can widen her perspective, so that remembering the Chinese poem she can see how often this observation of female suffering has been made before:

> Screens were drawn around the new girl's bed, nothing was allowed out but her high moaning. Presently, when the doctor had gone away, enamel basins slammed and nurses scurried. 'Nurse, Nurse, look at this floor.' Minna Craig whispered, 'It's blood. It's soaked right through the mattress and made a pool on the floor. Sister's not half wild.' The new girl's voice had grown dreamy and mechanical, she had nearly forgotten what she wanted to say.
>
> 'Doctor, I can't . . . oh, Doctor, dear, I can't . . .' Screens closed round her bed, wings folding, hard white wings of death.
>
> 'That's what you get for messing round with married men, me dear.'
>
> 'Yes,' thought Eliza, 'And Arthur Waley wrote in his translation of the little Chinese poem,
>
> 'How sad it is to be a woman,
> Nothing on earth is held so cheap.'
>
> The kind and the lovely . . . the kind and the lovely . . . their faces drift back through the twilight. Men, you have sentinelled your doors with them. It is a false judgment, the judgment you passed on them, and false the sentence of pain, and the base metal with which they were paid for living. But this is true. Their arms were white, their heavy hair fell back, wet as sickness had made it wet, their grey eyes kept a secret, and in twilight their mouths were kind. They did not remember to blame or to condemn you: if they spoke of you at all, it was quietly, with the old words of love. They were a flower that has spread itself too wide, and a moth that could not hate the flame. Grave-eyed they were garlanded; brave-winged they flew on into dust.
>
> There was something here about a bone that wouldn't set. The little old man who presided over the fizzling golden X-rays wouldn't have Eliza moved. Twice the big machine lumbered round to the side of her bed, and stood over her behind the screens. We're going to put you under. . . . Breathe deep, old girl, move your little finger if you can still hear me. She's off Sister. The rush of protest, the cry impossible to utter: 'No, no, I'm not off yet, Doctor.' Then nothing but wet blackness, and running, running along an endless stretch of sands.[85]

Eliza's eloquent but terrible description of women 'sentinelled at doors' and of a woman as 'a flower that has spread itself too wide' is influenced by the fact of her own feverish condition: 'There was something here about a bone that wouldn't set.' This juxtaposition serves to suggest – not that Eliza has grasped an ultimate truth – but that though women's lives could be otherwise, the seductiveness of suffering is very great, especially when one is at the lowest ebb. It tempts one to think that suffering for women is essential and has an essential dignity. The juxtaposition also indicates Eliza's problem of separating herself from events which get perceived as tragedy – a problem that intensifies later in the novel with the stillbirth of her own baby. [86]

The chapter 'Broken Trees' is about the kind of thoughtless male behaviour that has landed Kathleen in the hospital with 'appendicitis'. But this is not a display of conventional moralising. What is at stake is not simple. Men are not simply the guilty exploiters, and women are not simply the innocent victims. Timothy is also subject to being propositioned by his fellow worker Birkett – who 'tried to make up to Timothy after the others had doused the lights' and who advises against women: 'Don't go flossing around girls, they'll do you in.'[87] Even Timothy's sexual exploits in the paddock with Shelagh, the postmistress, provide little feeling of success. He longs for Shelagh's sexual enthusiasm: 'for it to happen of itself, because Shelagh said so.' But, even so, when she tells her sad story of a pregnancy, the child fostered out and with whom she has lost touch, his rejoinder – that he would love to have a child – is met with flat incomprehension:

> Queer, the premonitory pang that sometimes shot into his mind, the absurd thought, not to be exorcised until he had said it aloud. That lifted the Tapu.
> 'Somehow I don't think I'll ever have a son.'
> Shelagh said indifferently, 'Oh, go on,' but he could see she didn't care; that a man should actually *want* children was incredible to her.

Shelagh's blankness is an indication that it is difficult for men to change but it also shows her as alienated. Timothy is aware that he should have known better. The male thinker, the poet or intellectual, the unconventional one who wants freedom to experience the world has to identify when he really is tasting beautiful freedom, and when he is just following habitual patterns of male behaviour – 'scoring'. Timothy ponders this difference between freedom and insignificant exploitative moments. And when he does so he remembers (guiltily) the 'bitter lines' of a poet:

> Back in the saddle she swayed softly and drunkenly. She said good night at the door of the shack behind the post office, her mouth passive as a child's. The bitter lines of Iris Tree came into Timothy's mind:
>
> It yet is something to have cheated God
> And bored the Devil, with so easy prey.[88]

The chapter ends with Timothy awakening from a 'vague . . . nightmarish dream' – he was not sure what had aroused his terror. However, his sense of danger is averted by looking for Eliza's letter. It is as if he is saved by the fact that he has loved Eliza and refused to sleep with her. As in a fairy story, he is protected by his one good deed. However, Eliza has wanted his love, and his refusal has been tantamount to hypocrisy, using one woman and idolising another. Can just that be saving him? Perhaps it is Eliza's conversation (as recorded in her letter), her friendship and the equality of their intellectual exchange, that indicate a different possible relationship between men and women. Timothy puts Eliza's letter in his pyjama pocket and goes back to sleep 'quite happily having circumvented whatever danger was in the air'. However, the narrative is not quite finished. While he sleeps:

> Outside the trees glistened skeleton white, a ghostly army. It needed only one trumpet note to bring their silent company together, ready to march down for an inexorable revenge on the men who had murdered them and left their broken bodies standing, a mock for sun and moon.[89]

The political implications of this passage are interesting. It has the form of a revolutionary prediction. And I am struck with its similarity to the last pages of the novel *Potiki* by Maori writer Patricia Grace. That passage recounts a vision of weapons of revenge being prepared underwater, unbeknown to those who are threatened.[90] Timothy is similarly unconscious of the threat. How does one read this passage? A feminist explanation must see the assembled trees as the women threatening to assemble on behalf of the woman he has wronged, but also in this chapter the cleared land has symbolised the alienation of both men and women (a nationalist reading). The bush has its own revenge to take – as would the *tangata whenua*, for the clearing of the bush and the loss of their land. I would suggest that the interpretation of this passage has again to be inflected in terms of the period and the typicality of the characters. Timothy is a 'modern' and a kind of socialist, as is Eliza.[91] It is in negotiation with men like him that new relations between the sexes may evolve. This is the hope for the future. This is why the trumpet note is not sounded.

Yet the 1930s socialist feminist is also wary of male smugness. Does Timothy's new concern for the people and the nation, or his new relationship with one woman, really protect him from a possible revenge? What if (in some sense) the trees or the women actually managed to combine and become a ghostly army'? The question is left suggestively open.[92]

Instead of seeing Hyde as a writer in a female tradition which aroused the ire of her male contemporary writers (a narrowly literary historical interpretation), one can alternatively see her work as an attempt to explore the complexities of the period by addressing the relations between men and women in a new way. For the women, the negotiation of relationships with likeminded men was a way of formulating a new version of what it could mean to be female, and a possible new future. But as the poem 'Husband and Wife' shows, this was by no means easy.

Hyde's need to make a living as a writer (having no independent income) may have contributed to her keeping closely in touch with all aspects of the pre-war period, since she was necessarily writing for newspapers and mass-circulation periodicals and knew her audience. Her particular ideal of female autonomy comes out of her time – the idea of a woman with a baby and a job. This is an ideal that fell into disrepute and disappeared in the 1950s and 1960s. Perhaps the Domestic Purposes Benefit, which was introduced in the early 1970s, fits in with Hyde's hopes for the future, but now at the end of the century, when that benefit is a subsistence income only and when politicians see social freedom as the opportunity to participate in the market economy, we can see Hyde's picture of society as significant again. We should also see Hyde's 1930s type of feminism as socialist and concerned with formulating ways of thinking about working-class women, Maori women, and the material situation of individuals, unlike much second-wave feminism, which has been middle-class and has focused on psychology and psychoanalysis.

The suggestion that autobiographies are constructed in a similar way to fiction – with choice of emphasis and similar selection of detail – allows one to think about lives themselves as narratively constructed. For example, to see Hyde's pregnancies, and her decision to go through with them, as not a matter of accident but as one of choice means we are able to 'read' Hyde's life not in terms of tragedy but as a gesture towards how she thought people should be able to live and how the structure of society should change. But, as I hope I have shown, what is a significant gesture changes from decade to decade – even what we think of as most personal is also historical. Events have a different significance at different times and thus are treated in different ways by the people that they 'happen to'.

CONCLUSION

•

Making the Knight's Move

In titling his 1923 study of conventionality in art *The Knight's Move* Shklovsky created an image rich in implications. One of them is the necessarily oblique development of art. Like the chess knight, art does not progress in a straight line. It gets deflected because it aims to be unpredictable in relation to reigning norms. Criticism can progress in a similar fashion. The greatest novelty, at the moment, will come not from new semantic fields (post modernism or whatever will follow) but from a sidestepped dislocation of interpretation itself. It is time for critics to make the knight's move.[1]

The above are Bordwell's concluding lines to *Making Meaning*. This book has aimed to make its own kind of 'knight's move' for criticism. In order to challenge an officially sanctioned aesthetic we need new critical approaches. Bordwell argues that interpretation has become predictable, an industry of 'application', and in the case of film criticism he cites disappointing failures of initiative. Even structuralism, he suggests, with its 'concept of the contradictory text' which was such a 'promising initiative' and could have 'spurred lively sceptical debate' has developed into 'a practical criticism that is never logically staked out', and which 'squeezes film after film into the same half-dozen molds, and refuses to question its own procedures'.[2] In this book I have suggested that more recent semantic approaches to interpretation, for example feminist or even postcolonial, can become equally routine unless they practice some critical innovations. And the first step in new practice is selfconsciousness about the social and institutional implications of ways of reading. This book then has aimed to be both an example of, and a proposal for, a more self-aware approach to the study of New Zealand literature and culture.

However, whereas Bordwell tends to question the very activity of interpretation I am more concerned about developing a kind of code of ethics (or protocol) for interpretation, one of the most important of which is to introduce a wider notion of historical context and of cultural production. New Zealand literature does not as yet have the large industry of critical writing that surrounds American film and literature – it would be useful to have more. In this spirit I have offered some new historical readings of my own. In doing so, however, I have tried to maintain as high a degree of self-awareness as possible. For example, I have tried to present each reading as a conscious construction. Where I have proposed new readings I have tried to build my interpretations, logically, around hypotheses and questions, so that I am able to ask: Is this a useful method? How does it stand in relation (or opposition to) other methods? I have tried to introduce dialogue, to invite my own readers to be sceptical, and to draw attention to contradictions in order to promote debate – assumimg that texts do not change but readers do, and all readers, more or less self-consciously, get excitement and clarity by conjoining texts with other discourses that interest them. I have also suggested that one can do more things with texts than simply dig 'inside' them for meaning. Extratextual elements, such as the processes of cultural production (of novels or films) are vital to what we make of a cultural product. This is particularly the case with my chapter on *The Piano*, which argues that the making of the film – especially the way its intertextual connection was suppressed – holds special implications for some New Zealand viewers. In this respect I have much sympathy for Robert Hodge's suggestion that 'the object of study is no longer the meaning of literary texts as such, but the processes by which meaning is produced and renegotiated and circulated around literary and other texts which perform analogous functions in contemporary culture'.[3]

Bordwell, too, emphasises an 'historical poetics'; he speaks of the surprise of discovering how differently a film may be understood in different periods. He does not want to erase such contrasts: 'We don't want a critical language to flatten out our predecessors' difference.'[4] Similarly I have suggested that attempts to reconstruct historical contexts can throw up unexpected ideas and highlight new aspects of a text – differences that can otherwise be swamped by the broad application of psychoanalytic, feminist or other approaches. (Though I have tried to present 'history' not as 'given' but as itself an ongoing investigation.) To offer an example outside my thesis, it is very interesting to re-read the work of Janet Frame in a feminist manner as Australian critic Gina Mercer has done, but it also seems to me important to realise how 'unfeminist' Frame's early writing was in some respects, with its emphasis on the freedom of the artist rather than on gender oppression. That emphasis was very much part of the years from the 1940s to the 1960s, a shift in priorities from the pre-war years of Robin Hyde.[5] It is not a question of 'repudiating interpretations' but of 'situating protocols within a broader historical enquiry'.[6] I see this historical enquiry as important for New Zealand readers today, particularly since the last ten years have seen a shift in the economic and ideological character of our society which makes it important to revise ideas about the past.

The debate between nationalism and feminism has become repetitive in our culture but perhaps by looking at the wider international context of, for example, the inter-war years, we can appreciate its origins. This is what I attempted in the last chapter – setting Hyde and her work within a more complex context. The topical relevance of this approach was reaffirmed as I finished a first draft by seeing others working in a similar vein on similar themes. For example, the television drama *Forgotten Silver,* which aroused much controversy when screened (purportedly as a documentary) in 1995, attempts a similarly parodic look at the way the discourse of nationalism and a particular idea of the artist are embedded in New Zealand cultural consciousness. Like the directors of that movie, I hope that some of my readers were seduced by the particular readings explored in this book, before those readings were challenged or subverted. This strategy both reveals cultural assumptions and challenges them.

In my readings I have also tried to capture the sensuous aspects of the experience of viewing a movie or reading a novel. I have kept in mind Susan Sontag's imperative that a critic should produce 'really accurate, sharp, loving descriptions of the appearance of a work of art.'[7] Always in my mind as I was writing was the sense that activities associated with reading of novels, of poems and films are not always interpretive. The 'loving descriptions' called for by Sontag are important but so are the strategies by which any reader gets involved. In my case, as a university teacher, I value strategies useful to engage students. This is why I have dedicated the book to the students in my first university tutorials who ate Caramello chocolate bars, smelt marigolds, stroked woollen socks and helped me paste gold stars on the wall in a memory game to assist our discussion of Janet Frame's *Faces in the Water*.

•

Notes

INTRODUCTION

1 Mario J. Valdes, *A Ricoeur Reader: Reflection and Imagination* (Hemel Hempstead: Harvester Wheatsheaf, 1991) p.11.

2 This is in spite of the fact that a number of the most important of these second-wave feminist texts (e.g. Kate Millet, Germaine Greer) focused on literary texts. My (woman) supervisor seemed surprised some years later that I considered any feminist consciousness to have been at work in this dissertation. This was a comment apropos the period; she did not recall feminsim entering the academic discourse (in New Zealand) until the late seventies.

3 Mary Paul, 'The Success and Failure of Elizabeth Gaskell', MA dissertation University of Auckland, 1975, p. 80

4 J.A.V. Chapple and A. Pollard, eds, *The Letters of Mrs Gaskell* (Manchester: Manchester University Press, 1966) p. 106.

5 I have written a short autobiographical account of my family 'The We of Me', *Landfall* 180 (December 1991): 412-417.

6 Juliet Mitchell, *Psychoanalysis and Feminism* (London: Vintage Books, 1975) p. xix.

7 Mitchell, p. xiv.

8 Helene Cixous, 'The Laugh of the Medusa', *Signs* 1 (Summer 1976): 875-893. Luce Irigaray, 'When Our Lips Speak Together', *Signs* 6 (Autumn 1980): 69-79. Julia Kristeva, 'Women's Time', *The Kristeva Reader*, ed. Toril Moi (London: Basil Blackwell, 1986).

9 See for example Dale Spender's *The Mothers of the Novel* (London: Pandora, 1986).

10 Mary Paul, review of *Yellow Pencils: An Anthology of New Zealand Women Poets*, ed. Lydia Wevers, *NZ Listener* 11 February 1989: 56.

11 Mary Paul and Marion Rae, eds, *New Women's Fiction 3* (Auckland: New Women's Press, 1989).

12 Angela Carter, *The Passion of New Eve* (London: Penguin, 1977).

13 Toril Moi, 'Feminism, Postmodernism and Style' *Cultural Critique* 9 (Spring 1988): 5-7.

14 Another important influence in my developing this emphasis on a feminist materialism was the introduction to Judith Newton and Deborah Rosenfelt, eds, *Feminist Criticism and Social Change: Sex, Class and Race in Literature and Culture* (New York: Methuen, 1985).

15 For another account of this exhibition see Linda Hutcheon, *The Politics of Postmodernism*, New Accents (London: Routledge, 1989) p. 21.

16 *AND* Magazine seems though to have been unsure about its relationship to feminism. Some of its editors obviously realised that feminist theory was opening up new ways of looking at culture but it appears that they were unsure how to incorporate such ideas, or indeed work by women, in their agenda. At least, this is what I take from the fact that the first issue included the name of an imaginary woman contributor 'Anne Bland' on its back cover. Issues 2-4 however did include a range of women contributors including several feminist writers.

17 Murray Edmond and Mary Paul, eds, *The New Poets: Initiatives in New Zealand Poetry* (Wellington: Allen & Unwin/Port Nicholson Press, 1987) p. xi.

18 Leigh Davis, '62' from 'Willy's Gazette', reprint in Edmond and Paul, eds, *The New Poets,* p. 21.

19 Edmond and Paul, eds, *The New Poets*, p. x.

20 Terry Sturm, Introduction to the First Edition, *The Oxford History of New Zealand Literature in English*, 2nd edn, ed. Sturm (Auckland: OUP, 1998) p. xii.

21 Alex Calder, Introduction, *The Writing of New Zealand: Inventions and Identities*, ed. Calder (Auckland: Reed, 1993) p. 10.

22 'Reader response' and 'reception theory' do not necessarily embrace pluralism and have sometimes meant a shift from one kind of determinacy to another. For an account of this see Robert C. Holub on determinacy and the Fish/Iser debate in *Reception Theory: A Critical Introduction* New Accents (London: Methuen, 1984) pp. 101-106.

23 David Bordwell, *Making Meaning: Inference and Rhetoric in the Interpretation of Cinema*, Harvard Film Studies (Cambridge: Harvard Univ. Press, 1989) p. 1.

24 Bordwell, p. 3.

25 Bordwell, p. 13.

26 Paul Ricoeur, interview, *A Ricoeur Reader: Reflection and Imagination*, ed. Mario J. Valdes, p. 444.

27 Bordwell, preface, p. xi.

28 Many others have made similar comments. See for example Leigh Dale who in 'Whose English – Who's English? Teaching Literature in Australia', *Meanjin* 51.2, 1992: 393-409, argues that we should 'open up the possibility of [a] kind of cacophony' in which 'both the teacher and student' can 'consider their own investments in particular texts'(p. 406).

29 Bordwell, p. 35.

30 Moi, p. 12.

CHAPTER ONE

1 'Against Interpretation', in *Against Interpretation and Other Essays* (London: Eyre and Spottiswoode, 1967) p. 13.

2 David Bordwell, *Making Meaning: Inference and Rhetoric in the Interpretation of the Cinema* (Cambridge: Harvard University Press, 1992) p. 250.

3 Janet Staiger, *Interpreting Film: Studies in the Historical Reception of American Cinema* (Princeton: Princeton University Press, 1992) p. xi.

4 David Bordwell, p. 250.

5 These responses are all recorded in Pamela Dunbar's essay 'What does Bertha Want? A Re-Reading of "Bliss"' in *Women's Studies Journal* (NZ) 4. 2. (December 1988): 18-31.

6 See Elaine Showalter's chapter on 'The Female Aesthetic', in *A Literature of Their Own* (Princeton: Princeton University Press, 1977) especially pp. 246-7; C. K. Stead 'Katherine Mansfield: "The Art of Fiction"' in *In the Glass Case*. (Auckland: AUP, 1981), pp. 37, 45 and 46 and Kate Fullbrook, *Katherine Mansfield*, Key Women Writers Series (Brighton: Harvester Press, 1986) pp. 9 and 95-102.

7 Pamela Dunbar finds in the story both Freudian principles and elements of feminist revisionist versions of Freud, which she pictures as unproblematically linked into a true picture of identity and sexuality. My approach challenges this. A later statement of a similar reading can be found in Dunbar's *Radical Mansfield: Double Discourses in Katherine Mansfield's Short Stories* (Basingstoke: Macmillan, 1997) pp. 104-113.

8 See the 'Neuro Psychoses of Defence', 1894, *The Standard Edition of the Complete Psychological Works of Freud* vol III (London: Hogarth, 1962) p. 47. Other relevant works include 'The Aetiology of Hysteria,' 1896 v. III; 'Fragment of an Analysis of Hysteria', 1905 v VII; and 'Three Essays on the Theory of Sexuality' 1905 v. VII (London: Hogarth:

1953). Translations into English generally followed five years or so after the original German editions. Pamela Dunbar (p.28) discusses Mansfield's possible familiarity with the works, and ideas, of Freud. Also see my Reading Four.

9   Katherine Mansfield, 'Bliss' in *The Stories of Katherine Mansfield*, definitive edition, ed. Antony Alpers (Auckland: OUP, 1989) pp. 305-315. This story was first published in the *English Review* in August 1918 and in book form as *Bliss and Other Stories* in 1920.

10 Mansfield, 'Bliss', p. 308.

11 Freud, 'Fragment of an Analysis', p. 34.

12 Mansfield, 'Bliss', p. 309.

13 Mansfield, 'Bliss', p. 308.

14 Mansfield, 'Bliss', p. 305.

15 Mansfield, 'Bliss', p. 308.

16 Mansfield, 'Bliss', p. 314.

17 Freud, 'Three Essays on Sexuality', p. 227.

18 Freud, 'Three Essays', p. 227

19 Freud, 'Fragment of an Analysis', p. 110.

20 Mansfield, 'Bliss', p. 313.

21 This interpretation compares interestingly with the Freudian implications in Elaine Showalter's description of Virginia Woolf: 'In fact Woolf was far from sexless, her view of the world seems to have been quite sensual, even erotic, until she was forced to translate her view of the world into sexual events' (p. 270).

22 Mansfield, 'Bliss', pp. 314-315.

23 Freud, 'Fragment of an Analysis', p. 110.

24 Ezra Pound, 'The Garden' (Lustra, 1916) in *Selected Poems* (London: Faber, 1948) p. 92.

25 Mansfield, 'Bliss', p.305.

26 Mansfield, 'Bliss', pp. 305-306.

27 Susan Gubar, 'The Birth of the Artist as Heroine' in *The Representation of Women in Fiction* ed. Carolyn Heilbrun and Margaret Higonnets (Baltimore: John Hopkins University Press, 1983) p. 39. This phrase is used with reference to Mansfield's story 'The Doll's House'.

28 Gubar, p. 26.

29 Dunbar comments: 'one or two critics have tentatively suggested that the two pyramid shapes might be intended to symbolise breasts but if this episode is considered in relation to the succeeding one . . . then this implication seems clear' (p. 22).

30 Mansfield, 'Bliss', p. 306.

31 Gubar, p. 45.

32 Gubar, p. 45.

33 Nancy Chodorow, *The Reproduction of Mothering: Psychoanalysis and the Sociology of Gender* (Berkeley: Univ. of California Press, 1978) pp. 109-10.

34 'Mansfield', p. 312.

35 Virginia Woolf, 'A Society' in *Monday or Tuesday* (New York: Harcourt Brace, 1921) pp. 38-39.

36 Philip Armstrong's '"Flying Leaves" – a glance at Katherine Mansfield's "Bliss" in the light of the "Seminar on 'the Purloined Letter'" by Jacques Lacan', MA essay, English Department, University of Auckland, 1990, p. 1. Also see Shoshana Felman 'Turning the Screw of Interpretation' in *Literature and Psychoanlysis: The Question of Reading Otherwise* (Baltimore: Johns Hopkins University Press, 1982) especially pp. 190-196.

37 Shoshana Felman, 'Turning the Screw of Interpretation', p. 119.

38 Shoshana Felman, 'Turning the Screw of Interpretation', p. 112 (Felman's italics).

39 Armstrong, p. 5. Also see Pamela Dunbar 'What does Bertha want?' and Barbara Johnson, 'The Frame of Reference', *Yale French Studies*, 55.56 (1977): 457-505.

40 See Pamela Dunbar.

41 Mansfield, 'Bliss', p. 305.

42 Armstrong, pp. 5-6.

43 Armstrong, p. 7

44 Armstrong, pp. 7-8.

45 Armstrong, p. 8.

46 Mansfield, 'Bliss', p. 308 and p. 312.

47 Armstrong, p. 14.

48 Elizabeth Wright, *Psychoanalytic Criticism: Theory in Practice,* New Accents (London: Methuen, 1984) p. 113.

49 Armstrong, p. 15.

50 Dunbar, p. 18.

51 Nancy Armstrong, *Desire and Domestic Fiction: A Political History of the Novel* (New York: OUP, 1987) p. 224.

52 See essays in Charles Bernheimer and Clare Kahane, eds, *In Dora's Case: Freud – Hysteria – Feminism* (New York: Columbia Univ. Press, 1985).

53 Clare Hanson, *The Critical Writings of Katherine Mansfield* (Basingstoke: Macmillan, 1987) p. 40.

54 Sydney Janet Kaplan, *Katherine Mansfield and the Origins of Modernist Fiction* (New York: Ithaca, 1991) p. 185

55 From letter to Sydney and Violet Schiff, 3 December 1921, Hanson, pp. 76-77.

56 See Vincent O'Sullivan and Margaret Scott, eds, *The Collected Letters of Katherine Mansfield*, v.1. (Auckland: OUP, 1984) pp. 261-262.

57 Mansfield, 'The Advanced Lady', *Collected Stories*, p. 80.

58 Hanson, p. 63.

59 Clare Hanson comes to a similar conclusion after a discussion of Mansfield's life: 'I would suggest that KM's fiction is strong in feminist terms because her estrangement from, yet identification with, the feminine enabled her to see it as something learnt, not something given; something chosen, not necessarily determined by biological or psychological fact. In this context I think it is reasonable to see KM's rejection of feminine prose as more than the self-protective strategy which Showalter describes: KM rejected the cultivation of the "feminine".' (Hanson p. 20) For a fuller discussion of Mansfield's attitudes to 'feminine prose' and her sense of her own difference from Woolf and Richardson, see Kaplan's chapter on 'The Feminine Aesthetic'.

60 Fullbrook writes: 'while she [KM] is attracted to the possibility of a unified self, even if knowable only in infinitesimal moments, there is a final hanging back. And it is this hesitation, this honest uncertainty in the face of desire and need, that makes Katherine Mansfield, at times, one of the toughest and darkest of the modernists' (Fullbrook, p. 19).

61 The tendency to assume that the feminine character is developed along Freudian lines or even to assume, as feminist revisionists do, a starting point of Freudian psychology is all part of the still persuasive influence that Freud has on much discussion of the psychology of women. For an impressive summary of this influence see Phyllis Grosskurth's 'The New Psychology of Women' in *New York Review of Books* 24 October 1991: 25-32. In her conclusion to a survey review of eight books, Grosskurth quotes Freud's argument in *Civilisation and Its Discontents* (1930) that women 'exercise a "retarding and restraining influence" on the progress of civilisation' and concludes that: 'Perhaps they [women] would strengthen their cause if they ceased reacting against this brilliant but drastically limited theorist and struck out on their own'. See also Frederick Crew's 'The Unknown

Freud' in *TLS* 18 November 1993: 55-65.

62 My approach can be seen as new historicist in its impulse to (as Terence Hawkes puts it) 'dissolve literature back into the historical complex that academic criticism has traditionally held at arm's length' (*TLS* 10 April 1987: 390-393).

My contention that in order to do this we need to work beyond feminist revisions (and totalising discourses/ways of reading) is echoed in other new historicist research. See for example Gillian Brown's introduction to *Domestic Individualism; Imagining Self in the Nineteenth Century Novel* (Berkeley: University of California Press, 1990). In addition see Bridget Orr 'Reading with the Taint of the Pioneer' in *Landfall* 172: (December 1989): 447-461 and Lydia Wevers 'How Katherine Beauchamp was Kidnapped' in *Women's Studies Journal* 4.2 (December 1988): 5-17. These essays suggest ways in which it may be interesting to read Mansfield as a colonial writer.

63 Rachel Blau du Plessis in 'Pater-Daughter: Male Modernists – Female Readers' from *The Pink Guitar: Writing as Feminist Practice* (New York: Routledge, 1990) pp. 44-45.

64 Dora Marsden quoted in Rachel Blau du Plessis, p. 46.

65 An earlier paper of mine 'Bluebeard's Bliss' (1989 unpublished) explores this angle on the story as well as the intertextual relationship between this story, Grimm's version of Bluebeard, and a Margaret Atwood story, 'Bluebeard's Egg'.

66 Jerome McGann, *The Romantic Ideology* (Chicago: University of Chicago Press, 1983) p. 160.

Chapter Two

1 See Bordwell's objections to Stanley Fish, David Bordwell, *Making Meaning: Inference and Rhetoric in the Interpretation of Cinema*, Harvard Film Studies (Cambridge: Harvard University Press, 1989) p. 5.

2 See Bordwell's comments on Roland Barthes, pp. 1 and 10.

3 Bordwell, pp. 8-9.

4 Ian Gordon, 'Katherine Mansfield, New Zealander', *New Zealand New Writing* 3, ed. Ian Gordon (Wellington: Progressive Books, 1944) p. 63.

5 Katherine Mansfield, 'Prelude' in *The Stories of Katherine Mansfield*, definitive edition, ed. Antony Alpers (Auckland: Oxford University Press, 1988) p. 249.

6 See Katherine Mansfield *The Aloe* (New York: Howard Fertig, 1974) and also *The Aloe with Prelude*, ed. Vincent O'Sullivan (Wellington: Port Nicholson Press, 1982). *The Aloe* was written before 'Prelude' in the spring of 1916. Most of it, rewritten and reshaped, was incorporated into 'Prelude' a year later, in 1917. It was first published with an introduction by Middleton Murry in 1930. One significant difference is that the parts of this first version were titled as four chapters: 'Last Moments Before', 'A Journey with the Storeman', 'The Day After', and 'The Aloe'.

7 Ian Gordon, p. 61.

8 Ian Gordon, p.61.

9 C. K. Stead, 'Katherine Mansfield: The Art of "Fiction"' in his *In the Glass Case: Essays on New Zealand Literature* (Auckland: Auckland University Press, 1981) p. 32.

10 Ian Gordon, p. 60.

11 Katherine Mansfield, 'Prelude', p. 244.

12 Katherine Mansfield, 'Prelude', p. 250.

13 Gordon, p. 60.

14 For a full discussion of the dispute around *New Zealand New Writing* see Chapter Five of Rachel Barrowman, *A Popular Vision, The Arts and The Left in New Zealand, 1930-1950* (Wellington: Victoria University Press, 1991) pp. 150-157.

15 Barrowman, p. 155.

16 Publisher's blurb, *Katherine Mansfield: The Collected Short Stories*, Penguin Modern Classics (Harmondsworth: Penguin, 1984).

17 Gordon, p. 61.

18 Gordon, p. 59.

19 Gordon, p. 65.

20 'Prelude', p. 232.

21 Katherine Mansfield's comments made in a review of Jane Mander's *The Story of a New Zealand River* are also interesting in this discussion. Mansfield cautions against using names of native trees because it will not be evocative: 'What picture can that possibly convey to an English audience?' Her perspective is significantly different from this reading of her own story. See Mansfield, review of *The Story of a New Zealand River*, in *The Critical Writings of Katherine Mansfield*, ed. Clare Hanson (Basingstoke: Macmillan, 1987) p. 102.

22 Gordon, p. 59.

23 Curnow, p. 41.

24 Mansfield, 'Ode to Stanislaw Wyspianski', *Penguin Book of New Zealand Verse,* ed. Curnow (Harmondsworth: Penguin, 1960) pp. 127-128.

25 Mansfield, 'Prelude', p. 224.

26 Mansfield, 'Prelude', p. 225.

27 Mansfield, 'Prelude', pp. 226-227.

28 Curnow, *Penguin Book of New Zealand Verse*, p. 40.

29 Allen Curnow's reading of R. A. K. Mason's 'Footnote to John ii, 4' is another example. Curnow reads the poem not as about a son's struggle between the need for independence and loving his mother but as about a struggle to find national identity and separate from the suffocating motherland ('certainly about a rejection of the mother(land)'). For the poem see *Penguin Book of New Zealand Verse*, p. 168, and for Curnow's comments, introduction p. 43.

30 Bordwell, p. 10.

31 Lydia Wevers 'The Sod Under My Feet', *Opening the Book: New Essays on New Zealand Writing*, ed. Mark Williams and Michele Leggott (Auckland: Auckland University Press, 1995) pp. 31-48.

32 Mansfield, 'Prelude', p. 225.

33 Mansfield, 'At the Bay,' *The Stories of Katherine Mansfield* ed. Antony Alpers (Auckland: OUP, 1988) p. 455.

34 Mansfield, 'Prelude,' p. 226.

35 Allen Curnow, 'Wild Iron', in *An Anthology of New Zealand Poetry,* ed. Vincent O'Sullivan (Auckland: Oxford University Press, 1983) p. 118.

36 Mansfield, p. 232.

37 Keith Sinclair, *A History of New Zealand* (Harmondsworth: Penguin, 1969) p. 175. Quoted in Wevers, pp. 45-46.

38 Wevers, p. 46.

39 Wevers, p. 40.

40 Wevers, p. 41.

41 Wevers, p. 43.

42 Wevers, pp. 43-44.

43 Wevers, p. 44.

44 Wevers, p. 45.

45 Mansfield, 'Prelude', p. 255.

46 For other feminist accounts see Susan Gubar, 'The Birth of Artist as Heroine,' in *The Representation of Women in Fiction*, ed. Carolyn Heilbrun and Margaret Higgonets

(Baltimore: Johns Hopkins University Press, 1983) and Sydney Janet Kaplan, *The Origins of Modernist Fiction* (New York: Ithaca, 1991).

47 For an interesting parallel discussion of a 'heritage version' of a prominent writer see Roger Sales, *Jane Austen and Representationss of Regency England* (London: Routledge, 1996).

48 See Chapter Three of Kate Fullbrook's *Katherine Mansfield,* Key Women Writers Series (Brighton: Harvester, 1986) pp. 77-78.

49 Fullbrook, p. 66.

50 Fullbrook, p. 67.

51 Fullbrook, p. 69.

52 Mansfield, 'Prelude', p. 225.

53 Fullbrook, p. 70.

54 Mansfield, 'Prelude', p. 235.

55 Mansfield, 'Prelude', p. 233.

56 Mansfield, 'Prelude', p. 254.

57 Fullbrook, p. 82.

58 Fullbrook, p. 82.

59 Fullbrook, pp. 82-83.

60 Fullbrook, p. 76.

61 Fullbrook, p. 85.

62 Paul Ricoeur, 'What is a Text,' *A Ricoeur Reader: Reflection and Imagination,* ed. Mario J. Valdes (Hemel Hempstead: Harvester Wheatsheaf, 1991) p. 57.

63 Edward Gibbon Wakefield from *A View of the Art of Colonisation* (London, 1849) quoted in Raewyn Dalziel 'The Colonial Helpmeet' in *Women in History: Essays on European Women in New Zealand,* ed. Barbara Brookes, Charlotte Macdonald and Margaret Tennant, (Wellington: Allen & Unwin, 1986) p. 57.

64 Raewyn Dalziel, 'The Colonial Helpmeet', *Women in History,* ed. Brookes, Macdonald and Tennant, p. 59.

65 See comment in 'Maori and Pakeha Women: Many Histories, Divergent Pasts?' Barbara Brookes and Margaret Tennant in *Women in History, 2: Essays on Women in New Zealand,* ed. Barbara Brookes, Charlotte Macdonald and Margaret Tennant (Wellington: Bridget Williams Books, 1992) p. 41.

66 See for example Renée's *Jeanie Once* (Wellington: Victoria University Press, 1991).

67 Charlotte Macdonald, *A Woman of Good Character: Single Women as Immigrant Settlers in Nineteenth Century New Zealand* (Wellington: Allen & Unwin/ Historical Branch, 1990).

68 In spite of rhetoric condemning birth control and fearing race extinction, the birth rate continued to decline until after the Second World War.

69 Charlotte Macdonald, p. 164.

70 It is interesting to note that Katherine Mansfield's 'Woman at the Store' was written in the same year that there was legislation prohibiting women from being barmaids.

71 Edward Said, *Culture and Imperialism* (New York: Knopf, 1993).

72 New Zealand has always been known for its modernity and progressiveness particularly in terms of individual consumption of new technologies, for example electricity, cars and more recently personal computers. Interest in new technologies of birth control may be comparable. Certainly the medicalisation of birth, the development of obstetric hospitals and the status given to doctors has been different in New Zealand, than, for example in England. See Joan Donley *Save the Midwife* (Auckland: New Women's Press, 1986) and also my discussion in Chapter Four.

73 Susan Gardner, 'Portrait of the Artist as a Wild Colonial Girl' in *Gender, Politics and*

Fiction, Twentieth Century Australian Women's Novels, ed. Carole Ferrier (St Lucia: University of Queensland Press, 1985) p. 27.

74 Michael Cannon, *Life in the Country: Australia in the Victorian Age*, Nelson, Melbourne, 1973, pp. 140-154.

75 This comment (described by Gardner as 'pseudo-analysis') is made by Colin Roderick in his biography *Miles Franklin: Her Brilliant Career,* (Adelaide: Rigby, 1982) pp. 64 and 70. Gardner observes of the biography: 'a depressing example of how access to considerable private material and even personal acquaintance can impede rather than foster understanding.' (Gardner, note 6, p. 266.)

76 Jean Devanny, *Point of Departure, An Autobiography of Jean Devanny,* ed. with an introduction by Carole Ferrier (St Lucia: University of Queensland Press, 1986) p. 45.

77 Devanny, pp. 41-42.

78 Devanny, p. 57.

79 Devanny, p. 57.

80 See Claire Tomalin's biography *Katherine Mansfield: A Secret Life,* London: Viking, 1987.

81 Devanny, p. 57.

82 Antony Alpers comments matter-of-factly that Linda is pregnant in the story and implies that Mansfield's contemporaries would have been well aware of this: 'Perhaps some present-day readers might not realize (so discreet are the numerous hints, beginning with the third line of the first paragraph) that Linda is meant to be pregnant in the story.' (Alpers, *Collected Stories,* p. 558.) The piece of textual evidence he cites, from the first paragraph, is of Linda not wanting to carry a child on her lap. The other 'hints' he refers to are probably the same elements of the story that many other readers have noted, things coming alive, buds swelling, baby birds, dream babies, etc. However, it would also be possible to see Alpers' comments as extremely reticent, and to see his description of Linda as pregnant as a kind of euphemism for talking about the conception that I 'find' in the story.

83 In order to calculate the possible time of conception and length of pregnancy, from 'after Easter' to February, see Antony Alpers *The Life of Katherine Mansfield* (New York: The Viking Press, 1980): 'the two families moved in the same week, just after Easter 1893.' (p. 11) And Leslie 'the longed-for blessing of a son' was born 21 February 1894 (p. 12). If they moved in mid-May and Leslie was conceived then, he could have been born, a little late, on 21 February 1894. Alpers' scenario of Linda being pregnant in the story fits less well. The important thing is that Mansfield could herself have calculated or contemplated this as the time of her mother becoming pregnant/ her brother's conception.

84 See C.K. Stead, *In the Glass Case,* p. 37.

85 See Antony Alpers, *The Life of Katherine Mansfield,* pp. 2 and 9.

86 Mansfield, 'Prelude', p. 228

87 Mansfield, 'Prelude', p. 230 (Mansfield's ellipses).

88 Mansfield, 'Prelude', p. 231.

89 Mansfield, 'Prelude', pp. 231-232.

90 Mansfield, 'Prelude', p. 233.

91 Nancy Armstrong, *Desire and Domestic Fiction: A Political History of the Novel* (Oxford: Oxford University Press, 1987) p. 231.

92 Armstrong, pp. 230-231.

93 Mansfield, 'Prelude', p. 233.

94 Mansfield, 'Prelude,' p. 234.

95 Mansfield, 'Prelude', p. 240.

96 Mansfield, 'Prelude', p. 242.

97 Mansfield, 'Prelude', p. 243.

98 Mansfield, 'Prelude,' p. 243.

99   Mansfield, 'Prelude', p. 244.

100 Mansfield, 'Prelude', p. 253.

101 Mansfield, 'Prelude', p. 254.

102 A.G. Stephens, review of *My Brilliant Career,* by Miles Franklin, *The Bulletin,* 28 Sept. 1901, Red Page, quoted in Marjorie Barnard, *Miles Franklin,* Twayne's Authors Series (New York: Twayne Publishers: 1967) p. 46.

103 Mansfield quoted in Antony Alpers *The Life of Katherine Mansfield* (New York: The Viking Press, 1980) p. 41.

104 Mansfield quoted in Antony Alpers, *Life of Katherine Mansfield*, pp. 55-56. Admittedly, these writings (poem and notebook entries) were written earlier than 'Prelude' (1917) but not so far from its earlier version 'The Aloe' (drafted in 1916).

CHAPTER THREE

1   I quote this as a typical response. 'Campion Film Saluted', *NZ Herald,* 26 May 1993, sec.1: 24.

2   'The Piano "too arty" for Oscars', *Evening Post* 16 March 1994: 27.

3   Jane Campion quoted in *The Piano* (Cannes: International Press, 1993) p. 15.

4   *NZ Herald* 26 May 1993: 24.

5   Suzanne Duncombe and Felicity O'Brien, eds *Piano Lessons* (Sydney: Currency Press, 1996) and *Garage* 2 (Milan) 1994.

6   *Victorian Studies Network* also contained much on this theme. See 27 July to 4 August 1994, VICTORIA@IUBVM. UC.

7   Stella Bruzzi, 'Jane Campion: Costume Drama and reclaiming women's past', *Sight and Sound* rpt. in *Women and Film: A Sight and Sound Reader*, ed. Pam Cook and Philip Dodd (London: Scarlet Press, 1995) pp. 232-242. Also see Jan Chapman and Jane Campion in *The Piano* (Cannes: International Press, 1993) pp. 13-14.

8   Pat Hilton, 'Ask Pat', TV Week, *Wisconsin State Journal,* 16 November 1986: 35. Quoted in David Bordwell, *Making Meaning: Inference and Rhetoric in the Interpretation of Cinema* (Cambridge: Harvard University Press, 1989) p. 12.

9   Bordwell, p. 13.

10 The fact of this connection was revealed to me in discussion in May 1993, before the film was released (and I outline this information, though not the name of my informant below). Latterly in late 1993 it was corroborated by a series of short articles and notices in New Zealand newspapers by journalist/writer Geoff Chapple. Chapple was one of the writers of the screenplay of the proposed film 'The River,' an adaptation of Jane Mander's 1920 novel *The Story of a New Zealand River* for which Brigid Ikin (Hisbiscus Films) and John Maynard Films had bought development rights. Chapple argued for close connections between his script and Campion's. He uncovered (under the Official Information Act) correspondence between the producers of 'The River', Australian funders of *The Piano* and the New Zealand Film Commission that further substantiated the connection. Interestingly his articles were turned down for syndication in the Australian press on grounds of the delicacy of the subject. The same decision was made by the Australian editors of the forthcoming 'Piano Lessons' *vis-à-vis* a version of my seminar. They were worried about legal repercussions of discussing a possible connection between novel and film despite the fact such claims had already been made publicly here in New Zealand. Chapple and others were also interviewed for a news item on television (*20/20* TV2), which appeared in the same week as I first gave a paper on the subject. Round the same time another published discussion of the link between novel and film appeared in a Wellington journal as a section in a larger article 'The Last Patriarch' by Ann Hardy. (*Illusions* 23 Winter (1994): 9-10.) For a more recent summary see Rae McGregor's

biography *The Story of a New Zealand Writer: Jane Mander* (Dunedin: University of Otago Press, 1998).

11 For a discussion of the notion of there being a mix or co-existence of contemporary or non-contemporary features in any historical moment see Robert Holub, *Reception Theory: A Critical Introduction*, New Accents (London: Methuen, 1984) p. 65.

12 *The Piano* dir. and screenplay Jane Campion, with Holly Hunter, Harvey Keitel and Sam Neill, Miramax, 1993. *The Story of a New Zealand River* (1920) by Jane Mander (London: Robert Hale, 1960). *The Piano: The Screenplay* by Jane Campion (London: Bloomsbury, 1993). *The Piano*, a 58 pp. publicity publication (Cannes: International Press 1993). *The Piano: A Novel* by Jane Campion and Kate Pullinger (London: Bloomsbury, 1994). Promotional videos for *The Piano* (the video) and for Michael Nyman's score on cassette and compact disk (Miramax, 1994). All quotations from Mander's novel are from the 1960 edition.

13 *End of the Golden Weather*, dir. and screenplay Ian Mune, with Steven Pappas, Paul Gittens and Gabrielle Hammond, prod. Christina Milligan, 1991.

14 For a description of the circumstances of filming, see Robert Mannion 'Hollywood Stars Shrouded during NZ film shoot', *Dominion Sunday Times* 12 March 1992: 1. Campion required greasy locks for an authentic 'look': see *The Piano* (Cannes) p. 15.

15 *Desperate Remedies*, dir. and screenplay Stuart Main and Peter Wells, with Jennifer Ward-Lealand, Kevin Smith, Lisa Chappell and Cliff Curtis, James Wallace Productions, 1994. *Desperate Remedies* unlike *The Piano* was shot entirely 'on set' in a converted warehouse on the Auckland wharves.

16 MA paper 18.433 New Zealand and Australian Women Writers, English Department University of Auckland.

17 The researcher was Daniele Pistone while Edmond de Goncourt baptised the piano in this way. Both references are from Chapter 10 'The Secret of the Individual', *A History: of Private Life, from the Revolution to the Great War*, ed. Michelle Perrot (Harvard: Bellknap, 1990) p. 531.

18 Michelle Perrot, ed., pp. 531-3.

19 Janet Frame, *The Carpathians* (Auckland: Century Hutchinson, 1988) p. 71. Also see David Eggleton's comments on pianos in 'Grimm Fairytale of the South Seas', *Illusions* 23 Winter (1994): 3.

20 The novel came back into print in a new edition in 1994 (Auckland: Godwit Press, 1994). Its introduction by Dorothea Turner was previously published in 1976 as an essay entitled '*The Story of a New Zealand River*: Perceptions and Prophecies in an Unfixed Society', see note 30.

21 Also see Rae McGregor's *The Story of a New Zealand Writer: Jane Mander.*

22 'The River' was the title of the unfinished and unproduced film on which Brigid Ikin and John Maynard had been working. Chapter Four discusses that script in more detail.

23 Letter from The Film Commission to Geoff Chapple dated 22 Dec, 1993.

24 Miriam Dixson, *The Real Matilda: Woman and Identity in Australia, 1788-1975* (Ringwood, Vic: Penguin, 1976). Anne Summers, *Damned Whores and God's Police: The Colonisation of Women in Australia* (Ringwood, Vic: Penguin, 1975).

25 Jock Phillips *A Man's Country: The Image of the Pakeha Male: A History* (Auckland: Penguin, 1987) and Miles Fairburn *The Ideal Society and Its Enemies: The Foundations of Modern New Zealand Society 1850-1900* (Auckland: Auckland Univ. Press, 1989) Also see Charlotte Macdonald's *A Woman of Good Character: Single Women as Immigrant Settlers in Nineteenth-Century New Zealand* (Wellington: Bridget Williams Books/ Historical Branch, 1990). This work suggests that middle-class planning of immigration put particular strictures on women. However it is not a polemical revision of history in the

way that the Australian accounts were, perhaps because it was written in the 1980s when it was almost already too late for identity politics, thus as an informed post-feminist account it avoids stressing any general thesis. See my discussion of similar themes in Chapter 2.

26 Jane Mander, 'The Making of an Authoress', from *The Lady's World,* London, date unknown, p. 863. The article is held in Auckland Public Library. See bibliographic entry in Rae McGregor's 'Jane Mander: Writer', MA thesis, Univ. of Auckland, 1995, p. 93.

27 Jane Mander, *The Story of a New Zealand River,* 1920 (London/ Christchurch: Robert Hale/ Whitcombe and Tombs, 1960) pp. 245-246.

28 Mander, *Story*, p. 6.

29 Mander, *Story*, p. 8.

30 Dorothea Turner, '*The Story of a New Zealand River*: Perceptions and Prophesies in an Unfixed Society', in *Critical Essays on the New Zealand Novel,* ed Cherry Hankin (Auckland: Heinemann Educational Books, 1976) p. 8. Also see Dorothea Turner, *Jane Mander* Twayne's World Author Series (New York: Twayne Publications, 1972).

31 Mander, *Story*, pp. 8-9.

32 Mander, *Story*, p. 19.

33 Mander, *Story*, p. 169.

34 Mander, *Story*, p. 51.

35 Mander, *Story,* p. 36.

36 Mander, *Story*, p. 206.

37 Jane Mander, letter to her sister, quoted in Dorothea Turner, *Jane Mander*, p. 27.

38 Jane Mander, 'The Making of an Authoress', p. 863.

39 Jane Mander, 'The Making of an Authoress', pp. 863-864.

40 Dorothea Turner, *Jane Mander*, p. 131.

41 Newspaper reviews quoted in Dorothea Turner, *Jane Mander,* pp. 130-131. The preference for this sort of material is interestingly close to Fiona Kidman's comments in her introduction to Lady Barker's *Station Life in New Zealand* (London:Virago, 1984) p. x.

42 Turner, *Jane Mander.* Dorothea Turner was connected in New Zealand literary and intellectual circles. Her mother was a university graduate and her father, Alan Mulgan, was a journalist and writer while her brother, John Mulgan, was the author of what was considered a seminal New Zealand novel, *Man Alone* (London: Selwyn and Blount, 1939). Turner's monograph is a model of the genre in that it works history, biography and critical commentary together smoothly and convincingly.

43 Turner, *Jane Mander,* p. 130.

44 Jane Mander, 'New Zealand Novels: The Struggle Against the Environment,' *Press* (Christchurch) 15 December 1934 quoted in Turner, p. 26.

45 Dorothea Turner '*The Story of a New Zealand River:* Perceptions and prophecies in an unfixed society', in *Critical Essays on the New Zealand Novel,* p. 4.

46 Jean Devanny, *Cindie: A Chronicle of the Cane Fields* (London: Virago, 1986) was first published in 1949. Katharine Susannah Prichard's *Coonardoo: the Well in the Shadow* (Sydney: Angus & Robertson) was first published in 1929.

47 Turner, *Jane Mander*, p. 23.

48 Katherine Mansfield (born 1888) was writing and publishing between 1910 and 1923. Jane Mander (though born earlier in 1877) was writing fiction from around 1915 and her novels were published (in New York and London) between 1920 and 1930.

49 See article in *Vogue Australia* April 1993: 140. Campion's previous movies were: *Peel* (drama) 1982, *Mishaps of Seduction and Conquest* (drama) 1983, *A Girl's Own Story* (drama) 1983, *After Hours* (drama) 1984, *Passionless Moments* (drama) 1984, *Two Friends* (drama) 1986, *Sweetie* (fiction feature) 1989, and *An Angel at My Table* (fiction feature)

1990, and *The Piano* 1993.

50 Jane Campion quoted in 'Playing from the Heart' article by Peter Calder, *NZ Herald* 16 September 1993, sec. 3: 1.

51 See *The Piano* (Cannes: International Press, 1993) p. 15.

52 *NZ Herald* 16 September 1993, sec. 3: 1.

53 *NZ Herald* 16 September 1993, sec. 3: p.1.

54 *The Piano* (Cannes: International Press, 1993) pp. 14 and 39.

55 Jane Campion in *The Piano* (Cannes: International Press) p.11 and *NZ Herald* 16 September 1993, sec. 3: 1.

56 Interestingly Jane Mander's next New Zealand-set novels were written with film in mind. The New Zealand/ Australian novelist Jean Devanny also recounts that the idea of writing for film started her career as a novelist.(Jean Devanny, *Point of Departure: The Autobiography of Jean Devanny* (St Lucia: University of Queensland Press, 1986) p. 79.

57 Conversation with Geoff Chapple, July 1994. (Of the four writers named on the script only Geoff Chapple has since discussed the film in public and is also the only one I have been able to interview.)

58 Russell Campbell *20/20*, news programme, Television 2, 19 July 1994.

59 Holly Hunter in *The Piano* (Cannes: International Press) p. 39.

60 Jane Campion quoted in *Sunday Star* 19 September 1993, sec. C: 1.

61 Selwyn Muru, visual artist and playwright, was the initial Maori adviser on the script. Waihoroi Shortland is named first in the credits. The actors also apparently made some alterations to the details of the Maori scenes. It seems that Campion consulted Muru (and Shortland) on the characters and dialogue within each scene but the relationship of those scenes to the whole action did not radically change from her first conception. (Telephone interview, Selwyn Muru, 19 July 1994.)

62 Sarah Kerr, 'Shoot the Piano Player', *New York Review of Books* 3 February 1994: 29.

63 'Holly Hunter Key Performer', *Style* Summer 1993/4: 126.

64 'The Piano "too arty" for Oscars', *Evening Post* 16 March 1994: 27.

65 'Beatson Doesn't Play the Piano', article by Deborah Hill in *National Business Review* 31 March 1994: 48.

66 'Movies with Russell Baillie', review *Sunday Times*

67 Advertisement, *Sunday Star Times* 27 March 1994: D6.

68 'Outdoors with Colin Moore', *New Zealand Herald* 6 July 1994, sec. 2: 1.

69 Raybon Kan 'Anna's Win Simply Awesome', *Sunday Star Times* 27 March 1994: A20.

70 Sarah Kerr's review in *The New York Review of Books* suggests that '"By 1860", according to the *Encyclopaedia Britannica* entry on New Zealand, "the land gripes only hinted at here broke into a fully fledged war that lasted ten years."' But she goes on: 'Campion avoids the usual traps, her Maori are neither especially savage or excessively innocent.' (*New York Review of Books* 3 February 1994: 29.)

71 John Pocock, letter, *New York Review of Books* 7 April 1994: 47-48.

72 Lynda Dyson, 'The Return of the Repressed? Whiteness, Femininity and Colonialism', unpublished paper delivered at London University, May 1995, p. 4. Also see Dyson, 'Post-Colonial Anxieties and the Represenattion of Nature and Culture in *The Piano*', *Sites : A Journal of South Pacific Cultural Studies*, 30 (Autumn 1995).

73 Lynda Dyson, 'The Return of the Repressed', p. 4.

74 *Once Were Warriors*, dir. Lee Tamahori, screenplay Riwia Brown, with Rena Owen, Temuera Morrison and Cliff Curtis, Communicado, 1993. Much was made in promotional material of the fact that this film was, unlike *The Piano*, released locally before being released overseas.

75 Jane Campion quoted in *New Zealand Herald* 16 September 1993, sec. 3: 1. Also see

Jane Campion, *Cinema Papers* 93 (May 1993): 6. Campion talks of her interest in a photo history of Maori and contemporary photographs as 'a graphic visual metaphor of how Maori culture was assimilated by European culture'.

76 'Shoot the Piano Player', *New York Review of Books* 3 February 1994: 30.

77 Also see 'The Piano Story,' dir. Greg Mayer, documentary item on Maori involvement in the making of *The Piano*, *Marae* Television New Zealand, 1994. Interviewed in this programme, Waihoroi Shortland states that the kindest thing he could say about the movie is that 'it brushes Maori at the time very gently', and that in it Maori are a 'backdrop against the main action of the movie'.

78 Stuart Dryburgh, *The Piano* (Cannes: International Press, 1993) p. 47.

79 Francis Pound, *Frame on the Land: Early Landscape Painting in New Zealand* (Auckland: Collins, 1983).

80 Jane Campion in *The Piano* (Cannes: International Press, 1993) p. 26-27.

81 For example see Velazquez 'Venus and Cupid' reproduced in *The Outline of Art*, ed. Sir William Orpen, revised by Horace Shipp (London: George Newnes Ltd, 1950) p. 478.

82 *The Piano* (Cannes: International Press, 1993) p. 27.

83 Edward Said, *Culture and Imperialism* (New York: Knopf, 1993) p. 222.

84 In his essay 'The Invention of New Zealand', Roger Horrocks points up this preoccupation in New Zealand poetry. *AND* 1 (1983): 9-30.

85 Most of these poems can be found in standard anthologies. *An Anthology of Twentieth Century New Zealand Poetry*, selected Vincent O'Sullivan, 2nd edn (Auckland: OUP, 1983) includes Charles Brasch 'Islands (ii)', p. 74; Ruth Dallas 'Deserted Beach', p. 177; Allen Curnow 'Spectacular Blossom', p. 132; and Alistair Campbell, 'At a Fishing Settlement', p. 245. Charles Brasch 'Forerunners' and 'Word by Night' *Collected Poems* (Auckland: OUP, 1984) p. 15 and p. 39.

86 See for example Robin Hyde *A Home in this World* and Elsie Locke *Student at the Gates* (Christchurch: Whitcoulls, 1981).

87 'Beatson Doesn't Play the Piano', *National Business Review* 31 March 1994: 48.

88 John Pocock, letter, *New York Review of Books* 7 April 1994: 47-48.

89 This comment is made of Sam Neill's *Cinema of Unease*. *Auckland International Film Festival Programme*, New Zealand Federation of Film Societies, 1995: 37, probably by its editor Bill Gosden. For similar comments see 'Cinema of Unease' in *NZ Listener* October 14-20 1995: 30.

90 'Battle on for a Slice of the World Movie Market,' KRT article, *Evening Post* 11 January 1994.

CHAPTER FOUR

1 Greenblatt, Stephen, *Renaissance Self-Fashioning from More to Shakespeare* (Chicago:University of Chicago Press, 1980). See Chapter One.

2 Ray Richards, conversation, 2 September 1995.

3 Wendy Harrex, publisher New Women's Press, Auckland; now publisher, University of Otago Press, conversation June 1994.

4 Geoff Chapple, conversation, 15 July 1994.

5 *20/20* Documentary, 19 July 1994. Confirmed in conversation September 1994.

6 'The River', John Maynard Productions, 1990 (105 pp).

7 The script of 'The River' is copyright to John Maynard Productions who will not allow it be quoted.

8 *Desperate Remedies,* dir. and screenplay Stuart Main and Peter Wells, with Jennifer Ward-Lealand, Kevin Smith, Lisa Chappell and Cliff Curtis, James Wallace Productions, 1994.

9 This aspect of similarity was the main one stressed by Geoff Chapple and Bob Harvey in the *20/20* documentary. Conversation with Wendy Harrex, publisher.

10 Jane Mander, *The Story of a New Zealand River* (London:Robert Hale, 1960) pp.13-14. and 'The River', pp. 8-9.

11 'The River', p. 11.

12 'The River', pp. 12-14.

13 'The River', p. 16.

14 An account of a very different response to similarly trying circumstances can be found in Lady Barker's 'Letter xi: Housekeeping and Other Matters' *Station Life in New Zealand* (1865; London: Virago, 1984) pp. 68-74.

15 Mander, *Story*, p. 9.

16 Mander, *Story*, p. 8.

17 'The River', p. 17.

18 'The River,' p. 17.

19 'The River', p. 21.

20 'The River,' p. 21.

21 'The River', pp. 103-105.

22 Paul Ricoeur. See Mario J. Valdes, introduction, *A Ricoeur Reader: Reflection and Imagination* (Hemel Hempstead: Harvester Wheatsheaf, 1991) p. 17.

23 See *Desperate Remedies*. Also see Stephen Eldred-Grigg, *Pleasures of the Flesh: Sex and Drugs in Colonial New Zealand, 1840-1915* (Wellington: Reed, 1984) and Miles Fairburn *The Open Society and Its Enemies: The Foundations of Modern New Zealand Society, 1850-1900* (Auckland: Auckland Univ. Press, 1989).

24 'The River', p. 87.

25 Dorothea Turner, '*The Story of a New Zealand River*; Perceptions and prophecies in an unfixed society,' in *Critical Essays on the New Zealand Novel*, ed. Cherry Hankin (Auckland: Heinemann Educational Books, 1976) p. 17.

26 Lawrence Jones, 'The Novel,' *The Oxford History of New Zealand literature,* ed. Terry Sturm (Auckland: Oxford Univ. Press, 1998) p. 135. Jones sees Mander's novels as having a 'nascent sense of historical development, a three stage process' (p.134) and as showing the second stage in New Zealand's development as 'a misapplication of the "feminine element", the imposition on the crude society of false secularised puritan code of respectability.' (p.135)

27 Michel Foucault, *The History of Sexuality Vol.1: An Introduction*, trans. Robert Hurley (New York: Vintage Books, 1980) p. 108.

28 Mander, *Story*, p. 311

29 Mander, *Story*, p. 311.

30 Lawrence Jones, 'The Novel', *The Oxford History of New Zealand Literature,* ed. Terry Sturm (Auckland:Oxford Univ. Press, 1998) pp. 134-137.

31 Dorothea Turner, *Jane Mander* Twayne's World Authors Series (New York: Twayne Publishers, 1972) p. 136.

32 Foucault, *The History of Sexuality, Vol. 1*, p. 122.

33 See also Mander's essay on 'The Sheltered Daughter' in *New Republic* 24 June 1916, quoted in Dorothea Turner *Jane Mander*, p. 49 and pp. 150-151.

34 See for example Sara M. Evans, *Born for Liberty* (New York: Free Press, 1985).

35 Mander, *Story,* p. 206.

36 Mander, *Story*, p. 181.

37 Mander, *Story*, p. 253.

38 Mander, *Story*, p. 255.

39 Mander, *Story*, p. 43

40 Mander, *Story*, p. 169.

41 Mander, *Story*, p. 44.

42 Mander, *Story*, p. 44.

43 Mander, *Story*, p. 44.

44 Terry Eagleton, *Myths of Power, A Marxist Study of the Brontes* (London: Macmillan Press, 1988) p. 32.

45 Nancy Armstrong, *Desire and Domestic Fiction: A Political History of the Novel* (Oxford: Oxford University Press, 1986) p. 200 and p. 121. Both novels could also be seen, in Nancy Armstrong's phraseology, as turning 'political information into a language of the modern self' and as 'displacing class conflict onto sexual relations and inscrib[ing] them within a modern institutional culture' (p. 200).

46 Eagleton, p. 95.

47 Eagleton, p. 32.

48 Armstrong, p. 201.

49 Mander, *Story*, p. 169.

50 See David Bordwell, p. 16.

51 Paul Ricoeur, 'Word, Polysemy, Metaphor,' *A Ricoeur Reader: Reflection and Imagination,* ed. Mario J. Valdes, p. 84. Seen in this way 'metaphor is no longer a rhetorical device, no longer a trope, it designates the general process by which we grasp kinship, break the distance between remote ideas, build on similarities and dissimilarities' (p. 83).

52 Angela Carter, *The Sadeian Woman: An Exercise in Cultural History* (London: Virago, 1987) p. 107.

53 Mander, *Story*, p. 203.

54 Mander, *Story*, p. 32.

55 Mander, *Story*, p.32.

56 Mander, *Story*, p. 30. In a review Katherine Mansfield comments negatively on this passage asserting that local references such as names of native trees make Mander's writing unintelligible to an international audience: 'What picture can that possibly convey to an English reader?' See *The Critical Writings of Katherine Mansfield*, ed. Clare Hanson (Basingstoke: Macmillan, 1987) p. 102.

57 Mander, *Story,* p. 31.

58 Mander, *Story*, p. 21.

59 Mander, *Story*, p. 155.

60 Guthrie Smith, W.H., *Tutira: The Story of A New Zealand Sheep Station,* preface, 2nd edn (Edinburgh: Blackwood and Sons, 1926) p.vii-viii.

61 Guthrie-Smith, preface, p. viii.

62 Guthrie-Smith, p.105.

63 Guthrie-Smith, p. 138.

64 Guthrie-Smith, *Tutira*, 3rd. ed., extract reprinted in *The Writing of New Zealand: Inventions and Identities*, ed. Alex Calder (Auckland: Reed, 1991) p. 111.

65 Guthrie-Smith, preface, p. viii.

66 Joan Donley, *Save the Midwife* (Auckland: New Women's Press, 1986).

67 Jane Mander's other New Zealand novels look at the 'failure' of New Zealand society to develop as she anticipated and hoped. See Lawrence Jones 'The Novel', *The Oxford History of New Zealand Literature,* p. 135.

68 Michel Foucault, *The History of Sexuality, Vol 1*, p. 159.

CHAPTER FIVE

1   See Robert C. Holub, *Reception Theory: A Critical Introduction* New Accents (London: Methuen, 1984), for a discussion of 'dominants' in literary history (p. 22) and also the relationship of biography to interpretation of literature (p. 20). Holub notes that 'the Formalists' rejection of traditional scholarship with its dependence on the "life-and-work"

method' does not actually mean that biography is 'banished from critical studies', but that the relationship of biography to literature is seen differently, not as 'a question of the genesis or description of the work, but rather of its reception'.

2   Paul Ricoeur, 'Between the Text and Its Readers', in *A Ricoeur Reader: Reflection and Imagination*, ed. Mario J. Valdes (Hemel Hempstead: Harvester Wheatsheaf, 1991) pp.401-402.

3   Ricoeur, p. 402.

4   When Hyde died in 1939 she left her mother and a close friend, Gwen Mitcalfe, in charge of her literary papers (literary executors). W.R. Edge, an Auckland lawyer and friend, was named her executor and guardian of her son, Derek Challis. Edge shared a residence with Rosalie Rawlinson and her daughter (Gloria), and when Hyde's mother, Annie Wilkinson, died in 1945 the literary papers were received by Edge and looked after by Gloria until Derek came of age.

5   See bibliography for publication details.

6   Allen Curnow, Introduction, *A Book of New Zealand Verse, 1923-45* (Christchurch: Caxton Press, 1945) p. 24. When Curnow was making his selection for the Caxton anthology, Hyde's last poems had not been collected and many, including the sequence 'Houses by the Sea', had never been published. His selection was therefore limited. The poems he chose were: 'The Thirsty Land', 'Ku Li', 'Journey from New Zealand' and 'The Balance'.

7   Allen Curnow, Introduction, *The Penguin Book of New Zealand Verse.* (Harmondsworth: Penguin, 1960) p. 57.

8   This is Hyde's own phrase, used in her autobiographical fragment of the same title. But I stress it as part of her reception because it has been associated at different times with both the version of her as a dysfunctional individual and with a feminist account of her as person and writer.

9   See for example 'The Final Word' by Susan Chenery, *The Australian Magazine* 6-7 August 1994: 30-34.

10 Curnow, *Penguin*, p. 58. The poem is Hyde's 'Prayer for a Young Country', from *Houses by the Sea*, ed. Gloria Rawlinson (Christchurch: Caxton, 1952) p. 150.

11 Curnow, *Penguin*, p. 58.

12 Hyde, 'What Is It Makes the Stranger,' *Houses by the Sea*,' pp. 142-143.

13 Curnow, *Penguin*, p. 58.

14 Curnow, *Penguin*, p. 58.

15 Curnow, *Penguin*, p. 17.

16 Hyde, 'The Wanderer', *Houses by the Sea*, pp. 37-8.

17 Hyde, 'The Dusky Hills', *Houses by the Sea*, p. 47.

18 Rawlinson, Introduction, *Houses by the Sea*, p. 19.

19 Curnow, *Penguin*, p. 57.

20 E. H. McCormick, *New Zealand Literature, A Survey* (Wellington: Oxford University Press, 1959) p. 127.

21 Curnow, *Penguin,* p. 56.

22 McCormick, p. 128.

23 Curnow, p. 57. See also Rawlinson's introduction to *Houses by the Sea,* especially pp. 16-19 and McCormick, p. 123 and p. 129.

24 McCormick, p. 128.

25 Robin Hyde, Author's Foreword, *The Godwits Fly,* ed. Gloria Rawlinson (Auckland: Auckland University Press/ Oxford University Press, 1970) p. xx.

26 McCormick, pp. 128-129.

27 Rawlinson, Introduction, *Houses by the Sea,* p. 19.

28 This means that Hyde also had the manuscript with her in China, an unintended destination

when she left New Zealand.

29 Rawlinson, Introduction, *Houses by the Sea*, p. 19.

30 Curnow, *Penguin*, p. 57.

31 McCormick, p. 124.

32 McCormick, p. 123- 4.

33 James K. Baxter, 'Symbolism in New Zealand Poetry,' in *James K. Baxter as Critic*, ed. Frank McKay (Auckland: Heinemann Educational, 1978) pp. 60-61.

34 Baxter, p. 60.

35 Baxter, p. 60.

36 Baxter, p. 60.

37 Nick Perry, *The Dominion of Signs: Television, Advertising and Other New Zealand Fictions* (Auckland: Auckland University Press, 1994) p. 123.

38 For instance poems anthologised have been her late poems and *Godwits Fly* was the one novel to remain fairly continuously in print. A paradigmatic example of accepted attitudes to Hyde's poetry is in Macdonald P. Jackson's essay on 'Poetry' in the *The Oxford History of New Zealand Literature*, 2nd edn, ed. Terry Sturm (Auckland: Oxford, 1998) pp. 432-433.

39 McCormick, p.129. Compare Curnow's 'peurilities of local origin' (p. 56).

40 Curnow, Introduction, p. 20.

41 See Roger Horrocks, 'The Invention of New Zealand' in *AND* 1, October 1983: 9-30, for a discussion along these lines of *The Penguin Book of New Zealand Verse*.

42 Ezra Pound, 'The Hard and the Soft in French Poetry,' *Literary Essays of Ezra Pound*, ed. T. S. Eliot. (London: Faber and Faber, 1963).

43 Hyde's own phrase for this kind of categorisation of women writers was 'First rate second raters'. See 'Women have No Star', *The Press* 5 June 1937 reprinted in *Disputed Ground*, p. 201.

44 Sandbrook, who began working on Hyde in the 1970s, became a good friend of Challis. Challis was also involved as an adviser in the making of the *Iris* telefeature – which seems to have drawn on the material Sandbrook was uncovering about Hyde's life, and its relation particularly to her writing, as well as on Challis's enthusiasm for the poetry. The film had powerful aspects but was at times difficult to follow – suggesting that the director and screenwriter were assuming a knowledge of Hyde not generally available to their audience. It was criticised (*Broadsheet*) for being poorly made and as a consolatory male fantasy because of its parallel love stories that seemed to appropriate the writer. (A frame narrative shows writer and director planning the movie and casting the actress who is to play Hyde, while within the action the same actor who plays the screenwriter also plays Hyde's doctor.) Unsatisfactory elements were redeemed by the performance of Australian actress Helen Morse and by the use of a strong selection of Hyde's poetry. Notable too is the appearance of Derek Challis, on location at Hokio Beach, discussing the difficulties of dramatisation. Tony Isaac died not long after the making of *Iris* – which he had intended to be the first in a series of television dramas. (For a full account of Tony Isaac's significance to television drama in New Zealand see Trisha Dunleavy, 'New Zealand Television Drama: The First Thirty Years, 1960-1990', PhD thesis, University of Auckland, 1999.)

45 The fullest description of Hyde's work, including unpublished papers, is in the bibliography and 'descriptive inventory of some of Hyde's manuscripts and drafts' an appendix to Patrick Sandbrook's 'Robin Hyde: A Writer at Work,' unpublished PhD thesis, Massey University, 1984. Also see Sandbrook, 'A Descriptive Inventory of Some Manuscripts and Drafts of the Work of Robin Hyde', *Journal of NZ Literature* 4 (1986): 21-47. Two NZ Library School bibliographies cover published work: Jennifer Walls, 'A Bibliography of Robin Hyde (Iris Wilkinson) 1906-39' (1960) and Margaret Scott, 'A Supplementary

Bibliography of Robin Hyde (Iris G. Wilkinson) 1906-39' (1965).

46 *Check to Your King* was also republished, in 1975, by Viking O'Neill, Australia, and reprinted in 1987. However, I do not include this as part of the reassessment of Hyde because it stands as the production of an interesting historical novel, in a series of historical novels, and was not published with an introduction.

47 *The Godwits Fly* had come out in a new edition in 1970 and been reprinted pretty continuously ('74, '80, '84, '93) since then. The 1993 reissue retained Gloria Rawlinson's 1970 introductory essay but instead of the cover illustration designed by Vanya Lowry, it uses a photograph of Hyde that matches the recent University of Otago Press editions. Publishers Wendy Harrex (UOP) and Elizabeth Caffin (AUP) worked together to achieve this series look.

48 See note 45.

49 This project was continued by Derek Challis after Rawlinson's death in July 1995. Challis is revising, rewriting and adding to Rawlinson's substantial but incomplete draft.

50 In addition to Sandbrook see Susan Ash, 'Narrating a Female (Subject)ivity in the Works of Katherine Mansfield, Robin Hyde, Janet Frame and Keri Hulme', PhD thesis, University of Otago, 1991. Elizabeth A. Thomas, 'Appropriation, Subversion and Separatism: The Strategies of Three New Zealand Women Novelists: Jane Mander, Robin Hyde, and Sylvia Ashton-Warner', PhD thesis, University. of Canterbury, 1990. A selection of significant recent theses include: Stephanie Pride, 'A Home in this World: The Representation of Location and Identity in the Prose Fiction Texts of Katherine Mansfield, Robin Hyde and Janet Frame', dissertation, Victoria University, 1993. Tracey Slaughter, 'The Illegitimate Artist: Marginality and Maternity in the Autobiography of Robin Hyde', University of Auckland MA thesis, 1995, and Jane Moloney 'Another Story: Locating Robin Hyde's "The Book of Nadath"', MA thesis, University of Auckland, 1996.

51 Robin Hyde, 'Women Have No Star: Questions Not Answers', *The Press* 5 June 1937 reprinted in *Disputed Ground*, p. 202. The comment is in quote marks because it is part of a dialogue Hyde is informally reporting with a 'redoubtable reviewer'. His final response to her remarks is: 'The conditions aren't under discussion. It's the results that count. The results aren't quite the same as the work of the best men writers' (p. 202).

52 Phillida Bunkle, Linda Hardy and Jacqueline Matthews, Introduction, *Nor The Years Condemn* by Hyde (Auckland:New Women's Press, 1986) p. v.

53 Bunkle, Matthews, Hardy, introduction, p. v.

54 Rawlinson, p.18.

55 Sandbrook, p.1.

56 Sandbrook, p.1.

57 Introduction, *Nor the Years Condemn*, by Hyde, pp xiv-xv.

58 See Susan Ash and Elizabeth Thomas above.

59 Derek Challis, introduction, *A Home in this World*, pp. vii-xxi. Challis had initially offered this manuscript for publication to Blackwood Paul but felt unable to provide the suggested sizeable introduction because of his commitment with Gloria Rawlinson to a biography. Subsequently Challis was approached by Phoebe Meikle (former editor for Paul's), who had apparently kept a copy of the manuscript, and John Barnett of Longman Paul. It was the publisher's suggestion that the fragment 'A Night in Hell' be included with *A Home in this World*.

60 This is true in 1999 but up until the mid 1980s a substantial number of papers were in the possession of Gloria Rawlinson, on loan from Challis to enable her to work on the biography. For more detailed information on the whereabouts of Hyde's papers and manuscripts see Patrick Sandbrook, 'Robin Hyde: A Writer at Work', PhD thesis, Massey University, 1985 and 'A Descriptive Inventory of Some Manuscripts and Drafts of the

Work of Robin Hyde', *Journal of New Zealand Literature* 4 (1986): 21-47. For whereabouts of poetry manuscripts see Michele Leggott, introduction to 'An Inventory of the Poetry Manuscripts of Robin Hyde ca. 1925-1937: Mss and Archives Collection 97/1'. Compiled Leggott and Lisa Docherty (Auckland University Library, 1996): 1-4. For a history of ownership of Hyde's papers see Leggott's introduction to Hyde's previously unpublished long poem *The Book of Nadath,* ed. Michele Leggott (Auckland: Auckland University Press, 1999).

61 Challis, *Home*, p. xii.

62 Challis, *Home*, p. xiii.

63 Derek Challis, introduction, *Dragon Rampant* by Hyde (New Women's Press, 1984); *Iris,* dir. Tony Isaac, screenplay Keith Aberdein, with John Bach, Philip Holder, and Helen Morse, prod. Tony Isaac and John Barnet, Endeavour Productions/Aotea Enterprises, telefeature, 1984. Those of the Hyde papers not already in libraries are, since Gloria Rawlinson's death, in Derek Challis's possession. Challis is working on the biography using the material researched by Rawlinson and himself, as Rawlinson's draft (handed over to Challis shortly before her death in July 1995) and subsequently willed to him after her death, proved to be substantial but incomplete.

64 Robin Hyde, 'Less Happy Parenthood' from *Woman Today,* June 1937, reprinted in *Disputed Ground: Robin Hyde, Journalist* ed. Gillian Boddy and Jacqueline Matthews (Wellington: Victoria University Press, 1991) pp. 198-9.

65 See *A Home in this World*, pp. 36-37 and p. 52.

66 Hyde, 'The Beaches IV' from the sequence 'Houses by the Sea,' *Houses by the Sea*, pp. 116-17.

67 Michele Leggott, '"Sometimes Fighting and Dying are Better Than Anything Else": The poetry of Robin Hyde.' Concert Programme, 1993, p. 4.

68 Michele Leggott, 'Opening the Archive: Robin Hyde, Eileen Duggan and the Persistence of Record', *Opening the Book: New Essays on New Zealand Literature*, ed. Mark Williams and Michele Leggott (Auckland: Auckland University Press, 1995) pp. 270-271.

69 Leggott, 'Something Coming the Other Way: The Distaff line in New Zealand Poetry', unpublished draft, p. 5.

70 Poem 16, from *DIA,* (Auckland:Auckland University Press) 1994, p. 25.

71 Hyde, *Houses by the Sea*, pp. 107-8.

72 Hyde, *A Home in this World*, p. 65.

73 Hyde, *Houses by the Sea*, p. 46.

74 Compare Leggott in 'Opening the Archive: Robin Hyde, Eileen Duggan and the Persistence of Record', p. 278.

75 The dialogue poem 'Husband and Wife' was, for example, published in the *Caxton Miscellany of Poems, Verse, etc*, ed. Denis Glover (Christchurch: Caxton, 1937).

76 Curnow, p. 12.

77 Curnow, p. 57.

78 This manuscript is held in the Auckland Public Library.

79 Curnow, p.12. Reviews of Glover, Curnow, Fairburn and Sargeson from the *Auckland Observer* are reprinted in *Disputed Ground*, pp. 211-212, pp. 228-231 and p. 327. Also see the article on Bastion Point pp. 319-322 and pp. 334-344.

80 Boddy and Matthews, *Disputed Ground*, p. 79.

81 Sandbrook, pp. 67-69.

82 Sandbrook, p. 68.

83 Hyde, from 'First Version' *Godwits Fly*, typescript, pp.145-146. Quoted in Sandbrook p. 67.

84 See Sandbrook, pp. 52-53. Hyde describes herself as about to 'have a shot at the

supernormal' (p. 53).

85 Sylvia Plath, letter to her mother, *Letters Home: Correspondence, 1950-1963* (London: Faber and Faber, 1977) p. 473.

86 Hyde quoted in Sandbrook, p. 52.

87 Sandbrook, pp. 51-52.

88 Undergraduate essays about this poem often suggest that it is addressed to the poet's mother. A longer manuscript version of the poem held in the Auckland University Library has an extra verse which does identify the 'you' as 'mother' in its last three lines: 'Mothers aren't old, and yet they think so old. / Anyhow, you were counting up a sleeve,/ Two plain, two purl . . . Therefore it wasn't told.' The Beaches, typescripts and worksheets, Poetry Manuscripts of Robin Hyde 1925–1937, Mss and Archive Collection 97/1, University of Auckland Library.

89 See for example James K. Baxter, 'Pig Island Letters' and 'The Succubus': *Collected Poems*, ed. J. E. Weir (Wellington: Oxford University Press) pp. 330-331.

90 See Elizabeth Thomas, 'Appropriation and Subversion', p. 174. For other related comments see the whole of her section 'The Misogynism of the Literary Establishment', pp. 172-185. See also Kai Jensen, *Whole Men: The Masculine Tradition in NZ Literature* (Auckland: AUP, 1996) and Stuart Murray, *Never a Soul at Home: NZ literary nationalism and the 1930s* (Wellington: VUP, 1998).

91 Charles Brasch, *Indirections: A Memoir* (Wellington: Oxford University Press, 1980) p. 340.

92 'Opening the Archive: Robin Hyde, Eileen Duggan and the Persistence of Record', pp. 272 and 274.

93 *Houses by the Sea*, p.133. Note that *Selected Poems* (ed. Lydia Wevers) prints this poem as 'young' rather than 'your' thus missing this particular irony. However, there are multiple versions of many of the poems and this is no exception. In *Art NZ* in 1938 and *NZ Best Poems* in 1939, both selections made by Charles Marris, it appears as "young"; this version is continued in Curnow's anthologies (1945 and 1960) but Gloria Rawlinson, presumably working from another typescript, prints 'your'. There is no copy of the poem held in the Auckland University archive.

94 It is on this basis that Michele Leggott argues that Hyde belongs to an older 'female tradition of poets whose stock in trade is cultural continuity. . . . Hyde, Duggan, Mackay, Baughan and Bethell all transmit a humanistic warmth'. See Leggott, 'Opening the Archive: Robin Hyde, Eileen Duggan and the Persistence of Record', p. 274.

95 Bunkle was to have been one of the editorial group in this third project which she had also initiated, but for personal and professional reasons Jacqueline Matthews took over Bunkle's role. Wendy Harrex of New Women's Press was also an important figure; she published, in the New Women's Classics Series, *Dragon Rampant, Nor The Years Condemn*, and *Wednesday's Children*, and encouraged Bunkle and Matthews to work on the biographical essay and journalism project.

96 Phillida Bunkle and Sandra Coney, 'An Unfortunate Experiment at National Women's', *Metro Magazine*, 1 June 1987: 46-65.

97 Stephen Danby, review of *Nor the Years Condemn*, *NZ Times* 11 May 1986: 13; review of *Passport to Hell*, *NZ Sunday Times* 1 February 1987: 15. Danby's reviews attempt to undermine and make more complex what he seems to perceive as Hyde's reputation for 'political correctness'.

CHAPTER SIX

1 John Dos Passos, quoted in Linda W. Wagner, *Dos Passos, Artist as American* (Austin: University of Texas Press, 1979) p. 30.

2 Ruth Park, *A Fence Around the Cuckoo* (Ringwood, Victoria: Viking, 1992) p. 224. Park

left New Zealand in the late 1930s to live in Australia where she had a successful career as a novelist, a happy marriage and five children.

3   This student seminar thus drew on material very similar to that used by Michele Leggott in the compilation of her poem sequence 'Blue Irises'. See particularly 'Poem 16', beginning 'Coming home like a derelict Egyptian, changing/worlds, a baby delivered in a jacaranda mist *just/ like mine . . .* ' from *DIA,* (Auckland: Auckland University Press) 1994, p. 25. The poems on her seminar handout were 'Running Water' (1927), 'In Memory' (1927), 'Ghosts' (1929), 'Division' (1929), and from the thirties: 'Jacaranda' (1935), 'Hillside'(1935), 'Absalom' (1936-7), and 'Isabel's Baby' (1937).

4   MacD. P. Jackson, 'Poetry', in *The Oxford History of New Zealand Literature,* ed. Terry Sturm (Auckland: OUP, 1998) p. 340. I would see this oversight as to do with what I have shown to be the original orthodoxy on Hyde, which meant that Jackson was not prompted to reassess Hyde's lesser known poems when planning his survey.

5   W.H. Oliver, 'The Awakening Imagination, 1940-1980,' in *The Oxford History of New Zealand,* ed. Geoffrey W. Rice, 2nd edn (Auckland: OUP, 1992) p. 541.

6   Oliver, p. 549.

7   Rachel Barrowman, *A Popular Vision: The Arts and the Left in New Zealand 1930-1950,* (Wellington: VUP, 1991). See also *Women in History: Essays on European Women in New Zealand,* ed. Barbara Brookes, Charlotte Macdonald and Margaret Tennant (Wellington: Allen and Unwin/Port Nicholson Press, 1986) and *Women in History 2: Essays on Women in New Zealand,* ed. Barbara Brookes, Charlotte Macdonald and Margaret Tennant (Wellington: Bridget Williams Books, 1992). Keith Rankin's 'Labour Supply in New Zealand and Australia: 1919-1939,' unpublished MA thesis, Victoria University, 1990, looks at the effects of the Great Depression on the supply of female labour and suggests (amongst other things) that the depression of the thirties and not the Second World War changed the pattern of female employment (see pp. 189-195).

8   Robin Hyde, 'The New Zealand Woman in Letters', *The Working Woman,* April, 1936 reprinted in *Disputed Ground: Robin Hyde, Journalist,* ed. Gillian Boddy and Jacqueline Matthews (Wellington: Victoria University Press, 1991) p. 190.

9   Robin Hyde, 'Rhythmn and Reality, Young New Zealanders' Verse,' review of *Six Easy Ways of Dodging Debt Collectors,* by Denis Glover, *New Zealand Observer* 26 October 1936, reprinted in *Disputed Ground,* pp. 211-12.

10 For discussions that tend to separate the social realist and visionary see Phillida Bunkle, Linda Hardy, Jacqueline Matthews, introduction, *Nor the Years Condemn* (Auckland: New Women's Press, 1986) pp xvii-xxvi on that novel, and Eric McCormick (*New Zealand Literature: A Survey*) on *Godwits Fly* versus *Wednesday's Children* (p. 128).

11 David Carter, 'Documenting and Criticising Society', *The Penguin New Literary History of Australia,* ed. Laurie Hergenhan (Ringwood, Vic: Penguin, 1988) p. 371.

12 See, for example, Patrick Sandbrook's chapter 'The Uses of Art,' pp. 28-78 and Michele Leggott, Introduction, *The Book of Nadath.* (Auckland: AUP, 1999).

13 Hyde, *Nor the Years,* p. 251.

14 Hyde, *Godwits,* p. 374.

15 In 1936, the year she began *The Godwits Fly* and the year of the first Starkie novel, *Passport to Hell,* Hyde made just such a prilgrimage 'in search of her own country'. See Gloria Rawlinson, Introduction, *Houses by the Sea* (Christchurch: Caxton, 1952) p. 17.

16 Hyde, 'The Singers of Loneliness', *T'ien Hsia Monthly* August 1938, reprinted in *Disputed Ground,* pp. 347-358.

17 See W.H. Oliver, 'The Awakening Imagination, 1940–1980', *The Oxford History of New Zealand,* pp. 539-541.

18 Hyde, *Nor the Years,* p. 163.

19 Hyde, *Nor the Years*, p. 165.
20 Linda Hardy, Introduction, *Nor the Years Condemn*, p xxv. Hardy's authorship of this section of the multi-authored introduction is not indicated in the essay but I know of it as I was an editorial adviser for New Women's Press at the time it was published.
21 Barrowman makes many comments on how writing that could be understood as internationalist is made to look nationalist. See for example her comments on the 'production' of Frank Sargeson (p. 154).
22 See Nick Perry, 'Flying by Nets' chapter 7 in *Dominion of Signs: Television, Advertising and other New Zealand Fictions* (Auckland: Auckland University Press, 1994) and David Carter 'Documenting and Criticising Society' in *The Penguin New Literary History of Australia*, pp. 370-389.
23 Carter, pp. 370-371.
24 Carter, p. 371.
25 W.H. Pearson, Introduction, *Frank Sargeson Collected Stories 1936-1963* (Auckland: Blackwood and Janet Paul, 1964) p. 9.
26 Perry, p. 117.
27 Hyde, letter to John Schroder, August 1934, quoted in Patrick Sandbrook 'Robin Hyde: A Writer at Work,' PhD thesis, Massey University, 1986, p. 93.
28 Robin Hyde, note dated July 22nd [1936], quoted in Gloria Rawlinson, Introduction, *The Godwits Fly* (Auckland: Auckland University Press/Oxford Univ. Press, 1980) p. xv.
29 John Dos Passos, quoted in Linda W. Wagner, *Dos Passos, Artist as American* (Austin: University of Texas Press, 1979) p. 48.
30 John Dos Passos, quoted in Wagner, p. 30.
31 Hyde, *Godwits Fly*, p. 119.
32 Hyde, *Godwits Fly*, p. 47.
33 John Dos Passos, *The Garbage Man* (1926) quoted in John H. Wren, *John Dos Passos*, Twayne's US Authors Series (New Haven: College Univ. Press, 1961) pp. 134-135.
34 Hyde, *Godwits Fly*, pp. 31-32.
35 Robin Hyde, letter to John Schroder, 12 Dec. 1933 (Letter 71) quoted in Sandbrook, p. 53.
36 Hyde, *Godwits*, p. 113.
37 Hyde, *Godwits*, p. 117.
38 Hyde, *Godwits*, p. 53.
39 Hyde, *Godwits*, p. 69.
40 Hyde, *Godwits*, pp. 137-38
41 Hyde, *Godwits*, p. 139.
42 Hyde, *Godwits*, pp. 140-41.
43 Robin Hyde, *Nor the Years Condemn*, p. 119.
44 Carter, p. 371.
45 Carter, p. 371.
46 Carter, p. 374.
47 Linda W. Wagner, *Dos Passos*, p. 47.
48 Ann Jefferson, 'To Think about Women' review of *Civilisation without Sexes: Reconstructing Gender in Postwar France* by Mary Louise Roberts (Chicago: University of Chicago Press, 1994) in *Times Literary Supplement* Jan 6 1995: 26.
49 Hyde, *Nor the Years*, p. 270.
50 Hyde, *Nor the Years*, pp. 269-270.
51 Ann Jefferson review, *Times Literary Supplement* 6 January 1995: 26.
52 Renée's play *Wednesday to Come* (Wellington: Victoria Univ. Press, 1985) and its sequels *Pass It On* (Wellington: Victoria Univ. Press, 1986) and *Jeanie Once* (Victoria University

Press, 1991) address episodes in New Zealand history where women have had an significant but unrecognised political role. Particularly relevant to my discussion is *Wednesday to Come* which is set in the depression during a protest march and tells the story of female endurance and male fragility under these intolerable stresses.

53 Barbara Brookes, 'Reproductive Rights: The Debate Over Abortion and Birth Control in the 1930s', *Women in History: Essays on European Women in New Zealand,* ed. Brookes, Macdonald and Tennant, p. 119.

54 See Anne Else, '"The Need is Ever Present": The Motherhood of Man Movement and Stranger Adoption in New Zealand', and Margaret Tennant, '"Magdalens and Moral Imbeciles": Women's Homes in Nineteenth Century New Zealand', both in *Women in History 2,* ed. Brookes, Macdonald and Tennnant, pp. 225-253 and 49-75.

55 The 'nearly-new New Zealand school' is a phrase of Hyde's in her reviews. 'New New Zealand' school I am assuming was probably the Caxton poets' self-description. See *Disputed Ground,* p. 228.

56 In *Houses by the Sea,* pp. 65-69. See Appendix.

57 A recent exception is Michele Leggott's feminist reading, 'Opening the Archive: Robin Hyde, Eileen Duggan and the Persistence of Record', in *Opening the Book: New Essays on New Zealand Writing,* ed. Mark Williams and Michele Leggott (Auckland: AUP, 1995) pp. 273-274.

58 Hyde, letter to John A. Lee, March 10 1936. (Transcribed by Lisa Docherty) Auckland Public Library, Letter 3. A version is also in Bridget Shadbolt, 'Commonplaces: the Letters of Robin Hyde and John A Lee 1935-1939', MA thesis, University of Auckland, 1995, pp. 19-21.

59 Hyde, letter 16 March 1936, Shadbolt, p. 23.

60 Patrick Sandbrook, p. 39.

61 Robin Hyde *A Home in this World,* (Auckland: Longman Paul, 1984) p. 12; also quoted in introduction to *Nor the Years Condemn,* p. xxiii.

62 In saying this I am querying the established designation of Hyde as liberal humanist and as a sentimental individual struggling to represent the world as she felt it, and also the perception of her as being old-fashioned and anti-avant garde. Seen in a less positivist historical perspective her correspondence with John A. Lee, for instance, can be understood as an opportunity for her to contemplate a development of a style sufficient to her socialism, and his incitements to her to create 'themes for poetry that have the hot news value of 1936' as useful rather than hackneyed (Letter 7 March 1936, Shadbolt, p. 17).
Another relevant angle may be Fredric Jameson's contention about Walter Benjamin and Bertolt Brecht and this period: '... Brecht and Benjamin had not yet begun to feel the full force and constriction of that stark alternative between a mass audience or media culture, and a minority elite modernism in which our thinking about aesthetics today is inevitably locked.' Afterword, *Aesthetics and Politics,* Verso (London: New Left Books, 1977) p. 207.

63 Sandbrook, p. 62.

64 Sandbrook, p. 43 and p. 54.

65 Michele Leggott, 'Opening the Archive: Robin Hyde, Eileen Duggan and the Persistence of Record,' pp. 273-274.

66 Robin Hyde, *Dragon Rampant* (Auckland: New Women's Press, 1984) p. 76.

67 Barbara Brookes in *Women in History: Essays on European Women in New Zealand,* ed. Brookes, Macdonald and Tennant, pp. 119-136.

68 See Brookes, p. 128.

69 Brookes, p. 131.

70 Brookes, p. 134.

71 Hyde, 'Less Happy Parenthood: The Problem of the Unmarried Mother,' *Woman Today* June 1937, reprinted in *Disputed Ground*, pp. 198-201.

72 Hyde, 'Less Happy Parenthood,' p. 200.

73 Hyde, 'Less Happy Parenthood,' p. 201.

74 John Dos Passos, *The Big Money*, Vol III of *USA*, The Modern Library, (New York: Random House, 1937) p. 127.

75 John Dos Passos, *The Big Money*, Vol III of *USA*, The Modern Library (New York: Random House, 1937) p. 148.

76 Robin Hyde, *A Home in this World*, p. 36. However, Lonnie did in fact send 'nearly all the money for nursing home and doctor, and a good deal it was'. *A Home in this World*, p. 50.

77 Hyde, *A Home in this World*, p. 61.

78 Hyde, *Godwits*, p. 191.

79 Robin Hyde, *Wednesday's Children* (Auckland: New Women's Press, 1989) p. 58.

80 Robin Hyde, *Dragon Rampant* (Auckland: New Women's Press, 1984) p. 139.

81 Angela Carter, 'Notes from the Frontline,' in *On Gender and Writing*, ed. M. Wandor (London/ Boston: Pandora Press, 1983) p. 71.

82 Hyde, *Nor the Years*, p. 300.

83 Hyde, *Nor the Years*, p. 316.

84 Hyde, *Godwits*, p. 169.

85 Hyde, *Godwits*, pp. 169-70.

86 Many passages from Hyde's *A Home in this World* indicate Hyde was looking for a way of describing her own life without being self-pitying. One strategy is humour – she contrasts her own experience with an idealised fairy-tale life: 'In films and novels, the mothers of illegitimate children invariably died; or, with a fade-out scene of sacrifice, went on the streets and passed unrecognised, their remarkably good-looking, intelligent and able children, who had meanwhile beeen adopted either by rich women or by famous scientists. I remained inconveniently half-alive with insurance policies of several hundred pounds, suicide proof. It wasn't natural.' (p.100)
Another strategy was to question the idea of 'fault' or cause so that possible bitterness is countered with humour and suggestions of frivolous as against sensible desires: 'Was it Lonnie's fault that I had a baby instead of an abortion, lost a job, hunted about like a vixen whose earths have been stopped up, got another job, found the work too much, would like to throw the social pages in the silly women's faces, tell them to tear them to pieces with their silly red talons, took morphia, read Swinburne, wanted love more than anything on earth and spent money on deep velvety purple gladioli, instead of devoting it decently to sensible purposes?' (pp. 99-100).

87 Hyde, *Godwits*, pp. 130 and 134.

88 Hyde, *Godwits*, pp. 133-34. Iris Tree was an English modernist poet of the 1920s.

89 Hyde, *Godwits*, p. 134.

90 Patricia Grace, *Potiki* (Auckland: Viking, 1986).

91 This incident can also be paralleled with the chapter on Australian city girls in *Nor the Years Condemn* (see p. 218 and pp. 230-31).

92 Though Timothy's socialism does not stop him acting as 'scab labour', replacing a jailed English seaman on the ship he sails on to England – one of the many contradictions Hyde seems to have created in this character.

Conclusion

1 David Bordwell, *Making Meaning: Inference and Rhetoric in the Interpretation of Cinema* (Cambridge: Harvard University Press, 1989) p. 274.

2 Bordwell, p. 262.

3   Robert Hodge, *Literature as Discourse: Textual Strategies in English and History* (Cambridge: Polity Press, 1990) p. 18.

4   Bordwell, p. 265.

5   Gina Mercer, *Janet Frame: Subversive Fictions* (Dunedin: University of Otago Press, 1994). Mercer's discussion of Frame's autobiographies and her later works is particularly interesting, bringing in the extratextual questions of Frame's public image and Frame's 'corrections' of it.

6   Bordwell, p. 266.

7   Susan Sontag, *Against Interpretation* (London: Eyre and Spottiswoode, 1967) p. 13.

Bibliography

BOOKS, THESES AND ESSAYS IN PERIODICALS

Alpers, Antony. *The Life of Katherine Mansfield*. New York: Viking, 1980.

— ed. 'Commentary.' *The Stories of Katherine Mansfield*. Definitive Edition. Auckland: Oxford University Press, 1988. 543-76.

Anderson, Benedict. *Imagined Communities: Reflections on the Origin and Spread of Nationalism*. London: Verso, 1983.

Armstrong, Nancy. *Desire and Domestic Fiction: A Political History of the Novel*. Oxford: Oxford University Press, 1987.

Ash, Susan. 'Narrating a Female Subject(ivity) in the Works of Katherine Mansfield, Robin Hyde, Janet Frame and Keri Hulme.' PhD thesis. University of Otago, 1991.

— Introduction and critical afterword. *Wednesday's Children*. By Robin Hyde. Auckland: New Women's Press, 1989. 5-8 and 289-96.

Ashcroft, Bill, Gareth Griffiths, and Helen Tiffin, eds *The Post-Colonial Studies Reader*. London: Routledge, 1994.

Atwood, Margaret. *Bluebeard's Egg and Other Stories*. London: Jonathan Cape, 1987.

Azim, Firdous. *The Colonial Rise of the Novel*. London: Routledge, 1993.

Barclay, Barry. *Our Own Image*. Auckland: Longman Paul, 1990.

Barker, Mary (Lady). *Station Life in New Zealand*. 1870. London: Virago, 1984.

Barnard, Marjorie. *Miles Franklin: The Story of a Famous Australian*. St Lucia: University of Queensland Press, 1988.

Barnard Eldershaw, M. *Tomorrow and Tomorrow*. Melbourne: Georgian House, 1947.

Barrowman, Rachel. *A Popular Vision: The Arts and the Left in New Zealand, 1930-1950*. Wellington: Victoria University Press, 1991.

Barthes, Roland. *S/Z*. Trans. Richard Miller. New York: Hill and Wang, 1987.

Bartlett, Alison. 'The Representation of History in Recent Fiction by Australian Women Writers.' *Southerly* 53 (March 1993): 165-79.

Baxter, James K. *Collected Poems*, ed. J. E. Weir. Wellington: Oxford University Press, 1979.

— 'Symbolism in New Zealand Poetry.' *James K. Baxter As Critic*. Selected J.E. Weir. Auckland: Heinemann Educational, 1978. 50-70.

Beatson, Peter. *The Healing Tongue*. Palmerston North: Massey University, 1989.

Belich, James. *Making Peoples: A History of the New Zealanders from Polynesian Settlement to the End of the Nineteenth Century*. Auckland: Allen Lane, 1996.

Bennett, Tony. *Formalism and Marxism*. New Accents. London: Methuen, 1986.

Bernheimer, Charles, and Claire Kahane, eds *In Dora's Case: Freud, Hysteria, Feminism*. London: Virago, 1985.

Bhabha, Homi K. 'Signs Taken for Wonders: Questions of Ambivalence and Authority under a Tree outside Delhi, May 1817.' *The Location of Culture*. By Bhabha. London, Routledge, 1994. 102-22.

— 'DissemiNation: Time, Narrative and the Margins of the Modern Nation.' in *Nation and Narration*. Homi K. Bhabha, ed. London: Routledge, 1990. 291-322.

Black, Max. 'Metaphor.' *Philosophical Perspectives on Metaphor*, ed. Mark Johnson. Minneapolis: University of Minnesota Press.

Blythe, Martin. *Naming the Other: Images of the Maori in New Zealand Film and Television*. Metuchen, N.J.: Scarecrow, 1994.

Boddy, Gillian and Jacqueline Matthews. Introductory essays. *Disputed Ground: Robin Hyde, Journalist,* ed. Boddy and Matthews. Wellington: Victoria University Press, 1991. 3-141.

Bordwell, David. *Making Meaning, Inference and Rhetoric in the Interpretation of Cinema*. Harvard Film Series. Cambridge: Harvard University Press, 1989.

Brasch, Charles. *Collected Poems*, ed. Alan Roddick. Auckland: Oxford University Press, 1984.

— *Indirections: A Memoir 1909-1947.* Wellington: Oxford University Press, 1980

Brontë, Charlotte. *Jane Eyre*. 1847. New York: Norton, 1987.

Brooks, Peter. *The Pursuit of Signs*. London: Routledge, 1981.

Brookes, Barbara, Charlotte Macdonald, and Margaret Tennant, eds *Women in History: Essays on European Women in New Zealand*. Wellington: Allen and Unwin/ Port Nicholson, 1986.

— Charlotte Macdonald, and Margaret Tennant, eds *Women in History 2: Essays on Women in New Zealand*. Wellington: Bridget Williams, 1992.

— and Margaret Tennant. 'Maori and Pakeha Women: Many Histories, Divergent Pasts?' *Women in History 2: Essays on Women in New Zealand*: 25-48.

Brooks, Cleanth, and Robert Penn Warren.*Understanding Fiction*. New York: Appleton-Century-Crofts, 1959.

Brown, Gillian. *Domestic Individualism: Imagining Self in the Nineteenth Century Novel*. Berkeley: University of California Press, 1990.

Brownstein, Rachel. *Becoming a Heroine: Reading about Women in Novels*. London: Penguin, 1984.

Bruzzi, Stella. 'Jane Campion: Costume Drama and Reclaiming Women's Past.' *Sight and Sound Reader*, ed. Pam Cook and Philip Dodd. London: Scarlet Press, 1995. 232-42.

Bunkle, Phillida, and Beryl Hughes, eds *Women in New Zealand Society*. Auckland: Allen and Unwin, 1980.

Bunkle, Phillida, Linda Hardy, and Jacqueline Matthews. Introduction. *Nor the Years Condemn*. By Robin Hyde. Auckland: New Women's Press, 1986. v-xxvi.

Butler, Judith. *Gender Trouble and the Subversion of Identity.* New York: Routledge, 1990.

Calder, Alex, ed. *The Writing of New Zealand: Inventions and Identities*. Auckland: Reed, 1993.

Campion, Jane. 'The Dent.' *Sport* 8 (1992): 15-28.

— Interview. *Cinema Papers* 93 (May 1993): 4-11.

— *The Piano: the Screenplay*. London: Bloomsbury, 1993.

— and Kate Pullinger. *The Piano: A Novel*. London: Bloomsbury, 1994.

Caughey, Angela. *Pioneer Families: The Settlers of Nineteenth Century New Zealand*. Auckland: David Bateman, 1994.

Carter, Angela. 'Notes from the Frontline.' *On Gender and Writing,* ed. Michelene Wandor. London/ Boston: Pandora Press, 1983. 69-77.

— *Nothing Sacred: Selected Writings*. London: Virago, 1982.

— *The Passion of the New Eve*. London: Penguin, 1977.

— *The Sadeian Woman: An Exercise in Cultural History.* London: Virago, 1979.

Carter, David. 'Documenting and Criticising Society.' *The Penguin New Literary History of Australia*, ed. Laurie Hergenhan. Ringwood, Vic.: Penguin, 1988. 370-89.

Carter, Paul. *The Road to Botany Bay: An Essay in Spatial History.* London: Faber, 1987.

Challis, Derek. Introduction. *A Home in this World.* By Robin Hyde. Auckland: Longman Paul, 1984. vii-xii.

Chatman, Seymour. *Story and Discourse: Narrative Structure in Fiction and Film.* Ithaca: Cornell University Press, 1978.

Chodorow, Nancy. *The Reproduction of Mothering: Psychoanalysis and the Sociology of Gender.* Berkeley: University of California Press, 1978.

Cixous, Helene. 'The Laugh of the Medusa', trans. Keith and Paula Cohen. *Signs* 1 (Summer 1976): 875-893.

Clement, Catherine. *The Lives and Legends of Jacques Lacan*, trans. Arthur Goldhammer. New York: Columbia University Press, 1983.

— *The Weary Sons of Freud.* Trans. Nicole Ball. London: Verso, 1987.

Clifford, James. *The Predicament of Culture: Twentieth Century Literature, Ethnography and Art.* Cambridge: Harvard University Press, 1988.

Coward, Rosalind and John Ellis. *Developments in Semiology and the Theory of the Subject.* London: Routledge, 1977.

Crews, Frederick. 'The Unknown Freud.' *Times Literary Supplement* 18 November 1993: 55-65.

Culler, Jonathan. *Structuralist Poetics: Structuralism, Linguistics and the Study of Literature.* Ithaca: Cornell University Press, 1975.

— 'Beyond Interpretation: The Prospects of Contemporary Criticism.' *Comparative Literature* 28 (1979): 244-56.

Curnow, Allen. Introduction. *A Book of New Zealand Verse: 1923-45*, ed. Curnow. Christchurch: The Caxton Press, 1945. 13-55.

— Introduction. *The Penguin Book of New Zealand Verse*, ed. Curnow. Auckland: Penguin, 1960. 1-77.

— *Collected Poems 1933-73.* Wellington: Reed, 1974.

Dalziel, Raewyn. 'The Colonial Helpmeet.' *Women in History: Essays on European Women in New Zealand*, ed. Brookes, Macdonald, and Tennant. Wellington: Allen and Unwin, 1986. 55-68.

— 'Women in New Societies.' *New Worlds? The Comparative History of New Zealand and the United States*, ed. Jock Phillips. Wellington: New Zealand/ United States Educational Foundation, Stout Centre, 1989. 9-27.

Davis, Leigh. *Willy's Gazette.* Wellington: Jack Books, 1983.

Davidoff, Lenore, Megan Doolittle, Janet Fink and Katherine Holden. *The Family Story: Blood, Contract and Intimacy, 1830-1960.* Women and Men in History Series. London: Longman, 1999.

Denis, Jonathan and Jan Bieringa. *Film in Aotearoa, New Zealand.* Wellington: Victoria University Press, 1992.

Derrida, Jacques. 'The Purveyor of Truth', trans. Alan Bass. *Yale French Studies* 52 (1975): 31-114.

Devanny, Jean. *The Butcher Shop.* 1926. Auckland: Auckland University Press, 1981.

— *Cindie: A Chronicle of the Canefields.* 1949. London: Virago, 1986.

— *Point of Departure: The Autobiography of Jean Devanny,* ed. Carole Ferrier. St Lucia: University of Queeensland Press, 1986.

Diamond, Irene, and Lee Quimby, eds *Feminism and Foucault: Reflections on Resistance.* Boston: Northeastern University Press, 1988.

Dixson, Miriam. *The Real Matilda: Woman and Identity in Australia, 1788-1975.* Ringwood, Vic.: Penguin, 1976.

Donley, Joan. *Save the Midwife.* Auckland: New Women's Press, 1986.

Dos Passos, John. *USA.* The Modern Library. New York: Random House, 1937.

Dunbar, Pamela. *Radical Mansfield: Double Discourses in Katherine Mansfield's Short Stories.* Basingstoke: Macmillan, 1997.

—'What Does Bertha Want? A Re-Reading of "Bliss".' *Women's Studies Journal* (NZ) 4.2 (December 1988): 18-31.

Dunleavy, Trish. 'New Zealand Television Drama: The First Thirty Years, 1960-1990.' PhD thesis, University of Auckland, 1999.

Dunscombe, Suzanne and Felicity O'Brien, eds *Piano Lessons.* Sydney: Currency Press, 1996.

du Plessis, Rachel Blau. 'Pater-Daughter: Male Modernists-Female Readers.' *The Pink Guitar: Writing as Feminist Practice.* New York: Routledge, 1990. 30-51.

Dyson, Lynda. 'Post-Colonial Anxieties and the Representation of Nature and Culture in the Piano.' *Sites* 30 (Autumn 1995): 119-130.

During, Simon. 'Towards a Revision of Local Critical Habits.' *AND* 1 (1983): 75-92.

— 'What Was the West? Some Relations Between Modernity, Colonisation and Writing.' *Sport* 4 (1990): 69-89.

Eagleton, Terry. *Literary Theory.* Oxford: Basil Blackwell, 1983.

— 'The End of English.' *Textual Practice* 1.1 (Spring 1987): 1-9.

— *Myths of Power: A Marxist Study of the Brontes.* London: Macmillan Press, 1988.

— 'Two Approaches in the Sociology of Literature.' *Critical Inquiry* 14. (Spring 1988): 469-76.

Eggleton, David. 'Grimm Fairytale of the South Seas.' *Illusions* 23 (1994): 3-5.

Edmond, Murray, and Mary Paul, eds *The New Poets: Initiatives in New Zealand Poetry.* Wellington: Allen and Unwin, 1987.

Eldred-Grigg, Stevan. *Pleasures of the Flesh: Sex and Drugs in Colonial New Zealand, 1840-1915.* Wellington: Reed, 1984.

Else, Anne. '"The need is ever present": The Motherhood of Man Movement and Stranger Adoption in New Zealand.' *Women in History 2,* ed. Brookes, Macdonald, and Tennant. Wellington: Bridget Williams, 1992. 225-53.

Ensing, Riemke. *Private Gardens: An Anthology of New Zealand Women Poets.* Dunedin: Caveman, 1977.

Evans, Patrick. *The Penguin History of New Zealand Literature.* Auckland: Penguin, 1990.

Evans, Sara M. *Born for Liberty: A History of Women in America.* New York: Free Press, 1985.

Fairburn, Miles. *The Ideal Society and Its Enemies: The Foundations of Modern Society 1850-1900.* Auckland: Auckland University Press, 1989.

Felman, Shoshana. 'Turning the Screw of Interpretation.' *Yale French Studies.* 55-56 (1977): 94-207.

Ferrier, Carole, ed. *As Good as a Yarn with You: Letters between Miles Franklin, Katherine Susannah Pritchard, Jean Devanny, Marjorie Barnard, Flora Eldershaw and Eleanor Dark.* Cambridge: Cambridge University Press, 1992.

— ed. *Gender, Politics and Fiction: Twentieth Century Australian Women's Novels.* St

Lucia: University of Queensland Press, 1992.

Fetterley, Judith. *The Resisting Reader: A Feminist Approach to American Fiction.* Bloomington: Indiana University Press, 1979.

Fish, Stanley. *Is there a Text in this Class? The Authority of Interpretive Communities.* Cambridge: Harvard University Press, 1980.

Flower MacCannell, Juliet. *Figuring Lacan: Criticism and the Cultural Unconscious.* London: Croom Helm, 1986.

Flynn, Elizabeth A., and Patrocinio P. Schweickart, eds *Gender and Reading: Essays on Readers, Texts and Contexts.* Baltimore: Johns Hopkins University Press, 1986.

Forerunners. Periodical. Havelock North and Hastings, 1912-20. Collection Alexander Turnbull Library.

Foucault, Michel. *The History of Sexuality.* Vol 1. Trans. Robert Hurley. New York: Vintage Books, 1980.

— *Power/ Knowledge: Selected Interviews and Other Writings 1972-1977*, ed. Colin Gordon. Brighton: Harvester Press, 1980.

Frame, Janet. *The Carpathians.* Auckland: Century Hutchinson, 1988.

Franklin, Miles. *My Brilliant Career.* 1901. North Ryde: Angus and Robertson, 1980.

Freud, Sigmund. 'The Aetiology of Hysteria.' 1896. 'The Neuro Psychoses of Defence.' 1894. *The Standard Edition of the Complete Psychological Works of Sigmund Freud.* Vol. 3. 2nd edition. London: Hogarth Press, 1962. 189-221 and 43-68.

— 'Fragment of an Analysis of Hysteria.' 1905. 'Three Essays on the Theory of Sexuality.' 1905. *The Standard Edition of the Complete Psychological Works*. Vol. 7. 1st edition. London: Hogarth Press, 1953. 3-112 and 135-244.

— *Civilisation and Its Discontents.* London: Hogarth, 1988.

Frost, Robert. *Poems.* New York: Washington Square, 1962.

Fullbrook, Kate. *Katherine Mansfield.* Key Women Writers Series. Brighton: Harvester Press, 1986.

Gallop, Jane. 'Keys to Dora.' *In Dora's Case: Freud, Hysteria, Feminism*, ed. Charles Bernheimer and Claire Kahane. London: Virago, 1985. 200-220.

Gardner, Susan. 'Portrait of the Artist as a Wild Colonial Girl.' *Gender, Politics and Fiction, Twentieth Century Australian Women's Novels*, ed. Carole Ferrier. St Lucia: Queensland University Press, 1985. 22-43.

Gilbert, Pam. *Coming Out from Under: Contemporary Australian Women Writers.* Australian Literary Heritage. London: Pandora, 1988.

Glover, Denis, ed. *Caxton Miscellany of Poems, Verse, etc.* Christchurch: Caxton, 1937.

Gordon, Ian. 'Katherine Mansfield, New Zealander.' *New Zealand New Writing 3*, ed. Ian Gordon. Wellington: Progressive Books, 1944. 58-63.

Grosskurth, Phyllis. 'The New Psychology of Women.' *New York Review of Books* 24 October 1991: 25-32.

Grosz, Elizabeth. *Sexual Subversions.* Sydney: Allen and Unwin, 1989.

Grace, Patricia. *Potiki.* Auckland: Viking, 1986.

Grimshaw, Patricia. *Women's Suffrage in New Zealand.* Auckland: Auckland University Press, 1972.

Gubar, Susan. 'The Birth of the Artist as Heroine.' *The Representation of Women in Fiction.* ed. Carolyn Heilbrun and Margaret Higonnets. Baltimore: John Hopkins University Press, 1983. 19-59.

Guthrie-Smith, W. H. *Tutira: The Story of a New Zealand Sheep Station.* 1921. 2nd edition. Edinburgh: Blackwood and Sons, 1926.

Hankin, Cherry, ed. *Critical Essays on the New Zealand Novel.* Auckland: Heinemann Educational, 1976.

Hanson, Clare, ed. *The Critical Writings of Katherine Mansfield.* Basingstoke: Macmillan, 1987

— and Andrew Gurr. *Katherine Mansfield.* Commonwealth Writers Series. London: Macmillan, 1981.

Hardy, Ann. 'The Last Patriarch.' *Illusions* 23 (1994): 6-13.

Hardy, Linda. 'The Ghost of Katherine Mansfield.' *Landfall* 172 (1989): 416-32.

Hawkes, Terence. *Times Literary Supplement* 10 April 1987: 390-93.

Hergenhan, Laurie, ed. *The Penguin New Literary History of Australia.* Ringwood, Victoria: Penguin, 1988.

Holub, Robert C. *Reception Theory: A Critical Introduction.* New Accents. London: Methuen, 1984.

Horrocks, Roger. 'The Invention of New Zealand.' *AND* 1 (1983): 1-30.

Hurst & Blackett's Spring Announcements, 1936. Advertisements in end papers. *Passport to Hell.* By Robin Hyde. London: Hurst and Blackett, 1936. 1-48.

Hurst & Blackett's Spring Announcements, 1939. Advertisement in endpapers. *Dragon Rampant.* By Robin Hyde. London: Hurst and Blackett, 1936. 1-16.

Hutcheon, Linda. *Parody: A Theory of the Teachings of Twentieth Century Art Forms.* New York: Methuen, 1985.

— *The Politics of Postmodernism.* London: Routledge, 1989.

Hyde, Robin. *The Desolate Star and Other Poems.* Whitcombe and Tombs, Christchurch, 1929.

— *Journalese.* Auckland: The National Printing Co., 1934.

— *The Conquerors and Other Poems.* London: Macmillan, 1935.

— *Check to Your King: The Life History of Charles Baron de Thierry, King of Nukahiva, Sovereign Chief of New Zealand.* 1936. Intro. Joan Stevens. Wellington: A.H. and A.W. Reed, 1960, 1975.

— *Passport to Hell.* 1936. Introduction. D. I. B. Smith. Auckland: Auckland University Press, 1987.

— *Wednesday's Children.* 1937. Introduction and afterword Susan Ash. Auckland: New Women's Press, 1989.

— *Persephone in Winter: Poems.* London: Hurst and Blackett, 1937.

— *Nor the Years Condemn.* 1938. Introduction Phillida Bunkle, Linda Hardy and Jacqueline Matthews. Auckland: New Women's Press, 1986.

— *The Godwits Fly.* 1938. Introduction Gloria Rawlinson. Auckland: Auckland University Press, 1993.

— *Dragon Rampant.* London: Hurst and Blackett. 1939. Introduction Derek Challis. Critical note Linda Hardy. Auckland: New Women's Press, 1984.

— *Houses by the Sea and Later Poems*, ed. and introduction Gloria Rawlinson. Christchurch: Caxton Press, 1952.

— *A Home in this World: An Autobiographical Fragment.* Introduction Derek Challis. Auckland: Longman Paul, 1984.

— *Selected Poems*, ed. Lydia Wevers. Auckland: Oxford University Press, 1984.

— *Disputed Ground: Robin Hyde Journalist,* ed. with introductory essays by Gillian Boddy and Jacqueline Matthews. Wellington: Victoria University Press, 1991.

— *The Victory Hymn 1935-1995*, ed. Michele Leggott. Auckland: University of Auckland: Holloway Press, 1995.

— *The Book of Nadath*. Edited with an introductory essay Michele Leggott. Auckland: Auckland University Press, 1999.

Irigaray, Luce. 'When Our Lips Speak Together.' Trans. Carolyn Burke. *Signs* 6.1 (Autumn 1980): 69-79.

Jackson, MacDonald P. 'Poetry: Beginnings to 1945.' *The Oxford History of New Zealand Literature*. 2nd edition, ed. Terry Sturm. Auckland: Oxford University Press, 1998.

Jacobus, Mary. *Reading Women: Essays in Feminist Criticism*. 1986. New York: Columbia University Press, 1986.

Jameson, Fredric. *Aesthetics and Politics*. London: Verso, 1977.

Jefferson, Ann. 'To Think About Women.' Review of *Civilisation Without Sexes*, by Mary Louise Roberts. *Times Literary Supplement* 6 Jan. 1995: 26.

Jensen, Kai. *Whole Men: The Masculine Tradition in New Zealand Literature*. Auckland: AUP, 1996.

Johnson, Barbara. 'The Frame of Reference: Poe, Lacan, Derrida.' *Yale French Studies* 55-56 (1977): 457-505.

Johnson, Mark, ed. *Philosophical Perspectives on Metaphor*. Minneapolis: University of Minnesota Press, 1981.

— Introduction. 'Metaphor in the Philosophical Tradition.' *Philosophical Perspectives on Metaphor*. 3-47.

— and George Lakoff. 'Conceptual Metaphor in Everyday Language.' *Philosophical Perspectives on Metaphor*. 286-325.

Jones, Lawrence. *Barbed Wire and Mirrors: Essays on New Zealnd Prose*. Dunedin: University of Otago Press, 1987.

—'The Novel.' *The Oxford History of New Zealand Literature*. 2nd edition, ed. Terry Sturm. Auckland: Oxford University Press, 1998.

Kaplan, Cora. *Sea Changes: Essays on Culture and Feminism*. London: Verso, 1986.

Kaplan, Sydney Janet. *Katherine Mansfield and the Origins of Modernist Fiction*. New York: Ithaca, 1991.

Kerr, Sarah. 'Shoot the Piano Player.' Review of *The Piano* and the screenplay. By Jane Campion. *New York Review of Books* 3 Feb. 1994: 29-30.

King, Michael. *Frank Sargeson: A Life*. Auckland: Viking, 1996.

Lacan, Jacques. *The Four Fundamental Concepts of Psychoanalysis*. Trans. Alan Sheridan. Ed. Jacques-Alain Miller. New York: Norton, 1981.

— *Ecrits: A Selection*, trans. Alan Sheridan. New York: Norton, 1977.

— 'Seminar on "The Purloined Letter"', trans. Jeffrey Mehlman. *Yale French Studies* 48 (1972): 38-72.

Leach, Edmund. *Levi-Strauss*. Fontana Modern Masters. London: Fontana, 1970.

Lee, John A. *Children of the Poor*. London: Werner Laurie, 1935.

Leggott, Michele, ed. with an introductory essay. *The Book of Nadath* by Robin Hyde. Auckland: AUP,1999.

—*DIA*. Auckland: Auckland University Press, 1994.

— 'Opening the Archive: Robin Hyde, Eileen Duggan and the Persistence of Record.' *Opening the Book: New Essays in New Zealand Literature*, ed. Mark Williams, and Michele Leggott. Auckland: Auckland University Press, 1993. 266-93.

— '"Sometimes Fighting and Dying are Better than Anything Else": The Poetry of Robin Hyde'. Concert Programme. Radio New Zealand, 29 July 1993.

Lerner, Gerda. *The Majority Finds Its Past: Placing Women in History*. Oxford: Oxford University Press, 1981.

Levi-Strauss, Claude. *Structural Anthropology,* trans. Claire Jacobson. Harmondsworth: Penguin, 1972.

Locke, Elsie. *Student at the Gates.* Christchurch: Whitcoulls, 1981.

Lovell-Smith, Margaret. *The Woman Question: Writings by Women Who Won the Vote.* Auckland: New Women's Press, 1992.

Macdonald, Charlotte. *A Woman of Good Character: Single Women as Immigrant Settlers in Nineteenth Century New Zealand.* Wellington: Allen and Unwin/ Historical Branch, 1990.

Mander, Jane. *The Story of a New Zealand River.* 1920. 1938. London: Robert Hale/ Christchurch: Whitcombe and Tombs, 1960, 1975. Introduction Dorothea Turner. Auckland: Godwit Press, 1994.

— *The Passionate Puritan.* London: Jonathan Lane, 1922.

— *Allen Adair.* 1925. Introduction Dorothea Turner. Auckland: Auckland University Press, 1984. Auckland: Godwit Press, 1995.

— *The Besieging City.* London: Hutchinson, 1926.

Maning, Frederick. *Old New Zealand: A Tale of the Good Old Times by a Pakeha Maori.* 1887. Auckland: Viking, 1987.

Mansfield, Katherine. *The Aloe.* New York:Howard Fertig, 1974.

— *The Aloe with Prelude,* ed. Vincent O'Sullivan. Wellington: Port Nicholson Press, 1982.

— *Bliss and Other Stories.* London: Constable, 1920.

— *Katherine Mansfield: The Collected Short Stories.* Penguin Modern Classics. Harmondsworth: Penguin, 1984.

— *The Stories of Katherine Mansfield,* ed. Antony Alpers. Definitive edition Auckland: Oxford University Press. 1988.

Marcus, Stephen. *The Other Victorians: A Study of Sexuality and Pornography in Mid-Nineteenth Century England.* London: Weidenfeld and Nicholson, 1966.

Marris, Charles, ed. *Lyric Poems of New Zealand: 1928-42.* Christchurch: Whitcombe and Tombs, 1944.

Matthews, Jill Julius. *Good and Mad Women: The Historical Construction of Femininity in Australia.* Sydney: Allen and Unwin, 1984.

McCormick, Eric. *Letters and Art in New Zealand.* Wellington: Department of Internal Affairs, 1940.

— *New Zealand Literature: A Survey.* London: Oxford University Press, 1959.

McGann, Jerome. *The Romantic Ideology: A Critical Interpretation.* Chicago: University of Chicago Press, 1983.

McGregor, Rae. 'Jane Mander: a Bibliography.' MA diss. University of Auckland, 1994.

— *The Story of a New Zealand Writer: Jane Mander.* Dunedin: University of Otago Press, 1998.

Melville, Herman. *Typee.* 1845. London: Penguin, 1986.

Minh-ha, Trinh T. *Woman, Native, Other.* Bloomington: Indiana University Press, 1989.

Mitchell, Juliet. *Psychoanalysis and Feminism: Freud, Reich, Laing and Women.* New York: Vintage Books, 1975.

— and Jacqueline Rose, eds *Feminine Sexuality: Jacques Lacan and the Ecole Freudienne.* London: Macmillan, 1982.

— *Women: The Longest Revolution: Essays in Feminism, Literature and Psychoanalysis.* London: Virago, 1984.

Modjeska, Drusilla. *Exiles at Home: Australian Women Writers, 1925-45.* Sydney: Angus and Robertson, 1992.

Moi, Toril. *Sexual/Textual Politics: Feminist Literary Theory*. New Accents Series. London: Routledge, 1985.

— 'Feminism, Postmodernism and Style.' *Cultural Critique* 9 (Spring 1988) 5- 7.

Morris, Meaghan. *The Pirate's Fiancée: Feminism, Reading, Postmodernism.* London: Verso, 1988.

Mulgan, John. *Man Alone*. London: Selwyn and Blount, 1939.

Murray, Stuart. *Never a Soul at Home: New Zealand Literary Nationalism and the 1930s.* Wellington: VUP, 1998.

Newnham, Tom. *New Zealand Women in China*. Auckland: Graphic Publications, 1995.

Newton, Judith, and Deborah Rosenfelt, eds *Feminist Criticism and Social Change: Sex, Class, Race in Literature and Culture*. New York: Methuen, 1985.

Olssen, Eric. 'Women, Work and Family: 1880-1926.' *Women in New Zealand Society*, ed. Phillida Bunkle and Beryl Hughes. Auckland: Allen and Unwin, 1980. 159-83.

Orpen, Sir William, ed. *The Outline of Art*. Revised by Horace Shipp. London: George Newnes Ltd, 1950.

Orr, Bridget. 'Reading with the Taint of the Pioneer.' *Landfall* 172 (1989): 447-482.

O'Sullivan, Vincent. *An Anthology of Twentieth Century New Zealand Poetry*. Auckland: Oxford University Press, 1983.

— and Margaret Scott, eds *The Collected Letters of Katherine Mansfield*. Vol.1. Auckland: Oxford University Press, 1984.

Park, Ruth. *Fence Around the Cuckoo*. Ringwood, Vic.: Viking, 1992.

Parry, Benita. 'Problems in Current Theories of Colonial Discourse.' *Oxford Literary Review* 9.1-2 (1987): 27-58.

Paul, Mary Eleanor. 'The Success and Failure of Elizabeth Gaskell.' MA dissertation. University of Auckland, 1975.

— and Marion Rae, eds *New Women's Fiction 3*. Auckland: New Women's Press, 1989.

— 'The We of Me.' *Landfall* 180 (1991): 412-17.

— '"Bliss," and Why Ignorance Won't Do: The Use of Criticism and Theory in Current Reading Practices.' *Opening the Book: New Essays on New Zealnad Writing*, ed. Williams and Leggott. 211-31.

Pearson, W. H. Introduction. *Collected Stories, 1936-1963*. By Frank Sargeson. Auckland: Blackwood and Janet Paul, 1964. 7-19.

— *Fretful Sleepers and Other Essays*. London: Heinemann, 1974.

Perry, Nick. *The Dominion of Signs: Television, Advertising and Other New Zealand Fictions*. Auckland: AUP, 1994.

Perrot, Michelle, ed. *A History of Private Life: from the Revolution to the Great War*. Harvard: Bellknap, 1990.

Phillips, Jock. *A Man's Country? The Image of the Pakeha Male: A History*. Auckland: Penguin, 1987.

The Piano. Promotional publication. Cannes: International Press, 1993.

Plath, Sylvia. *Letters Home: Correspondence, 1950-1963*. London: Faber and Faber, 1977.

Pocock, John. Letter. *New York Review of Books*. 7 April 1994: 47-48.

Pope, Quentin, ed. *Kowhai Gold: An Anthology of Contemporary Verse*. London: Dent, 1930.

Pound, Francis. *Frame on the Land: Early Landscape Painting in New Zealand*. Auckland: Collins, 1983.

Pound, Ezra. 'The Hard and the Soft in French Poetry.' 1918. *Literary Essays of Ezra Pound*, ed. T. S. Eliot. London: Faber and Faber, 1963.

— *Selected Poems*. London: Faber, 1948.

Pratt, Mary Louise. *Imperial Eyes: Travel Writing and Transculturation*. London: Routledge, 1992.

Rankin, Keith. 'Labour Supply in New Zealand and Australia, 1919-1939.' MA thesis, Victoria University, 1990.

Rawlinson, Gloria. Introduction. *The Godwits Fly*. By Robin Hyde. Auckland: Auckland University Press, 1980. ix-xviii.

— Introduction. *Houses by the Sea and Later Poems*. By Robin Hyde. Christchurch: Caxton Press, 1952. 11-34.

Renee. *Jeannie Once*. New Zealand Playwrights Series. Wellington: Victoria University Press, 1991.

— *Pass It On*. New Zealand Playwrights Series. Wellington: Victoria University Press, 1986.

— *Wednesday to Come*. New Zealand Playwrights Series. Wellington: Victoria University Press, 1985.

Rich, Adrienne. *Of Woman Born: Motherhood as Experience and Institution*. New York: Norton, 1976.

Richards, I.A. 'The Philosophy of Rhetoric.' *Philosophical Perspectives on Metaphor*. Ed. Mark Johnson. Minneapolis: University of Minnesota Press, 1981. 48-62.

— *Practical Criticism: A Study of Literary Judgement*. 1929. New York: Harcourt Brace, 1935.

Rose, Jacqueline. *Sexuality in the Field of Vision*. London: Verso, 1986.

Ricoeur, Paul. *The Philosophy of Paul Ricoeur: An Anthology of his Work*, eds Charles E. Reagan and David Stewart. Boston: Beacon Press, 1978.

— *A Ricoeur Reader: Reflection and Imagination,* ed. Mario J. Valdes. Hemel Hempstead: Harvester Wheatsheaf, 1991.

— *The Rule of Metaphor: Multi-Disciplinary Studies Of the Creation of Meaning in Language*. Trans. Robert Czerny. Toronto: University of Toronto Press, 1977.

Roberts, Heather. *Where Did She Come From? New Zealand Women Novelists, 1862-1987*. Wellington: Allen and Unwin/ Port Nicholson, 1989.

Said, Edward. *Culture and Imperialism*. New York: Knopf, 1993.

Sandbrook, Patrick. 'Robin Hyde: A Writer at Work.' PhD thesis, Massey University, 1984.

Schaffer, Kay. *Women in the Bush: Forces of Desire in the Australian Cultural Tradition*. Cambridge: Cambridge University Press, 1988.

Scholes, Robert. *Textual Power: Literary Theory and the Teaching of English*. New Haven: Yale University Press, 1985.

Schreiner, Olive. *The Story of an African Farm*. 1883 New York: Oxford University Press, 1992.

Segal, Lynne. *Is the Future Female? Troubled Thoughts on Contemporary Feminism*. London: Virago, 1987.

Seigel, Jerrold. *Bohemian Paris: Culture, Politics and the Boundaries of Bourgeois Life, 1830-1930*. New York: Viking, 1986.

Shadbolt, Bridget. 'Commonplaces: The Letters of Robin Hyde and John A. Lee.' MA thesis, University of Auckland, 1995.

Showalter, Elaine. *A Literature of Their Own*. Princeton: Princeton University Press, 1977.

— ed. *The New Feminist Criticism: Essays on Women, Literature and Theory*. London: Virago, 1986.

Silverman, Kaja. *The Subject of Semiotics.* New York: Oxford University Press, 1983.

Sinclair, Keith. *A History of New Zealand.* Harmondsworth: Penguin, 1988.

Sontag, Susan. 'Against Interpretation.' *Against Interpretation and Other Essays.* London: Eyre and Spottiswoode, 1967. 3-36.

Spender, Dale. *Mothers of the Novel.* London: Pandora, 1986.

Spivak, Gayatri. 'Three Women's Texts and a Critique of Imperialism.' *'Race', Writing and Difference.* Ed. Henry Gates. Chicago: Chicago University Press, 1986. 262-80.

Staiger, Janet. *Interpreting Film: Studies in the Historical Reception of American Cinema.* Princeton: Princeton University Press, 1992.

Stead, C. K. 'Katherine Mansfield: The Art of the "Fiction".' *In the Glass Case: Essays on New Zealand Literature.* Auckland: AUP, 1981. 29-46.

Sturm, Terry. Introduction to the First Edition. *The Oxford History of New Zealand Literature.* 2nd edition, ed. Terry Sturm. Auckland: Oxford University Press, 1998. ix-xviii.

Summers, Anne. *Damned Whores and God's Police: The Colonisation of Women in Australia.* Ringwood, Vic.: Penguin, 1975.

Thomas, Elizabeth. 'Appropriation, Subversion and Separatism: the Strategies of Three New Zealand Women Novelists: Jane Mander, Robin Hyde and Sylvia Ashton-Warner.' PhD thesis. University of Canterbury, 1990.

Tomalin, Claire. *Katherine Mansfield: A Secret Life.* London: Viking, 1987.

Tompkins, Jane, ed. *Reader Response Criticism: From Formalism to Post-Structuralism.* Baltimore: Johns Hopkins University Press, 1983.

Turner, Dorothea. *Jane Mander: A Monograph.* Twayne's World Authors Series. New York: Twayne Publishers, 1972.

Turner, Dorothea. '*The Story of a New Zealand River:* Perceptions and Prophecies in an Unfixed Society.' *Critical Essays on the New Zealand Novel,* ed. Cherry Hankin. Auckland: Heinemann Educational Books, 1976.

Vlades, Mario J., ed. *A Ricoeur Reader: Reflection and Imagination.* Hemel Hempstead: Harvester Wheatsheaf, 1991.

Wagner, Linda. *Dos Passos: Artist as American.* Austin, University of Texas Press, 1979.

Wandor, Michelene, ed. *On Gender and Writing.* London/ Boston: Pandora Press, 1983.

Webby, Elizabeth, and Lydia Wevers, eds *Goodbye to Romance: Stories by New Zealand and Australian Women Writers, 1930-1980s.* Sydney: Angus and Robertson, 1989.

— and Lydia Wevers, eds *Happy Ending: Stories by Australian and New Zealand Women Writers, 1850s-1930s.* Sydney: Angus and Robertson, 1987.

Wedde, Ian, and Harvey McQueen, eds *The Penguin Book of New Zealand Verse.* Auckland: Penguin, 1985.

Wevers, Lydia. 'Pioneer into Feminist: Jane Mander's Heroines.' *Women in New Zealand Society,* ed. Bunkle and Hughes. Auckland: Allen and Unwin, 1980. 244-60.

— ed. *Robin Hyde: Selected Poems.* Auckland: Oxford University Press, 1984.

— 'How Katherine Mansfield was Kidnapped.' *Women's Studies Journal* (NZ) 4. 2 (1988): 5-17.

— *Yellow Pencils: Contemporary Poetry by New Zealand Women.* Auckland: Oxford University Press, 1989.

— 'The Sod Under My Feet.' *Opening the Book: New Essays on New Zealand Writing,* ed. Mark Williams and Michele Leggott. Auckland: Auckland University Press, 1995.

Williams, Mark. *Leaving the Highway: Six Contemporary New Zealand Novelists.* Auckland: Auckland University Press, 1990.

Williams, Raymond. *Marxism and Literature*. Marxist Introductions. Oxford: Oxford University Press, 1977.

Woolf, Virginia. 'A Society.' *Monday or Tuesday*. New York: Harcourt Brace, 1921. 9- 40.

Wren, John H. *John Dos Passos*. Twayne's US Authors Series. New Haven: College University Press, 1961.

Wright, Elizabeth. *Psychoanalytic Criticism: Theory and Practice*. New Accents Series. London: Methuen, 1984.

ARTICLES IN MAGAZINES AND NEWSPAPERS

Baillie, Russell. 'Jane Campion: Storyteller supreme.' *Sunday Star* 19 September 1993: C1.

Baillie, Russell . 'Movies with Russell Baillie.' *Sunday Star* 19 September 1993: C5.

Recent Books. Bridget Williams Books Catalogue. 1995: Cover.

Bunkle, Phillida and Sandra Coney. 'An Unfortunate Experiment at National Women's.' *Metro* 1 June 1987: 46-65.

Bunkle, Phillida and Linda Hardy and Jacqueline Matthews. 'Who is the Real Robin Hyde? *Iris* Reviewed.' *Broadsheet* Jan-Feb 1985: 22-6.

Calder, Peter. 'Playing from the Heart.' *New Zealand Herald* 16 September 1993, sec. 3: 1.

'Campion Film Saluted.' *New Zealand Herald* 26 May 1993, sec.1: 24.

Chenery, Susan. 'The Final Word.' *The Australian Magazine* 6-7 August 1994: 30-34.

'*Cinema of Unease.*' *Auckland International Film Festival Programme* June-July 1995: 37.

'*Cinema of Unease.*' *New Zealand Listener* 14-20 October 1995: 30.

Danby, Stephen. Review of *Nor the Years Condemn* by Robin Hyde. *New Zealand Sunday Times* 11 May 1986: 15.

Danby, Stephen. Review of *Passport to Hell* by Robin Hyde. *New Zealand Sunday Times* 1 February 1987: 13.

Hill, Deborah. 'Beatson Doesn't Play the Piano.' *National Business Review* 31 March 1994: 48.

Kan, Raybon. 'Anna's Win Simply Awesome.' *Sunday Star Times* 27 March 1994: A20.

Langley, Kim. 'Dark Talent.' *Vogue Australia* April 1993: 138-142

McDonald, Bernard. 'Holly Hunter Key Performer.' *Style* Summer 1993-4: 126.

Mannion, Robert. 'Hollywood Stars Shrouded During NZ Film Shoot.' *Dominion Sunday Times* 12 March 1992: 1.

Moore, Colin. 'Outdoors with Colin Moore.' *New Zealand Herald* 6 July 1994, sec. 2: 1.

'*The Piano* "too arty" for Oscars.' *Evening Post* 16 March 1994: 27.

'Waitakere City Congratulates . . . Jane Campion for Making Our Beach the Most Famous in the World.' Advertisement. *Sunday Star Times* 27 March 1993: D6.

MANUSCRIPTS AND OTHER UNPUBLISHED MATERIAL

Armstrong, Philip. '"Flying Leaves" – a glance at Katherine Mansfield's "Bliss" in the light of the "Seminar on 'the Purloined Letter'" by Jacques Lacan.' MA essay, 1990.

Batten, Kim. 'Seminar on Robin Hyde.' Paper delivered to MA class. University of Auckland, 1995.

Dyson, Lynda. 'The Return of the Repressed? Whiteness, Femininity and Colonialism.' Paper delivered in 'Reading New Zealand' Lecture Series. University of London May 1995.

Hardy, Linda. 'James Heberley, "On the Beach": high and vernacular colonialisms in the Pacific.' Paper delivered at the David Nicoll Smith Seminar XI, University of Auckland, 26 August 1993.

Hyde, Robin. (Iris Wilkinson) 'Autobiography.' MSS 412. Auckland Public Library.

Hyde, Robin. 'The Beaches.' Typescript worksheets. Auckland University Library.

Leggott, Michele. 'Something Coming the Other Way: The Distaff Line in New Zealand Poetry.' Unpublished draft, 1993.

'The River.' Unfinished screenplay. 'Adapted by Debra Daley, Geoff Chapple, Pat Murphy and Helen Hodgman from the novel by Jane Mander *The Story of a New Zealand River*.' Auckland: John Maynard Productions. 1990.

Victorian Studies Network. Correspondence on *The Piano*, 1994.

Zimmerman, Anne. 'Research notes on Robin Hyde's "Autobiography." October, 1991.' Held with Hyde manuscripts at Auckland Public Library.

INTERVIEWS

Chapple, Geoff. Personal interview. 15 July 1994.

Chapple, Geoff. Telephone interview. 20 October 1994.

Harrex, Wendy. Personal conversation. June 1994.

Muru, Selwyn . Telephone interview. 19 July 1994.

Sandbrook, Patrick. Personal conversation. July 1987.

FILMS AND TELEVISION PROGRAMMES

An Angel at My Table. Dir. Jane Campion. Screenplay Laura Jones. With Kerry Fox, Alexia Keogh and Karen Ferguson. Prod. Brigid Ikin, 1990.

Desperate Remedies. Dir. and screenplay Stuart Main and Peter Wells. With Jennifer Ward-Lealand, Kevin Smith, Lisa Chappel and Cliff Curtis. Prod. James Wallace, 1993.

Forgotten Silver. Dir. Peter Jackson. Written Costa Botes and Peter Jackson. Montana Sunday Theatre. Prod.Peter Jackson and Sue Rogers. Television One, 29 Oct. 1995.

Heavenly Creatures. Dir. Peter Jackson. Screenplay Peter Jackson and Frances Walsh. With Melanie Lynskey, Kate Winslet and Sarah Peirse. Prod. Jim Booth, 1994.

Iris. Dir. and screenplay Tony Isaacs. With John Bach, Philip Holden and Helen Morse. Prod. John Barnett. Telefeature, 1984.

Once Were Warriors. Dir. Lee Tamahori. Screenplay Riwia Brown. With Rena Owen, Temuera Morrison and Cliff Curtis. Prod. Robin Scholes, 1994.

The End of the Golden Weather. Dir. and screenplay Ian Mune. With Steven Papps, Paul Gittens and Gabrielle Hammond. Prod. Christina Milligan, 1991.

The Piano. Dir. and screenplay Jane Campion. With Holly Hunter, Harvey Keitel, Sam Neill and Anna Paquin. Prod. Jan Chapman, 1993.

'The River Story.' Dir. Greg Mayer. Documentary item. *Marae.* Television New Zealand 1 Oct. 1993.

Sweetie. Dir. Jane Campion. Screenplay Jane Campion and Gerard Lee. With Genevieve Lemon, Karen Colston and Tom Lycos. Prod. John Maynard, 1991.

'Variations on a Theme.' Reporter Keith Davis. Documentary item. *20/20.* Television New Zealand, 19 July 1994.

Wuthering Heights. Dir. William Wyler. With Merle Oberon and Lawrence Olivier. Prod. Samuel Goldwyn, 1939.

Index